MW00563735

READING THE NEWSPAPER

Margery Staman Miller, Ed.D./Karen Kuelthau Allan, Ph.D.
LESLEY COLLEGE GRADUATE SCHOOL

Jamestown Publishers/Providence, Rhode Island

The basis of our government being the opinion of the people, the very first object should be to keep that right; and were it left to me to decide whether we should have a government without newspapers, or newspapers without a government, I should not hesitate a moment to prefer the latter.

Thomas Jefferson

READING THE NEWSPAPER
Advanced Level

Catalog No. 571
Copyright © 1989 by Jamestown Publishers, Inc.

Cover and Text Design by Deborah Hulsey Christie
Cover painting by Bob Eggleton
Front page courtesy of The Washington Post

Printed in the United States KI

89 90 91 92 93 94 10 9 8 7 6 5 4 3 2 1

ISBN: 0-89061-500-4

To our respective spouses, Lee and Andy, who have provided the necessary quiet support that allows a project like ours to reach completion.

C O N T E N T S

UNIT THREE: HOW WE USE THE NEWS

Introduction

Reading the Newspaper was created to promote secondary students' critical thinking skills while reinforcing skills needed to read the newspaper effectively. Students are also encouraged to apply those skills to the process of writing as well as reading.

Unit Organization

Reading the Newspaper is divided into three units, each representing a way to critically analyze the newspaper and the news. We recommend that the student read the book unit-by-unit to gain full understanding of the major concepts developed in one unit before moving on to the next. Each unit is introduced by a Unit Overview that should be the basis for prereading discussion by the students and the teacher. The lessons in each unit are arranged to go from simpler to more complex subject matter, and the student is sometimes referred to information presented in prior lessons within the unit or lessons in prior units. Such connections will help increase the student's level of comprehension as he or she progresses through the book.

Unit One, What Makes News, deals with the news values and guidelines that newspaper publishers and editors follow in deciding what news to print. The five guidelines are introduced in the Unit Overview and are dealt with in detail in the eight lessons that make up the unit. The two stories in each lesson exemplify one of the guidelines, giving the student an opportunity to read and study material that, for a set of reasons applied by journalists, is deemed newsworthy. For example, Lesson 1 examines the influence of the news value proximity on news stories about a disastrous tornado in Texas and the attack on the USS *Stark* in the Persian Gulf. In like manner, a lesson covering the influence of recency on the news includes a story on AIDS.

Unit Two, Who Reports the News, focuses on the journalists who write for a newspaper and on some non-writers such as photographers, artists, and cartoonists. The writing roles highlighted are those of reporter, feature writer, editorial writer, critic, news columnist, and how-to columnist. The non-writing roles are those of the photographer, the artist, and the cartoonist.

Unit Three, How We Use the News, focuses on ways that the newspaper influences our daily lives in both overt and subtle ways. Lessons deal with reader appeal, special papers, news datelines, the newspaper as a daily record, and the newspaper as a historical record.

Lesson Organization

The lessons within each unit are arranged by complexity, from the simplest to the most difficult. Each lesson is based on two closely connected news stories and comprises five components: instructional lesson material; two newspaper stories; two sets of six multiple choice comprehension questions; an exercise based on a specialized newspaper reading skill requiring varied short answers; and one or two extension activities designed to involve students in reading and understanding specific elements of their own news-papers and in writing their own newspaper-style stories in various forms and on various topics.

Instructional Lesson Material

Each lesson opens with instructional lesson material that establishes a purpose for the lesson, explains the lesson's role in the development of the unit, and gives background information needed to read the first story. Between the two newspaper stories is a continuation of the lesson material—usually one or two paragraphs—that reiterates the major purpose of the lesson and sets a purpose for reading the second story. A final, summary section of lesson material directly follows the second story.

It is important that students be reminded to read the lesson material and be encouraged to refer to it as often as necessary while working the lesson. It is also important that students understand the information and be encouraged to pose questions before they begin work on the specialized reading skill or Using Your Newspaper and Practicing Newspaper Skills.

Newspaper Stories and Checking Your Comprehension

Each lesson contains two actual newspaper stories taken from major local or national newspapers.

Six multiple choice comprehension questions follow each story. There are two vocabulary, two literal, and two inferential questions directly related to the story's main points. The vocabulary questions are designed to give the students practice in determining word meanings using context clues. The words are considered key words necessary to the understanding of the story; their selection is determined by the story's purpose and topic. The literal questions are designed to focus the student's attention on the story's main idea and important supporting details; they address the traditional Five W's—*Who? What? Where? When? Why?*—and *How?* Finally, the inferential questions, or critical thinking questions, are built on the vocabulary and literal questions; they are designed to give the students practice in reading between the lines to make inferences and draw conclusions.

Students should be encouraged to answer the questions without looking back at the stories. Rereading should, however, be permitted when a student realizes he or she does not know an answer. Students are to check their own work using the Answer Key that begins on page 137. The consistent format of two vocabulary, two literal, and two inferential questions allows teacher and student alike to see whether a particular type of question is giving a student difficulty. For example, a number of errors with the vocab-ulary questions might indicate that a student should receive direct instruction on using context clues to determine word meaning.

Specialized Reading Skill

The specialized reading skill exercises are designed to give students practice in applying specific reading skills to a variety of newspaper topics and formats. Each specialized reading skill is directly related to the purpose and writing style of the newspaper story it accompanies. For example, in a lesson based on two opinion columns, the specialized reading skill is Evaluating Comments in an Editorial. Similarly, in a sports news story that uses lively, descriptive language, the specialized reading skill is Interpreting Colorful Language in Sports Stories.

The specialized reading skill exercises offer instruction and practice with four major reading comprehension skills at a critical level: recognizing the main idea and supporting details; arranging events in chronological order; distinguishing between fact and opinion; analyzing cause-and-effect relationships. There is a balance of these skills throughout the text. If a student has difficulty with one in particular it is important to go over the lesson and perhaps do some direct instruction on the skill before allowing the student to go on to future lessons where he or she will again be required to use the skill.

Using Your Newspaper/ Practicing Newspaper Skills

These two extension activities offer the student the opportunity to apply what he or she has learned about the focus of the lesson in two distinct ways. In Using Your Newspaper, the student is asked to find an article in his or her own newspaper that is similar to a story used in the lesson. In other words, if the focus of a lesson is on proximity, as it is in Unit One, Lesson 1, the student is asked to conduct a survey of his or her newspaper to see how it treats important events from different places in different ways.

In the second activity, Practicing Newspaper Skills, the student is asked to extend his or her thinking and to demonstrate in writing the ability to produce newspaper-style stories that replicate either the form or the content of one of the newspaper stories in the lesson. In these activities, which connect the reading process to the writing process, students are encouraged to practice various writing techniques and research and data-collecting techniques employing a range of language arts skills. The emphasis in the activities is on moving the student into a writer's role parallel to the role of the person who produced the stories in the lesson.

We recommend that teachers invest the time required for Using Your Newspaper and Practicing Newspaper Skills. They are an integral part of each lesson and will help students using this book become active readers whose response to the newspaper is thoughtful and critical.

Introducing the Book to the Student

Students and teachers should begin work in *Reading the Newspaper* by completing a sample lesson together. Additionally, it would be worthwhile to schedule time for class reading and discussion of each Unit Overview to lay a firm foundation for studying the lessons that make up the unit. In order to work through a lesson with the students we recommend the following steps:

1. Read the To the Student section as a class. Review the organization of the book and discuss what it is about.

2. Read silently and then discuss the ideas found in the Unit Overview. Take the time needed to discuss the concepts and to set a clear purpose for the unit.

3. Have the students read the instructional lesson material at the beginning of Lesson 1. This material introduces the

subject of the first story and sets a purpose for reading. It will also start the students thinking about the focus of the lesson.

4. Have the students read the first story silently, keeping the focus of the lesson in mind.

5. Introduce the six comprehension questions and make sure all students understand the three different types of questions. Work the questions as a class. Be sure to have students correct their answers using the Answer Key which begins on page 137 in the worktext. Encourage them to reread the story for verification or support of answers.

6. Have a student read aloud the continuation of the lesson material. Discuss how the material reiterates the focus of the lesson. Point out how it sets the purpose for reading the second story.

7. Follow steps 4 and 5 for the second story in the lesson.

8. Read aloud the summary lesson material that follows the second story and its comprehension questions. Use this as a review and as a time for clarification of concepts with the students.

9. Go on to the specialized reading skill. Have a class member read the title of the exercise and the directions to the class. Discuss these before having the students actually work the exercise. After working the exercise, have the students correct their work using the Answer Key. Allow them to discuss and verify answers by rereading appropriate parts of the stories.

10. Turn to the extension activities. Point out to students that they can choose to complete Using Your Newspaper, Practicing Newspaper Skills, or, in some cases, both. Point out that these activities give them an opportunity to apply what they have learned about the focus of the lesson.

In Using Your Newspaper the students will be asked to find an article in their own newspaper that is similar in content to a story in the lesson. Inform students that they must have access to a daily newspaper to work the extensions. Begin making arrangements to assist the class members in obtaining newspapers. The second extension activity, Practicing Newspaper Skills, is designed to link reading of the newspaper to writing a variety of newspaper-style pieces. It will be important to talk with students about the need to collect data by going to libraries, attending local events, or interviewing people in their school or community. Equally important is the need to discuss guidelines for time management so that students can complete the activities within specified times. You will also want to remind students that their written products will vary from lesson to lesson as they assume various journalistic roles to work in a variety of styles and forms. Offer guidelines in the presentation of the products of completed activities. The students will need an entire class period to complete a Using Your Newspaper activity, and one to two periods as well as time outside of class to complete a Practicing Newspaper Skills activity.

11. Allow time for sharing of the products from the two extension activities.

12. Conclude the lesson by discussing with students the connection of the particular lesson to the focus of the entire unit as it is described in the Overview.

13. It is recommended that students, after having completed a sample lesson with the teacher, should work through the units one lesson at a time. We estimate that each

lesson will take approximately one week or five periods of class work.

14. Each unit should be introduced in the same manner, with time for guided discussion and clarification. The concepts increase in complexity from Unit One to Unit Two to Unit Three. The clearer the ideas and the purposes for reading, the more success and growth each student can be expected to experience.

Reading the Newspaper is designed so that it can be incorporated into a secondary program in three ways. First, it can be used as a regular part of the reading/language arts curriculum. The stories, comprehension questions, specialized reading skills, and extension activities support a variety of reading and writing skills.

Second, the worktext can be part of the curriculum devoted exclusively to newspaper study. As such, the emphasis would fall on an understanding of the focus of Unit One, What Makes News, and a concentration on studying the journalistic and non-writing roles covered in Unit Two, Who Reports the News. The Practicing Newspaper Skills activities reinforce this understanding by giving the student the opportunity to write in a variety of styles exemplified by the different writers of the newspaper.

Third, *Reading the Newspaper* can be used as a tool for connecting different curriculum areas. Many of the stories are germane to the social sciences covered in the secondary grades—history, sociology, economics. The students can be encouraged to use the newspaper as a daily record of events happening in their own communities and in their own lifetime, events that can be connected to content they are studying. This is an excellent way to increase their interest in and their understanding of complex concepts mandated in the curriculum.

It is our hope that whatever way you choose to use this worktext, the newspaper and its varied contents will become an important and rich part of your curriculum.

Introduction

If you are like many people, you may glance at the headline of a newspaper and think about the news-making event that inspired it. You may pick up the paper to learn more of the facts about the event. You might not, however, think about why that particular story was considered newsworthy enough to be in the paper and why it occupies the place it does on the page. In other words, you might think about the news itself, but not about *what makes news.*

Likewise, you may immediately turn to the sports page for the latest information about your team without noticing the reporter's name or the credit for the photographer who took the great action shot accompanying the story. You might be caught up in reading about your favorite team without thinking about who wrote and illustrated the story or *who reports the news.*

Finally, you might skim the newspaper to learn about the day's events without thinking about how the newspaper affects your daily life. You might not consider the notion that the newspaper serves its readership in many ways. Perhaps you have never stopped to think about *how we use the news.*

This book is designed to help you evaluate these three facets of the newspaper and the news. In addition, *Reading the Newspaper* will aid you in building critical newspaper reading skills, thereby enhancing your understanding and enjoyment of the newspaper.

The playwright Arthur Miller said that a good newspaper is a "nation talking to itself." To reap the full benefits of the newspaper—to take part in the dialogue—you must be able to use and comprehend this important source of information. To do so will make you not only a better reader but also a more informed member of society.

How to Use This Book

This book is divided into three units—What Makes News, Who Reports the News, and How We Use the News. We recommend that you read the units of the book in order. At the beginning of each unit is a Unit Overview that is designed to introduce you to the contents of the unit.

Unit One, What Makes News, teaches some of the guidelines that a newspaper's staff follows in deciding what stories to run. The unit contains examples of stories that illustrate the use of guidelines based on proximity, names in the news, recency, discovery and invention, and trends.

In Unit Two, Who Reports the News, you will learn about the journalists who work on a newspaper. There are stories by reporters, feature writers, editorial writers, critics, columnists, and how-to writers. The roles of the people who illustrate the news—photographers, artists and cartoonists—are included as well.

Unit Three, How We Use the News, considers how the newspaper may influence our daily lives. Featured in the unit are stories with different reader appeal, stories from special papers, and stories with different news datelines. There are also examples of the newspaper as a daily record of events and as a historical record of past events.

Completing the Lessons

Every lesson in the book contains the same five elements and should be worked through in the same manner.

1. Lesson Material. The first thing you will read in each lesson is a paragraph that directly precedes the newspaper stories. This first paragraph of lesson material has two purposes: to start explaining the main topic of the lesson and to set a purpose for reading the newspaper stories.

After you have read the first newspaper story you will come to a continuation of the instructional lesson material. The material—usually one or two paragraphs—leads you to the second newspaper story. After you have read the second news story, you will come to the last section of instructional lesson material.

Read the lesson material surrounding the newspaper stories carefully. Return to any part of the material as often as you need to while reading the articles.

2. Two Newspaper Stories. Each lesson contains two stories taken from actual newspapers. Read them carefully, keeping the lesson material in mind.

3. Checking Your Comprehension. Six multiple choice questions follow each newspaper story. Questions 1 and 2 are vocabulary questions that test your ability to determine the meanings of words taken from the story. Questions 3 and 4 test your ability to recall facts from the story. Questions 5 and 6 ask you to draw inferences about ideas implied in the story.

Try to answer the comprehension questions without looking back at the story. If you cannot answer a question, return to the appropriate part of the story and reread it. Then answer the question.

Check your answers in the Answer Key that begins on page 137. The answers for the first set of comprehension questions will be in the left-hand column under the heading *Checking Your Comprehension.* The answers for the second set of comprehension questions will be in the right-hand column under the same heading. Examine any wrong answers. Then look back at the article. Try to figure out why you were wrong.

4. Specialized Reading Skill. This is a short-answer activity. It focuses on the specialized reading skill necessary for a complete understanding of the two stories.

Carefully read the directions that introduce the activity— they explain how to complete the activity as well as teaching you more about the skill involved. Once you are sure you understand the directions, proceed with the activity.

After you have completed the specialized reading skill activity, check your answers against the Answer Key in the back of the book. Examine any wrong answers. Then look back at the two stories. Try to figure out why you were wrong.

5. Using Your Newspaper/Practicing Newspaper Skills. These two activities offer you the opportunity to apply what you have learned about the focus of the lesson. In Using Your Newspaper, you will be asked to find a story in your own newspaper that is similar to one or both of the stories in the lesson. For example, after the lesson on names in the news, your task will be to collect, and categorize stories about well-known people in your paper.

Practicing Newspaper Skills is designed to link your reading of the newspaper to the writing of your own newspaper-style reports. Many of these writing activities will require you to collect data. You may, for example, need to go to the library, or attend a local event, or interview a person in your school or town. You will be asked, in other words, to assume the role of a journalist.

We recommend that you take about four or five periods for each lesson. You will probably complete the opening lesson material and one newspaper story and its comprehension questions in one period. In the second period, you could complete the second story and its comprehension questions, the continuation of the instructional material, and the specialized reading skill activity. You may choose to complete either Using Your Newspaper or Practicing Newspaper Skills or both. You will probably need one period for the Using Your Newspaper assignment and one or two periods for the Practicing Newspaper Skills assignment. You may find that some of the activities, interviewing, for instance, are easier to complete outside of school.

What Makes News

UNIT OVERVIEW

The publishers and editors of newspapers must constantly balance the twin goals of informing readers and selling papers. Newspapers have a responsibility to furnish the reading public with news, but as private business organizations, they must be operated with profit in mind, too. That means printing relevant, meaningful information in a compelling, attractive manner that attracts and holds readers.

In making information available to the public, publishers and editors follow certain guidelines. In this first unit we will learn about five of the news values that play a part in defining those guidelines—proximity, names in the news, recency, discovery and invention, and trends.

The first news value we will look at is *proximity,* which has to do with the nearness of news-making events to the places where people live. Here is an example. An important news event happens in close proximity to your town, in a neighboring community, let's say. The newspaper in your town would probably devote a great deal of space to the story. It might run follow-up stories for several days. On the other hand, newspapers in places other than your town might not cover the story at all, or they might run only one story, possibly buried on a back page. Of course, that is a basic example. The effect of proximity is exerted on national and world reporting also, as national and world events affect readers everywhere. A newspaper will cover those events in spite of the distance at which they are playing themselves out. Some news events—nuclear arms talks, for instance—make neighbors of us all.

Publishers and editors also guide news selection according to the luster lent to a story by famous names, what we call in this book *names in the news.* Many readers are interested in famous people and will buy newspapers to learn even trivial things about their lives. So, if the president of the United States has a cold, that is news. If a major TV personality comes to town, that is news. But if your friend from down the street has the sniffles or if you make a trip to a different state, neither event would likely be considered news. True, "ordinary" people can become names in the news by accomplishing something unique. Unknown inventors and scientists, for example, can become instant celebrities through their work. But their day in the sun may be short, whereas a famous person with a continuing career will be a magnet for readers for a long time.

The third news value that we will consider in Unit One is *recency.* While newspapers are not as immediate as TV or radio, they must report up-to-date information that readers will be interested in. Additionally, the newspaper is expected to report information in more depth than do TV and radio. Thus, to report on an event from the day before, newspapers must include the most current facts as well as details that readers might not have heard the night before on the evening television news or on radio reports. Often, a development in a news story will break just as the newspaper is going to print. Then the editors and writers scramble to update the story in an effort not to send out an edition with anything but the most current information.

In this unit we will also evaluate the effect of *discovery and invention* on the selection and reporting of news stories. The category of discovery and invention often overlaps with the celebrity and recency factors. Stories on recent discoveries and new inventions often satisfy the demands of readers who want to know as quickly as possible about the "latest things" and the people behind them. Interestingly, discoveries and inventions are usually the culmination of efforts that newspapers do not report. The scientist or inventor may labor in obscurity for years. Then comes the breakthrough, and suddenly the invention or discovery is news and the creator or discoverer is newsworthy.

Finally, *trends* provide editors with a guideline to follow. Many readers are curious about the newest fads, fashions, and leisure-time activities, for example. Newspapers try to cover these fads just as they are at the peak of popularity. As with outdated news, outdated trends are nearly meaningless.

Some values may be intrinsically linked to certain types of stories more than to others. Naturally, editors apply guidelines connected to those values more rigorously in certain sections of the newspaper than in others. For example, discovery tends to be the major criterion in a science section, just as trends tend to be more suited to the living and fashion sections. Names in the news in business will naturally be reported in the business section; names in the news in entertainment will be found in the entertainment section. Guidelines applied in connection with recency and proximity dominate the major news sections and the sports sections.

As you read the lessons in Unit One consider which of the guidelines led to the selection of each story. Also think about why each story is written as it is and why it contains the information it does.

As you have learned in the introduction to this unit, the editors of a newspaper often pay as much attention to where a news event takes place as they do to what that news event is. That is because most people find events that occur nearby to be especially compelling. The nearness, or *proximity,* of the event to the readers, then, is a factor nearly as important as news content. The two stories you will read in this lesson are an example of that double focus. Each story reports an event in detail, emphasizing the event's impact on the people in a specific locale.

Both events were disastrous and unexpected. Both were reported in newspapers throughout the country and on national television news. The first, the tornado in Saragosa, Texas, caused many deaths and injuries in West Texas. The *Dallas Morning News* carried a range of in-depth stories for days following the storm, long after papers elsewhere in the country had stopped reporting the story. The pieces in that Texas newspaper were of particular interest to the people in the area. The follow-up story below appeared two days after the tornado had struck.

In a more complicated example of proximity, the people of Jacksonville, Florida, were greatly affected by the attack on the USS *Stark,* a Navy frigate in the Persian Gulf. Despite the distance, the attack hit close to home for Jacksonville residents, for many of them had relatives and loved ones aboard the ship. Jacksonville, it turns out, is the *Stark*'s home port. For that reason, the *Jacksonville Journal* reported on stories about the attack for a longer time and in greater depth than did other newspapers around the country. As you can see from the picture on page 17, the people of Jacksonville were quite aware of their close connection to the *Stark*.

SARAGOSA TORNADO

Tornadoes rare in stricken area, forecasters say

By CURTIS RIST
Staff Writer of The News

A violent tornado that ripped a half-mile swath through the town of Saragosa on Friday occurred in an area of Texas that meteorologists considered practically immune to twisters.

Although Texas has an average of 119 tornadoes a year—killing an average of 11 people—none has caused any serious damage in recent years west of the Pecos River, meteorologists said Saturday.

"I do not know when we had a killer tornado west of the Pecos River," said George Bomar, a climatologist for the Texas Water Commission who has written a book called *Texas Weather.* "It probably is the most protected area in terms of tornado occurrence."

But the ingredients for a deadly storm—warm, moist air from the Gulf of Mexico and cool, swift-moving air above it—converged Friday night in an unlikely area, forming a tremendous thunderstorm that from satellite photographs looked "like a huge marshmallow sticking out of the state of Texas," Bomar said.

This massive storm, which punched upward from the ground to a height of more than eight miles and stretched more than 30 miles wide, spawned a tornado of disastrous proportions, Bomar said.

Continued on following page

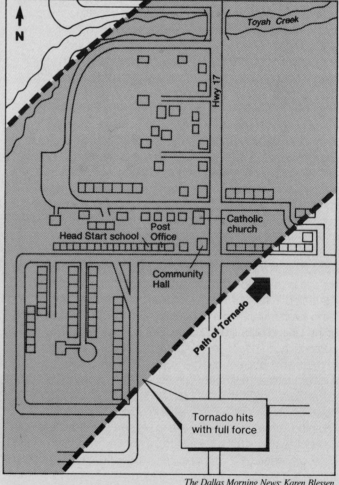

The Dallas Morning News

SARAGOSA: MOMENTS BEFORE DESTRUCTION

The Dallas Morning News: Karen Blessen

Continued from preceding page

"The fuel was there for a horrendous thunderstorm to happen, and that's exactly what happened," Bomar said. "This thing mushroomed like a nuclear explosion."

The thunderstorm that spawned the tornado began about 3 p.m. Friday, about 20 miles northeast of Balmorhea in Reeves County, said Constantine Pashos, a meteorologist with the National Weather Service in Midland. Most thunderstorms dissipate within an hour, but this one lingered and grew quickly in intensity.

At 7:54 p.m., the weather service issued a tornado warning, and less than 10 minutes later, two spotters reported seeing a "rotating wall cloud," a precursor to a tornado, about four miles west of Balmorhea, Pashos said.

Buddy McIntyre, a meteorologist with the National Weather Service in Fort Worth, said rotating storms become concentrated, and work their way down to the ground with wicked force. He compared the process to a twirling ice skater, who speeds up by pulling in his arms.

Of the 700 tornadoes that form each year in the United States, about 98 percent dissipate soon after they touch the ground. But meteorologists said the tornado that struck the West Texas town of Saragosa was characterized as a "violent" one, a term that indicates winds as high as 300 mph traveling in a swath up to a mile and a half wide.

A tornado of this magnitude moves along the ground an average distance of 26 miles, compared with an average of three to nine miles for lesser ones, McIntyre said.

The tornado that hit Saragosa touched ground at 8:16 p.m. Friday about 10 miles west of the town. Its circular winds skimmed along the ground eastward at about 30 mph, then hit with full force at Saragosa, about 15 miles northeast of Balmorhea, about 8:30 p.m., Pashos said. The thunderstorm turned northeast toward Midland and began to break up about 11 p.m., eight hours after it had formed.

McIntyre said a group of meteorologists with the weather service in Lubbock had converged on Saragosa, and were studying the tornado and ways to improve storm warnings. The warnings, he said, are sent by teletype to sheriff's departments, which then notify local police. He said the weather service also sends the warnings to radio and TV stations.

"They'll want to find out how people responded to the warning: Did they act on it, or did they ignore it?" McIntyre said. "There's always room for improvement."

Bomar said the warm, moist Gulf air —described by meteorologists as "fuel" for thunderstorms and tornadoes— normally flows to the north. But beginning early Friday morning, McIntyre said, the moist air unexpectedly took a turn up the Rio Grande, and flowed into West Texas.

"They don't see that kind of moisture out there very often," Bomar said.

The "line of demarcation" for tornado-prone areas, which normally runs east of Abilene and San Angelo, was pushed southwest into Mexico, Bomar said.

At the same time, a cooler high-level storm moved in from California over West Texas. It sucked up the warm, moist air from the Gulf, which caused condensation and released tremendous amounts of heat that "just fueled the storm more," Bomar said.

"This was one of the largest thunderstorms I've seen this year," he said.

The storm was the only one reported in the area at the time, which contributed to its severity, McIntyre said. Had other storms formed nearby, the amount of warm air flowing into one thunderhead would have been less, decreasing the chances of a violent and deadly tornado forming.

Staff writer Marice Richter contributed to this report.

INJURED IN TORNADO

This is a list of the 30 people still hospitalized Saturday evening in five medical facilities near Saragosa:

1. REEVES MEMORIAL HOSPITAL, Pecos (eight hospitalized, 81 treated and released):
- Tomas Martinez, 54, Saragosa, stable condition
- Roberta Natividad, 86, Pecos, stable
- Carlotta Nunez, 86, Pecos, stable
- Billy Gallegos (brother), 5, Pecos, stable
- Ringo Gallegos (brother), 8, Pecos, stable
- Adelia Lopez, 30, Saragosa, stable
- Octavio Muniz, 21, Saragosa, stable
- Olga Mendoza, 23, Balmorhea, stable

2. PECOS MEMORIAL HOSPITAL, Fort Stockton (four hospitalized, one treated and released):
- Richard Avalos, 5, Saragosa, stable
- Manuela Casillas, 11, Balmorhea, stable
- Leticia Martinez, 22, Saragosa, stable
- Corina Brijalba, 48, Balmorhea, serious condition with internal injuries

3. BREWSTER MEMORIAL HOSPITAL, Alpine (six hospitalized):
- Linda Briceno, 38, Saragosa, good
- Embur Briceno, 9 months, Saragosa, fair
- Amparo Gallego, 58, Saragosa, good
- Regina Gallego, 18, Saragosa, fair
- JoGina Gallego, 6 months, Saragosa, fair
- Belia Rodriguez, 50, Saragosa, fair

4. ODESSA MEDICAL CENTER, Odessa (11 hospitalized, five treated and released):
- Adrian Casias, 10, Saragosa, stable
- Lisa Carillo, 31, Saragosa, stable
- Raul Lopez, critical in intensive care unit
- Juana Bejurano, critical in intensive care unit
- Artia Hildago, undergoing surgery Saturday afternoon
- Dorothy Berdon, critical in intensive care unit
- Aurora Bricanico, 75, Saragosa, stable
- Murian Mondrheon, 17, Saragosa, stable
- Ramon Meneses, critical in intensive care unit
- Socorro Vasquez, 55, Pecos, stable
- Teresa Bejaro, 7, Saragosa, stable

5. WARD MEMORIAL HOSPITAL, Monahans (one hospitalized):
- Rachel Carrillo, 9, stable

The Dallas Morning News

Checking Your Comprehension

Read the following questions. Put an x in the box beside the answer that best completes each one.

1. The *Morning News* story states, "Of the 700 tornadoes that form each year in the United States, about 98 percent dissipate soon after they touch the ground." To *dissipate* is to
   - ☐ a. break up and disperse.
   - ☐ b. destroy and cause ruin.
   - ☐ c. distill.

2. The tornado struck in an area that was thought to be "practically immune to twisters." *Immune* means
   - ☐ a. subject to.
   - ☐ b. at ease with; familiar.
   - ☐ c. free from; not susceptible to.

3. All of the following are ingredients for a heavy storm like the one that converged on Saragosa on May 22, 1987, *except*
   - ☐ a. warm, moist air.
   - ☐ b. polluted air.
   - ☐ c. cool, swiftly moving air.

4. Each of the following people studies weather conditions and forecasts weather occurrences except a
   - ☐ a. geologist.
   - ☐ b. climatologist.
   - ☐ c. meteorologist.

5. A weather occurrence that would have helped decrease the chances for a violent tornado in Saragosa would have been
   - ☐ a. a tornado on the same day somewhere else in the world.
   - ☐ b. a series of smaller storms in nearby Texas locations.
   - ☐ c. more cool air coming into Texas from California.

6. The National Weather Service wants to find out if people actually responded to their warning in order to
   - ☐ a. improve the warning system.
   - ☐ b. see if the local police were to blame for so many deaths.
   - ☐ c. determine if their teletype was working.

☆　☆　☆

The *Dallas Morning News* story is not a typical front page disaster piece filled with quotes from witnesses, descriptions of fatal storm-related mishaps, and human-interest items. That was the report—in many places other than Texas—the day after the storm. But in the *week* following the storm, papers around the country moved on to other stories while the Texas paper continued to run news items on the tornado and its aftermath.

Some elements of the *Dallas Morning News* story emphasize the fact that the tornado was a local disaster.

Would anyone but local residents be served by a list of injured people and the hospitals they are in? Would the town map showing major buildings and roads interest people who do not know Saragosa? As we can see, the proximity of a news event to readers not only affects how long a newspaper continues to report a story, it affects what information the newspaper chooses to print as well.

Read the following story about a disaster that holds significance for the people of Jacksonville, Florida, despite the fact that it happened halfway around the world from them.

TUESDAY

May 19, 1987 — 4 Sections, 38 Pages

Vol. 100A, No 139 Copyright 1987 Florida Publishing Co.

FINAL EDITION

JACKSONVILLE Journal

B   25¢

Stark death toll rises to 37

U.S. wants answers on attack by 'trigger-happy' Iraqi pilot

WASHINGTON (AP)—The death toll climbed to 37 today in the missile attack on the USS Stark as White House Chief of Staff Howard Baker asked why a "trigger-happy" Iraqi pilot had launched a deadly missile into the Stark's crew quarters.

Defense Secretary Caspar Weinberger said the ship's 185 other crew members "are fine," but did not elaborate.

Baker, interviewed on the NBC-TV show *Today,* said, "I think we should understand that free transit on the high seas, and the Persian Gulf is international water, . . . is

Continued on following page

Continued from preceding page

absolutely essential to the vital interests of the United States and the free world.

"I would certainly like to know why a trigger-happy pilot decided to fire on the basis of radar signals, why there wasn't more identification."

He said the United States had listened in on radio communications from the Iraqi Mirage fighter that launched the missile against the U.S. frigate in the Persian Gulf. Baker did not elaborate.

Weinberger, testifying before a Senate Appropriations subcommittee, said the ship was carrying a total of 222 officers and sailors when it was attacked by a single missile Sunday.

Of the 37 dead, he said, 24 have been identified and their families notified. The remaining 13 have not been identified. A Pentagon spokesman said earlier that 15 sailors had been washed overboard or were still trapped in the wreckage.

Weinberger did not elaborate on the condition of the survivors, beyond saying they "are fine."

He also said a board of inquiry has been convened and will arrive tomorrow in Bahrain, where the Stark is expected to arrive under tow later today.

The secretary said one Exocet missile was launched from 12 miles away, giving the Stark 60 to 80 seconds to respond with its defensive weapons.

But Weinberger noted that the missile defenses were not used and added, "We do not know why. . . . The most likely explanation, it seems to me, is that there was no reason to believe an Iraqi plane would attack."

On the Senate floor, meanwhile, Minority Leader Bob Dole, R-Kan., said, "we need to rethink exactly what it is we are doing in the Persian Gulf. What are our goals? What is our strategy? What are the risks? And how much cost are we willing to pay?"

But the first need, he said, is "to find out why this ship—equipped with some of our most modern and effective defensive weaponry—was not able to, or just did not, use any of it to defend itself."

Appearing earlier on ABC-TV's *Good Morning America,* Weinberger said it was impossible to prejudge why the ship's captain did not respond to the attack.

He also disputed an explanation by the Iraqi ambassador to the United States, Nizar Hamdoon, that Iraqi warplanes had

JOHN PEMBERTON/staff

Londie Rhoden completes a sign at the Homestead Restaurant in Jacksonville Beach that expresses the area's sentiments after the attack on the *Stark.*

targeted a suspected Iranian ship 20 miles from the Stark.

"I think he was aiming at that ship," Weinberger said. "I think the real situation is he did not know it was an American ship. And that's why, as I've called it, it was a ghastly error on his part."

Iraqi warplanes hit another ship 40 to 60 miles away from the Stark earlier in the day and missed another one in roughly that same area, Weinberger said.

The Pentagon said yesterday that most of the sailors who died had been trapped by intense fire in one compartment.

As a result of the Iraqi missile attack, President Reagan upgraded the alert status and warned both Iran and Iraq their jets will be shot down if they threaten other U.S. ships.

Reagan's response was coupled with a demand that Iraqi president Saddam Hussein's government immediately explain, apologize and compensate the victims' families and the U.S. Navy.

Hussein, in a letter to Reagan delivered to the State Department yesterday, expressed "deepest regret over the painful incident." Presidential spokesman Marlin Fitzwater said: "We feel it does represent an apology. It does not address the matter of compensation."

The White House and Pentagon said the attack was inadvertent and unexplained.

It was the first attack on a U.S. warship in the gulf since U.S. ships began operating in the area in 1949, and the deadliest attack on shipping of the seven-year-old Iran-Iraq war. The war has posed a constant threat to commerce in the oil-rich gulf.

The Stark, a 453-foot guided-missile frigate, was being towed by the USS Conyngham, as firefighters continued to battle stubborn fires around a 10-to-15-foot hole in its port side.

A top Pentagon officer said the Stark would likely be able to return to the United States under its own power after temporary repairs.

The initial response in Congress was subdued, while Reagan himself held to a schedule calling for a flight to Chattanooga, Tenn., today to deliver a high school commencement address. He expressed "concern and anger" over the attack and met for nearly two hours with his national security advisers.

Reagan and top Pentagon officers promised a full investigation of the attack.

"We're not treating it lightly," Weinberger said yesterday. "We're not treating it as a mere accident." But he added, "We

Continued on following page

Continued from preceding page
have no evidence to indicate that it was anything other than an accident, a ghastly accident."

Weinberger said U.S. ships would remain in the area. "They should be there because these are international waters, and we cannot be driven out of international waters by anyone," he said.

Iranian Prime Minister Hussein Musavi, in a radio broadcast monitored in Cyprus, said the gulf is not a safe place for the superpowers and said about the attack on the U.S. ship, "The great Satan has been trapped."

Fitzwater said Iran and Iraq, the two belligerents, had been officially notified of the "higher state of alert for U.S. vessels in the area."

Fitzwater's statement also warned the two sides that "aircraft of either country flying in a pattern which indicates hostile intent will be fired upon unless they provide adequate notification of their intentions."

Earlier, the United States registered bitter protests with Iraqi diplomats here and in Baghdad and swept aside an early Iraqi claim that perhaps another nation had struck the American guided missile frigate.

The attack jolted a diplomatic campaign by the administration to repair relations with Baghdad after secret U.S. weapons purchases by Iran.

But the American objectives—an end to the gulf war and promoting Arab-Israeli peace talks—remain in place.

"Those basic interests are still there," State Department spokesman Charles E. Redman said.

He said the United States would continue discussions with Kuwait about putting an American flag and an American captain on some of the country's tankers for protection. This followed an offer to escort ships to Kuwait, which is situated in the head of the gulf and has sustained at least 16 attacks by Iranian planes.

Iran has launched 20 attacks this year on ships in the gulf, hoping to frighten off countries that have assisted Iraq in their war.

"I think it happens in every air force in the world, in every army in the world, that mistakes do happen," he said, expressing condolences to the families of those killed.

U.S. officials also quickly attributed the missile strike to inadvertence or accident, while acknowledging they were not certain what happened.

"I don't know all of the reasons," presidential spokesman Fitzwater said, "except for we believe it was inadvertent. We know no motive for this kind of action."

Similarly, Air Force Lt. Gen. Richard Burpee, director of operations for the Joint Chiefs of Staff, said, "We have no reason to believe there was hostile intent."

The frigate, part of a U.S. naval task force in the gulf, was hit by one or two French-made Exocet missiles while on routine patrol about 85 miles northeast of Bahrain.

The U.S. ambassador to Bahrain, Sam Zakhem, and marine salvage representatives in the gulf area said two Exocets struck when the frigate was 45 miles northeast of the emirate of Qatar,

Continued on following page

Associated Press

The USS *Stark* limps toward the port of Bahrain in the Persian Gulf with the missile damage on the hull forward of the bridge.

Continued from preceding page
punching two holes in the port side and starting a huge fire.

Two of the wounded who had suffered burns were expected to remain at the military hospital in Wiesbaden, West Germany, for several days before being transferred to the Brook Army Medical Center in Texas, a spokesman said.

On Capitol Hill, meanwhile, the administration sent Richard Murphy, assistant secretary of state for Near Eastern affairs, to brief the Senate Foreign Relations Committee today on the military measures ordered by the White House.

Murphy had just completed a visit to Iraq, partly to explain the surreptitious U.S. weapons deal with Iran but primarily to extend assurances that the United States intends to protect oil shipments through the Strait of Hormuz.

Checking Your Comprehension

Read the following questions. Put an x in the box beside the answer that best completes each one.

1. Defense Secretary Caspar Weinberger called the attack a "ghastly error." *Ghastly* means
   - ☐ a. ghostly.
   - ☐ b. horrible.
   - ☐ c. cowardly.

2. Marlin Fitzwater said, "Iran and Iraq, the two belligerents, had been officially notified of the higher state of alert for U.S. vessels in the area." By *belligerents*, Fitzwater means
   - ☐ a. those waging war.
   - ☐ b. neighbors.
   - ☐ c. competitors.

3. The subhead under the main headline features a quote from
   - ☐ a. the Defense Secretary.
   - ☐ b. the White House Chief of Staff.
   - ☐ c. a Pentagon spokesman.

4. When the story was written, it was believed that most of the sailors who died had
   - ☐ a. tried to escape in lifeboats.
   - ☐ b. been hit directly with the missile.
   - ☐ c. been trapped by fire in one compartment.

5. When this May 19 front page article appeared in the *Jacksonville Journal,* only twenty-four families had been notified even though thirty-seven sailors were known dead. That was because
   - ☐ a. thirteen bodies had not yet been identified.
   - ☐ b. the State Department had not yet been able to reach the other thirteen families.
   - ☐ c. they couldn't find the bodies of those washed overboard.

6. According to the State Department officials, American ships are in the Persian Gulf area for all of the following reasons except that
   - ☐ a. these are international waters.
   - ☐ b. the Iran-Iraq war is a constant threat to oil commerce.
   - ☐ c. they are secretly taking weapons to Iran.

☆ ☆ ☆

Proximity has to do with more than physical distance. A tornado in a Texas town is naturally the main concern of local residents and just as naturally becomes the major story in the local newspaper. But for the people of Jacksonville, Florida, proximity was a mental and emotional phenomenon. Because their town was the home of the USS *Stark,* the attack on the ship touched their lives directly—family members, loved ones, and friends were in danger. That made the reports as urgent, if delayed, as if the attack had happened in the Gulf of Mexico or off the east coast of Florida. The editors of the newspaper, aware of the pressing local impact of the news reports, gave the *Stark* story top priority for a longer time than did editors at other papers in other places.

☆ ☆ ☆

Recognizing Cause and Effect

It is not uncommon for a reporter to use a cause-and-effect writing pattern to emphasize key points in a news story. Such a pattern is apparent in each of the stories you have read in this lesson.

In the tornado story, the writer draws attention to the causes of the storm. In the *Stark* story, the reporter places emphasis on the effects of the Iraqi missile attack. Listed on the next page are statements from both stories. For the tornado story, the tornado's effect is given, followed by statements that may or may not express what caused the storm. In the space provided, write *cause* before each statement that expresses a cause.

For the *Stark* story, the cause of the disaster is given, followed by statements that may or may not express effects of the attack. In the space provided, write *effect* before each statement that expresses an effect.

Saragosa Tornado

Effect: A violent tornado ripped a swath through the town of Saragosa on Friday.

_____ 1. The thunderstorm lingered and grew in intensity.

_____ 2. Texas has an average of 119 tornadoes a year.

_____ 3. Warm, moist air and cool, swiftly moving air converged.

_____ 4. Circular winds hit full force in Saragosa.

_____ 5. People ignored the warning from Lubbock, Texas.

_____ 6. This was the only storm in the area.

Stark Missile Attack

Cause: An Iraqi pilot launched a deadly missile into the U.S. Navy frigate *Stark*.

_____ 1. Thirty-seven crew members of the *Stark* were killed.

_____ 2. A board of inquiry was sent from the State Department to Bahrain to investigate the tragedy.

_____ 3. America hopes to end the Gulf War and to promote Arab-Israeli talks.

_____ 4. President Reagan upgraded the alert status of all U.S. boats in the Persian Gulf.

_____ 5. The President received a letter of apology from Iraqi President Saddam Hussein.

_____ 6. Iran and Iraq have been at war for seven years.

Using Your Newspaper

Survey your newspaper for a week or more for a collection of stories about disastrous events from a variety of places. Look for everything from extensive front page stories to more modest reports inside the paper to single paragraph accounts buried in the paper's back pages. (In many newspapers, single paragraphs describing far-off events are to be found in a special section with a title like "News Around the World" or "World News at a Glance.")

The purpose of the survey is to see how your paper treats disastrous events that have varying degrees of proximity to your area. A full-scale disaster in your town or the next town is obviously going to merit front page attention. The same goes for a national disaster like the explosion of the space shuttle Challenger. But what about, say, a major fire two states away? Would that be reported on the front page or the inside pages? Perhaps it would be reported in a brief summary in the news section's back pages. Or, if the day of the fire was a busy news day in your locale, your newspaper might not report it at all.

Cut the stories out of the newspaper and staple a blank sheet of paper to each one. On the sheet of paper, list the proximity considerations that you think caused the editors of the newspaper to place the story where they did. For a front page story you might write, "This story was on the front page because it tells of a plastics plant on the outskirts of town that exploded, injuring ten local residents." Or, "This single paragraph was placed on page eleven. It recounts a bus accident in India that killed forty people. It might not have made the paper at all except for the fact that three of those killed were Americans and two were Canadians."

You might also want to indicate which stories interest you more. Do you find yourself less caught up in events that occurred at some distance than those that happened in your own area?

Many newspapers carry a daily column that serves up tidbits on the doings of famous people. The short news items offered in such sections often deal with an insignificant episode in the daily life of a celebrity. Readers who care about such things—and there are many—can learn that Princess Di has bought six new hats or that Madonna has been seen having lunch with Michael Jackson. Celebrity items like those attract a lot of newspaper buyers.

But not all famous people appear in the newspaper simply because they have a name or a face that attracts readers. Many people who are names in the news are involved in newsworthy activities that are meaningful. These activities will not be reported in the daily column. They will be reported as feature stories or even as straight news stories. Perhaps the ultimate example of such an activity is the chock-full-of-celebrities Live Aid concert intended to help feed Africa's hungry. For the newspaper, such stories are a blessing, because they have substance *and* the allure of celebrity.

Read the story from the *Atlanta Constitution Journal* that follows. Is the well-known subject of the story doing something newsworthy, or was the story printed mainly because she is considered a famous person with reader appeal?

Tempestt Bledsoe of 'Cosby' raising awareness about food

By GERRY YANDEL
Staff Writer

It was somewhat ironic that Tempestt Bledsoe was applying makeup before her interview. As Vanessa Huxtable on tonight's episode of "The Cosby Show," that's exactly what she gets in trouble for doing.

But the 13-year-old wasn't in Atlanta this week to talk about makeup or the television series. She was here to address the "unfit generation"—America's teenagers.

Tempestt made an early morning appearance at Northside High School to talk about nutrition on behalf of the California Raisin Advisory Board and the President's Council on Physical Fitness and Sports.

As Vanessa, Tempestt is often in the midst of sibling frays—but she gets a lot of laughs. On the fitness tour without her writers, however, she is given to talk peppered with puns about raisins—as in "raisin people's awareness"—which get a lot of groans.

After stressing the virtues of vegetables —her favorite is broccoli—and the evils of fast foods, Tempestt led a group of students and teachers in a stretching and exercise demonstration.

"We are fatter, weaker and slower," she told the students. "Most of us think physical fitness is hopping in the car and going to McDonald's."

Tempestt only recently discovered the joy of sweat herself, but she now can run a mile in 9½ minutes and has an honorary Presidential Physical Fitness Patch of her own. She failed the pullup test because she practiced it with an underhand grasp and had to take the test with an overhand grasp, which she said was much more difficult.

When she isn't pushing push-ups, Tempestt works with Bill Cosby on television's No. 1 rated prime-time show. "Bill is wonderful. He's very easy to work with," Tempestt said. "And he also finds time to exercise."

Cosby taught Tempestt a lot about acting and how to be serious about it. "He told me, 'Be proud of what you do, and don't do anything you wouldn't enjoy watching yourself,' " she said.

The rest of the Cosby kids are also "wonderful," Tempestt said—just like a real family. "We all meet up with each other sometimes if we're both doing the same things," she said. "We might go play cards or something, or go outside and run or whatever."

Tempestt got her start on the small screen singing jingles for commercials, such as Applejacks and Good 'n' Plenty, and modeling. She also will star, with Della Reese, as a 17-year-old member of a gospel singing family on an upcoming ABC Afterschool Special titled "Amazing Grace." Ms. Reese also offered professional

Continued on following page

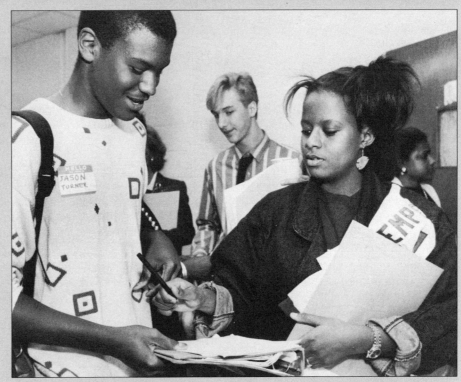

Tempestt Bledsoe gives Jason Turner her autograph at Northside High School.

Continued from preceding page
advice to the young actress. "She told me, 'Be nice to your fans, don't lose yourself and don't do anything you won't be proud of because it will always come back,' " Tempestt said.

Besides acting on television, Tempestt also watches it. "Moonlighting" is her personal favorite, besides, of course, "Cosby." "I think David Addison is *the most . . . the ultimate*—gorgeous, funny, hilarious," she said. "And I love 'L.A. Law.' That show is a *stone trip.*"

Tempestt is the youngest of three children and travels with her mother, Willa, while her father, Keith, is in Chicago. One brother, James, is a television writer in Los Angeles and her other brother, Wayne, lives in Colorado.

She is tutored by teachers from Manhattan's Professional Children's School on the set of "The Cosby Show," which is taped in Brooklyn, and she also has a full day of school on Friday, her day off.

In her off time, she said, "I read a lot, write poetry, write short stories, and, um, read a lot." She recently had an essay about children and cartoon violence published in a teachers' trade newsletter.

Checking Your Comprehension

Read the following questions. Put an *x* in the box beside the answer that best completes each one.

1. The story begins by saying that it was "somewhat ironic that Tempestt Bledsoe was applying makeup." The word *ironic* is used to mean
   - ☐ a. irritating and deliberately confounding.
   - ☐ b. inconsistent with expected actions.
   - ☐ c. silly.

2. The reporter says Tempestt is "given to talk peppered with puns about raisins." A *pun* is
   - ☐ a. a play on words.
   - ☐ b. an exaggeration.
   - ☐ c. a riddle.

3. Tempestt says America's teenagers are called unfit because they are all of the following, compared to teens in other countries, except
   - ☐ a. fatter.
   - ☐ b. weaker.
   - ☐ c. more tired.

4. Tempestt Bledsoe is a name in the news because of her recognition as a TV personality. Until recently she had done all of the following except
   - ☐ a. singing jingles for Applejacks and Good 'n' Plenty ads.
   - ☐ b. performing as one of the kids on "The Cosby Show."
   - ☐ c. taking part in the Presidential Physical Fitness Program.

5. Tempestt used the word *raisin* in her pun because
   - ☐ a. raisins are her favorite snack.
   - ☐ b. one of the sponsors of her tour is the California Raisin Association.
   - ☐ c. raisins are an important part of any nutritious diet.

6. The reporter says the joy of sweat was only recently discovered by Ms. Bledsoe. The reporter means that
   - ☐ a. Tempestt herself is new to exercise.
   - ☐ b. in addition to her role on TV, Tempestt likes to wear and sell sweatpants and exercise tops.
   - ☐ c. Tempestt was the first thirteen-year-old to wear the honorary patch of the Presidential Commission on Physical Fitness.

☆ ☆ ☆

Famous names make news because some readers enjoy hearing every scrap of information about the lives of important people, especially those in government, entertainment, and sports. On many newspapers, certain reporters are assigned to write about the current celebrities in each of those areas.

The writer of the *Atlanta Constitution Journal* story followed Tempestt Bledsoe to Northside High School to hear her talk about nutrition and fitness for young people. Tempestt was no doubt selected as spokesperson for the California Raisin Advisory Board and the President's Council on Physical Fitness and Sports because she holds appeal for teens, and teens were targeted for the fitness message. The newspaper, in turn, carried the story of her talk because she is a famous person who was visiting town. Such a story might pull in readers who are "Cosby" fans or who are interested in famous people in general.

Now read the following story from *USA TODAY* about a young member of what is arguably the best-known political family in the United States. Try to decide why Ted Kennedy, Jr. qualifies as a name in the news.

☆ ☆ ☆

CANCER and COURAGE
TV film tells of triumph amid tragedy

'When you're 12, you don't think about death and dying,' says Ted Jr.

By GREGORY KATZ
USA TODAY

By GREGORY KATZ
USA TODAY

Ted Kennedy Jr. was just a kid in 1973—a scared, 12-year-old kid whose leg problems were diagnosed as bone cancer.

Sen. Edward Kennedy, D-Mass., broke the bad news, telling his son the diseased right leg would have to be removed. Even after amputation, there was an 80 percent chance the cancer would spread to Kennedy's lungs—and kill him.

The crisis came at a terrible moment. His mother, Joan, was drinking heavily and her marriage to Sen. Kennedy was coming apart.

But Kennedy pulled through. Now 25, he's a man with a message. He's cooperated with producers of a TV movie—Monday on NBC—about his triumph. His goal is to change the way disabled people are viewed.

"Losing a leg is not a tragedy," he said. "The tragedy is that when people come back into society, it's often a hostile and cold place to live because of peoples' misconceptions."

The vigorous, athletic young man with the broad, Irish smile and the "stay tough, don't let it defeat you" attitude believes the movie will give him a forum to talk about the handicapped. He's written a cover story for Sunday's *Parade* magazine about their need for independence.

"I really wasn't that crazy about the idea of making a movie," said Kennedy, who walks with a slight limp and has some trouble climbing stairs. "I didn't want to put my family through it, but I felt it would give me a chance to speak about these issues."

To be realistic, the movie had to deal

PROUD PAPA: Says Ted Sr. of Ted Jr., 'He's taken adversity and turned it back.'

with his parents' problems. Kennedy said he and his parents agreed they had nothing to fear from an accurate portrayal.

"It's no mystery to anybody that my parents took two different directions in their lives and that my mother was drinking heavily," said Kennedy. "But there's no family in America that hasn't been touched either by drugs or alcohol or cancer. We weren't hiding anything."

Sen. Kennedy acknowledges that his prominence and wealth helped him get the finest medical care for his son. But nothing could shield the boy from trauma.

"When you're 12, you don't think about death and dying, you think about wanting to do the things you've always done," Kennedy said. "I had moments of self-pity, of 'Why did it have to happen to me?' Times when I felt lousy about wearing this wooden leg. But I tried to concentrate on the things I could still do."

His father remembers the crisis as a time of turmoil.

"I was full of crashing emotions," said Sen. Kennedy. "Anger, frustration, hope, bitterness, hostility and an outpouring of love. Determination that nothing's going to happen to him. You get some good news but it's tentative. The early tests look good but you can't be sure. There's never a time when you're sure."

After doctors told Sen. Kennedy his son's leg needed to be amputated, he waited a few days to tell his boy. "There's no easy way, but the words have to come. It takes time, it creates a climate where there's perhaps some acceptance, he sort of knows it and senses it before you tell him, but he doesn't believe it."

The amputation was followed by experimental chemotherapy to keep the cancer from spreading—and months of

Continued on following page

UNIT ONE/LESSON 2   **23**

Continued from preceding page

physical rehabilitation. "Teddy was very courageous and very cheerful," said Dr. Emil Frei III, chief physician at the Dana Farber Cancer Institute in Boston, who set up the treatment. "His mental outlook and positive outlook were important—he's indeed a role model."

Kennedy's chemotherapy regimen, said Frei, "has raised the survival rate (of that type of bone cancer) from 20 percent to 60-70 percent. It was an important advance."

Kennedy's full-time job today: using his Boston-based foundation, *Facing the Challenge,* to push for better enforcement of laws providing jobs and access for the handicapped. He speaks for a sizable group: 36 million people in the USA suffer physical or mental disabilities, according to the President's Committee on Employment of the Handicapped.

"Teddy's role in our movement is to raise consciousness," said Mary Jane Owen, a blind woman who directs Disability Focus, an advocacy group in Washington, D.C.

"He knows what it's like to have a body that has revealed its vulnerability. He can sit down and joke with a mentally retarded adult and treat her with respect and not be patronizing. There are very few people who have the wit and sensitivity to be able to do that."

Kennedy also skis and sails to demonstrate that a one-legged person can pursue excellence. He races sailboats off Cape Cod and—aided by special ski poles with runners on the bottom—races with the National Disabled Ski Team.

"People with disabilities live in a slow motion world and you have to get used to that," he said. "But skiing unlocks the cage. I ski downhill at 65 miles per hour. When I ski, I'm not impaired. I'm not slow at all. It's freedom, it's liberty."

Sailing and skiing are liberating for a man who remembers the agony of watching his buddies play sports he could no longer handle.

Today Sen. Kennedy beams at his son's accomplishments. "He's taken adversity and turned it back, and that's a central challenge of everyone's life."

Since graduating from Wesleyan University two years ago—he majored in history and literature—Kennedy has lived in Boston near his mother. Older sister Kara just moved into the neighborhood from New York; younger brother Patrick is away in prep school.

Besides his foundation work, Ted Jr. has toured famine areas in Africa and testified on Capitol Hill.

As he matures, he looks more and more like his father. The two have an easy friendship, kissing each other on the cheek as a greeting and working out and swimming together when they're in the same city. But Kennedy's not sure whether he'll follow his dad into politics.

"I've come to really believe that you don't have to run for office to make a difference," he said. "Look at my Aunt Jean (Kennedy Smith) who runs arts programs for kids with disabilities, or my Aunt Eunice (Shriver), who runs the Special Olympics. Look how many lives she's touched."

His cousin, Rep.-elect Joe Kennedy, this month won the seat left vacant by retiring house Speaker Thomas P. O'Neill. Before Joe announced, there were widespread reports that Ted Jr. would run.

"I was flattered by the speculation, and there were a number of people trying to convince me to do it," said Kennedy. "But you listen to 100 different people, then decide for yourself, and my decision was clear. It's no surprise that I'm interested in politics. Am I going to be actively involved in things during my lifetime? The answer is yes."

That sounds good to Owen, who hopes Kennedy's involvement leads him to run for Congress.

"I think he needs time to mature. He's still a very young man with a lot to learn," she said. "But what impresses me is how open he is to other people and how interested he is in other peoples' experiences and how relaxed he is. He can help a lot."

Asked what he would tell young people disabled by cancer, Kennedy replied:

"I'd tell them, 'Listen, life is not fair. But the fact is, there are so many people who are worse off. Just take it, stay tough, and don't let it defeat you.' "

Checking Your Comprehension

Read the following questions. Put an *x* in the box beside the answer that best completes each one.

1. Senator Kennedy recognizes that what the reporter calls his "prominence and wealth" enabled him to obtain the best medical care for his son. *Prominence* is
   ☐ a. the state of being widely known.
   ☐ b. seriousness.
   ☐ c. the quality of being influential in politics.

2. Mary Jane Owen says that the younger Kennedy "knows what it's like to have a body that has revealed its vulnerability." The word *vulnerability* means
   ☐ a. virility.
   ☐ b. openness to attack or injury.
   ☐ c. sensitivity to the needs of others.

3. Kennedy's Boston-based foundation, *Facing the Challenge,* helps handicapped people by
   ☐ a. working for better laws.
   ☐ b. giving them money for treatment and housing.
   ☐ c. sponsoring the Special Olympics.

4. The story says Kennedy enjoys skiing and sailing for the following reasons except that
   ☐ a. he feels liberated.
   ☐ b. he likes to win medals and trophies.
   ☐ c. he's not slow when he skis.

5. Kennedy's major reason for supporting the idea of a movie about his triumph over cancer is that he
   □ a. feels that people should know the truth about his parents' problems.
   □ b. sees it as a vehicle to change society's negative view of disabled people.
   □ c. hopes to run for political office.

6. Eunice Shriver and Jean Kennedy Smith are mentioned in this article because they
   □ a. are close family members.
   □ b. have also worked for the disabled.
   □ c. will also be in the TV film.

☆ ☆ ☆

Tempestt Bledsoe and Ted Kennedy, Jr. are both names in the news. Bledsoe's recognition stems from her role on Bill Cosby's successful television show. Kennedy's comes with being a member of a high-profile American family. Each is in the newspaper for an additional reason, Bledsoe because she is speaking on health and fitness, Kennedy because he has overcome a disability and the story of his personal victory is being made into a TV movie.

To most people, the activities of Bledsoe and Kennedy would seem laudable and newsworthy—they make for good, even inspiring, news stories. Be that as it may, those stories probably would not have been reported if both had not been well known in the first place. For example, if an unrenowned teenager gave a speech promoting health and fitness, would that speech make the paper? Likewise, how many disabled people who are not well known have the story of their struggle filmed and televised? Bledsoe and Kennedy visibly represent two groups, the young and the disabled, because their names attract and hold attention. And that is precisely why they are in the newspaper.

☆ ☆ ☆

Recognizing Supporting Details in News Stories

Each of the stories you have just read focuses on a name in the news, a person who is written about because many readers recognize the name. Tempestt Bledsoe is recognized primarily as a TV personality. Ted Kennedy, Jr. is known because his whole family is known.

Reread each story to find four details that support each person's name-in-the-news status. Then, in the spaces provided, use those details to complete the sentences given below. Use details other than, in Bledsoe's case, her weekly TV show, and in Kennedy's case, the television movie about his triumph over bone cancer. Begin with the sentence describing Tempestt Bledsoe. Then complete the sentence describing Ted Kennedy, Jr.

Tempestt Bledsoe is a name in the news who

1. _____

2. _____

3. _____

4. _____

Ted Kennedy, Jr. is a name in the news who

1. _____

2. _____

3. _____

4. _____

Using Your Newspaper

Survey your newspaper for a week. Collect stories on people who qualify as names in the news, people who are known for something in public life.

When you have collected a week's worth of stories, organize them into two groups. The first group should be stories that are about a famous person doing what he or she is famous for. A story on a singer giving a concert will belong in this category. The second group of stories will be those that are about a famous person doing something *other than* what he or she is famous for. A story about a major league baseball player visiting children in a hospital would belong in this category, as would the story on Tempestt Bledsoe.

Which group has the most stories?

Practicing Newspaper Skills

The *Boston Globe* runs a daily column called "Names and Faces" that presents brief stories on people in the public eye. Many other major dailies feature similar columns. There are also two magazines, *Us* and *People,* that are devoted entirely to stories about public personalities. The celebrity business, in other words, is thriving. Here are two examples from the *Globe*'s "Names and Faces":

Defaming the realm?

■ Lurid headlines yesterday blared forth allegations of further friction in the marriage of **Prince Charles** and **Princess Diana**, but a backlash is beginning, with critics of the rumor-mongers saying the two are victims of a boorish battle for readers. "Some newspapers . . . devote more and more space to fantasies willfully invented by themselves, many concerning the royal family," editorialized the Daily Telegraph. "Constant media mauling of their relationship must become close to intolerable." **Harold Brooks-Baker,** senior editor of Burke's Peerage, the British aristocracy guide, said: "The tabloids made this marriage into the romance of the century, which it wasn't. Now they or their readers are tired of it so they're trying to do the opposite."

Roots of rock

■ *Dick Clark,* host of television's "American Bandstand" for three decades, won a spot on the Walk of Fame of music yesterday in the city where the show began introducing music talent and dances to the nation. The Philadelphia Music Foundation unveiled a bronze plaque on the Walk of Fame outside the Academy of

Dick Clark

Music, where **Frankie Avalon** and **Chubby Checker** joined Clark. Clark took over as host of the local "Bandstand" show in 1956, the next year selling the idea to ABC for "American Bandstand."

Using these stories as models, create a small names-and-faces column geared to a teenage readership. Begin by selecting three stars of stage, screen, music, or sports who interest teens. Then research all three people. You might want to check the *World Almanac* for birthdates and other vital facts, and the *Readers' Guide to Periodical Literature* for information on background stories. Then check newspapers, magazines, and television for an up-to-date story that would serve you well in your column. An upcoming marriage, a baby on the way, an honorary degree, an industry award—all would make good, brief stories.

Limit each story to no more than 130 words. An account that abbreviated must of necessity be densely written. You must get to the point quickly—in the first sentence—and each description must be something that is necessary to the story. Your background research may not mean much in the way of a word count, but the facts should show through just the same. Look again, for instance, at the Dick Clark paragraph above. Every sentence is jam-packed with facts. Try to make your brief paragraphs convey as much information.

Write a catchy blurb for each story and assemble them in an imitation of a newspaper column. If you can find pictures in magazines, paste them near the stories they accompany. Give your names-and-faces column a title of your own.

When the Statue of Liberty turned one hundred years old in 1986, newspapers across the United States ran front page stories describing local celebrations as well as the major birthday party in New York City. In addition, many newspapers carried related stories on the immigration process and the variety of immigrant groups who have settled in the United States.

The Liberty celebration was a big story for a couple of weeks, and the immigration pieces were the latest chapters in a continuing American story. News stories on either subject were compelling, then, because of their recency— people like knowing about what is current.

The first story in this lesson is an immigration piece from the *Boston Globe*. The second is an editorial from *USA TODAY* on the Liberty celebration. Both stories were written to ride the wave of interest in the Statue of Liberty and the freedom the statue represents.

Liberty at 100: Changing faces of immigration

Shifts in a continuous thread

First in a three-part Sunday series, on the occasion of the 100th anniversary of the Statue of Liberty, that will consider the past and future of immigration to America.

By SUSAN TRAUSCH
Globe Staff

LIBERTY AT 100

AMERICA EVOLVING

Immigrants raise their right hands as they take an oath during a naturalization ceremony at a U.S. District Court in Brooklyn, less than a mile from Ellis Island.

LOS ANGELES—It was the immigrant experience in microcosm: Dino Hirsch, a German Jew with an Italian first name, sat in a Central American refugee center in west Los Angeles speaking rapid-fire Spanish to a man from El Salvador.

Where else but in America?

The year was 1986 but the feelings in that small, messy office with the second-hand furniture were as old as the country itself.

Hirsch, 73, a counselor at the center, had escaped Nazi Germany, had spent time in an Italian concentration camp, and had come to the United States through Ellis Island in 1941. He got his first view of the United States from the deck of a crowded ship, leaning against a railing as fellow passengers pressed forward to see the Statue of Liberty rising above the waves in New York Harbor.

The Salvadoran refugee, who was in his late 20s and wished to be known only as "Elias," had fled his country and slipped over the Mexican border into California last March after three members of his family had been killed by government troops.

He had come by himself, paying off the "coyotes" who feed on the illegal immigrant trade. He had pushed through the honky-tonk of Tijuana, kept to the shadows, dodged the US border patrol, and got his first view of the American dream in the form of a cityscape rising above the edge of a field as he walked to San Diego.

The two men were generations apart, cultures apart and yet the same. One was "an American," and the other was "a foreigner," but the American had been a foreigner once, and the foreigner would, legally or illegally, most likely become an American, learning the language, raising his children on US television programs, mixing the strict patriarchal family values of his homeland with L.A. punk, eating the old-country bean and rice dishes along with the Big Macs and washing them down with Pepsi.

The two men looked at each other with understanding eyes, although one has been completely assimilated into his adopted country and the other stands warily

Continued on following page

Manhattan, as seen from Ellis Island

Immigrants wait to become U.S. citizens.

Continued from preceding page

on the ragged edges of a new life. Hirsch got his foothold in the tight little streets of 1940s Manhattan in the Big Band Era, while Elias was grappling with the wide-open freeway life of rock video 1980s Los Angeles—a city dubbed "the new Ellis Island" because of the thousands of people pouring into it every year. (During one week last November, 39,000 people were naturalized in ceremonies at the Los Angeles Convention Center.)

The older man and the younger man, separated by nearly 50 years, leaned forward intently as they spoke across the decades, knowing instinctively that they were part of a continuous thread. They were immigrants. They had made the journey. They had gathered as many belongings together as they could carry, closed the door on the place they had called home, and walked away to start a new life somewhere else.

A constant quest

Whether the year is 1986, 1941, 1910 or 1840, the central emotional core of such a trip remains constant. Society changes, the political climate changes, the world hot spots change, the accents of the newcomers change, the ports of entry change, the academics argue about the economic effects and the demographics, the government wrangles back and forth about quotas and laws, but the basic human experience is the same—people travel to America to find something better.

It started with the Pilgrims and hasn't stopped. Immigration officials say the country is undergoing its biggest wave of entrants since the decade of 1900 to 1910 when a record eight million plus people came into the United States. In the 1980s, seven million immigrants are expected to enter, and that doesn't count the illegal aliens coming over the borders. The United States, hated in many parts of the world, targeted by terrorists, often disillusioned about itself, still beckons to the masses. My grandparents made the journey and maybe yours did too. Maybe your parents paid the $10 to get a place in steerage and maybe you went with them, rocking with the waves for 14 days as Peter DiFoggio did, although he was one of the few passengers who didn't get seasick.

"I remember all these people puking their guts out," said DiFoggio, who came from Italy with his mother in 1920 when he was 6 years old. He is a retired quality control engineer who is now in the nursing home business and lives in Newtonville.

"I saw this huge structure rising up out of the water," recalled DiFoggio. "My mother told me it was the Statue of Liberty and explained that it meant we had freedom and were welcome. I remember that made a hell of an impression on me."

Next month the country will remember its various impressions of that statue in a July Fourth Liberty Weekend celebration in New York City, held to mark the newly renovated statue's 100th anniversary.

It will be a time of political speeches, emotional reactions, family gatherings and reflections on the country's roots. It will also be a time for thinking about the present and the future of the unique American experiment that has been built by a nation of immigrants.

Still a melting pot?

Is the melting pot still the melting pot? Although the experts argue the ins and outs of that one, immigrants themselves present a continuing saga. Interviews with people who came through Ellis Island from Germany, Italy, Poland or Ireland strike similar themes with those who have recently left Vietnam in a crowded boat or who have landed at airports from China, or who have crossed the border at night from Mexico.

They talk of not knowing the language, of the difficulty of getting used to new foods, of seeking out a community of their own in a strange city street, of feeling the prejudice often directed against newcomers, of missing home, and of their hopes, dreams, fears and courage.

"I was afraid," said Victoria Sarfatti Fernandez, 74, of Chicago, who left Macedonia in 1916, crossed the Mediterranean Sea to Italy and came to the United States. "I remember hiding in the bottom of the ship. There was so much water everywhere."

Seventy years later, in the Phuoc Chau jewelry store in Westminster, a suburb of Southern California near Anaheim, Dung

Continued on following page

Continued from preceding page

Mai, a 30-year-old refugee from Vietnam, seems to pick up the story.

"The sea was black and I was afraid," she said, explaining in her careful English that she had left Vietnam in a small boat loaded with 40 people in 1981. "I thought the sea was blue, not black. In pictures it is blue. We were three days on the sea without food. The sea stayed calm. I was lucky."

Victoria Sarfatti Fernandez lived in New York, became an American citizen, went to school and had a career as a teacher. Dung Mai spent six months in a refugee camp in Indonesia, flew to California to join a sister and brother, attended the City College of San Francisco and is now saving to start a career in fashion design. She will become a citizen next year.

Both women found a community in their adopted land. For Fernandez, it was a neighborhood on New York's Lower East Side, where she would walk on the strange new streets, shadowed under the tall buildings, listening to the Italian bakers and Polish grocers.

She watched the signs go up in English on the store fronts, and heard the children pick up American slang as they slipped easily back and forth between their native language and their new one.

Dung Mai works in the "Today Plaza" where signs are written in three languages —Chinese, Vietnamese and English. Near her jewelry store, which she runs with her husband, is a video tape store featuring current US movies in Asian languages.

Signs of times

Across the way is the Man Wah Supermarket, where the satay seasoning and pickled bamboo shoots sit on a shelf next to the Betty Crocker cake mixes. Early one recent Friday morning, two women speaking in German accents could be seen reading the French labels on the jars of mushrooms as recordings of Asian artists singing American soft rock tunes were played over the public address system.

Out along Bolsa Street, the main thoroughfare running past the shopping center are the signs of the times—"Ngo Binh Fast Food," "Du Thi My Lan, DDS," "Do Mat Contact Lenses," "Khai Thue' Income Tax," and under a line of Vietnamese characters, the words, "Unisex Hair Design."

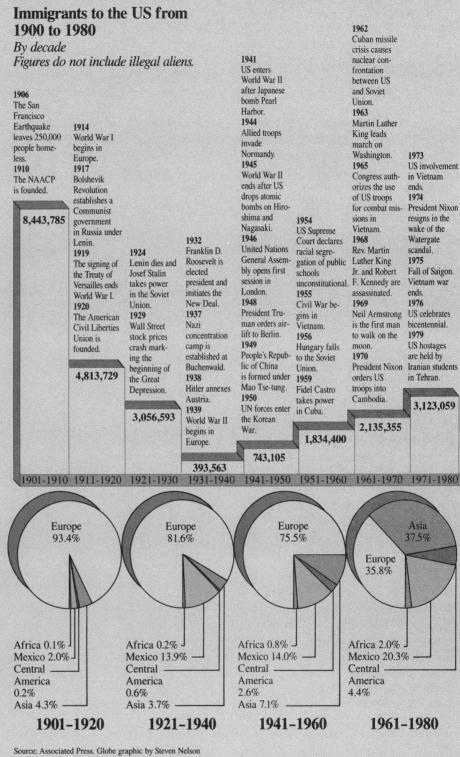

Immigrants to the US from 1900 to 1980

By decade
Figures do not include illegal aliens.

1906 The San Francisco Earthquake leaves 250,000 people homeless.
1910 The NAACP is founded.

1914 World War I begins in Europe.
1917 Bolshevik Revolution establishes a Communist government in Russia under Lenin.
1919 The signing of the Treaty of Versailles ends World War I.
1920 The American Civil Liberties Union is founded.

1924 Lenin dies and Josef Stalin takes power in the Soviet Union.
1929 Wall Street stock prices crash marking the beginning of the Great Depression.

1932 Franklin D. Roosevelt is elected president and initiates the New Deal.
1937 Nazi concentration camp is established at Buchenwald.
1938 Hitler annexes Austria.
1939 World War II begins in Europe.

1941 US enters World War II after Japanese bomb Pearl Harbor.
1944 Allied troops invade Normandy.
1945 World War II ends after US drops atomic bombs on Hiroshima and Nagasaki.
1946 United Nations General Assembly opens first session in London.
1948 President Truman orders airlift to Berlin.
1949 People's Republic of China is formed under Mao Tse-tung.
1950 UN forces enter the Korean War.

1954 US Supreme Court declares racial segregation of public schools unconstitutional.
1955 Civil War begins in Vietnam.
1956 Hungary falls to the Soviet Union.
1959 Fidel Castro takes power in Cuba.

1962 Cuban missile crisis causes nuclear confrontation between US and Soviet Union.
1963 Martin Luther King leads march on Washington.
1965 Congress authorizes the use of US troops for combat missions in Vietnam.
1968 Rev. Martin Luther King Jr. and Robert F. Kennedy are assassinated.
1969 Neil Armstrong is the first man to walk on the moon.
1970 President Nixon orders US troops into Cambodia.

1973 US involvement in Vietnam ends.
1974 President Nixon resigns in the wake of the Watergate scandal.
1975 Fall of Saigon. Vietnam war ends.
1976 US celebrates bicentennial.
1979 US hostages are held by Iranian students in Tehran.

Bar chart values:
8,443,785 (1901-1910)
4,813,729 (1911-1920)
3,056,593 (1921-1930)
393,563 (1931-1940)
743,105 (1941-1950)
1,834,400 (1951-1960)
2,135,355 (1961-1970)
3,123,059 (1971-1980)

Pie charts:

1901–1920
Europe 93.4%
Africa 0.1%
Mexico 2.0%
Central America 0.2%
Asia 4.3%

1921–1940
Europe 81.6%
Africa 0.2%
Mexico 13.9%
Central America 0.6%
Asia 3.7%

1941–1960
Europe 75.5%
Africa 0.8%
Mexico 14.0%
Central America 2.6%
Asia 7.1%

1961–1980
Asia 37.5%
Europe 35.8%
Africa 2.0%
Mexico 20.3%
Central America 4.4%

Source: Associated Press. Globe graphic by Steven Nelson

"The first year is culture shock," said Quen-Fen Chen, an immigrant from Taiwan, who owns a dress shop in Westminster and now goes by the name Ellen. "You go to the bank and you don't know how to cash a check. You go to the market and there are rows and rows of food and nobody helps you. Everything is so free and open and there is so much. But you learn. You have to learn."

Rose Vanger had to learn fast too, coming alone to the United States from Russia at age 14. The year was 1910. She was supposed to connect with an aunt when the boat made a stop in England, but they missed each other and Vanger made the trip by herself, knowing no one

Continued on following page

Continued from preceding page

on board and having no money since she had spent all she had—25 rubles—on the ticket for passage. When she got to Ellis Island she was kept there for 35 days because no relatives were there to meet her.

"I didn't cry," said Vanger, who is 91 years old now and living in New York. "I remember thinking, 'Whatever happens to me I'm going to go through with it. . . .' One woman gave me a jacket and said it would keep me warm on the trip back. I hoped I wouldn't need it."

Vanger's relatives learned of her whereabouts as many relatives learned they had family waiting on Ellis Island—through an ad in a newspaper. She lived with an aunt and uncle, did the washing in the house and got a factory job.

"It wasn't easy," she recalled. "The kids called me 'kike.' "

When Carmen Lima came to Los Angeles from Mexico 14 years ago she and her family were called "beaners" and "greasers."

"It has been the same for all immigrant groups," said Lima, sitting in Our Lady of the Angels Church in downtown Los Angeles. "Americans were afraid of the Irish and Chinese taking the jobs. Then the Italians were the problem, then the Germans and the Japanese and now the Latin Americans. It's a tradition."

Illegal alien

Lima, 40, has been living in the United States illegally for the past 15 years. In 1971 she came in on a 36-hour visa from Tijuana and never went back. Her husband crawled through a drainage pipe at night. They have four sons, three of them born here. She works as a cleaning woman, but has an associate arts degree from a local community college and is taking graduate courses so she can work with the deaf. Her husband is a parking lot attendant.

"I tell my kids they have nothing to be ashamed of because their parents are undocumented workers," said Lima, who is slim and articulate with short, reddish-blond hair. She is involved in organizing for the rights of illegal aliens and also volunteers to work on voter registration campaigns, urging her American citizen neighbors to vote although she cannot.

"I feel I am a part of this country," Lima said. "My husband and I work hard. We don't want something for nothing. He has

a Social Security card and pays income taxes."

She bristled at a comment indicating that she is unusual.

"There are hundreds like me," she said. "People think all Mexicans are fat and lazy and sit around eating burritos. I came here for economic reasons. It was not a life-and-death situation, but if we had stayed in Mexico our kids would not be getting a good education and we would be earning very little money. We aren't special. We're like everybody who has ever come to America. We want a better life."

Arnold Ambler wanted a better life too when he left England in 1920 with his bride of two days. He was 20 years old and came to Springfield, Mass., where he worked as a machinist for 46 cents an hour.

"My mother wanted me to stay in Yorkshire so she could set me up in a little variety store," said Ambler, now 86 years old and living in a nursing home in Concord. "But I wanted adventure. I wanted the freedom of a place with no class structure. This is the greatest country in

the world. And when you see how people are still flocking here to live you realize that we must have something the rest of the world doesn't have."

Rose Vanger stands near portraits of her husband and herself.

The waiting area of Ellis Island

Checking Your Comprehension

Read the following questions. Put an x in the box beside the answer that best completes each one.

1. The situation described in the first paragraph is called "the immigrant experience in microcosm." The word *microcosm* means
   □ a. a little world that represents the big world.
   □ b. something that is looked at under magnification.
   □ c. a life form of microscopic size.

2. The feature writer describes Dino Hirsch as being "completely assimilated into his adopted country." As it is used here, *assimilated* means
   □ a. rejected.
   □ b. encouraged or welcomed.
   □ c. incorporated or absorbed.

3. The author states that the basic human yearning associated with an immigrant trip to America is to
   □ a. find something better.
   □ b. see the Statue of Liberty.
   □ c. get rich quick.

4. At present the United States is accommodating its biggest wave of immigrants since the
   □ a. Pilgrims landed in 1620.
   □ b. first decade of the twentieth century.
   □ c. decade following the end of WWII.

5. The writer talks about the Salvadoran refugee paying off the "coyotes" who feed on illegal immigrant trade. Who or what are the coyotes?
   □ a. small western wolves
   □ b. bandits
   □ c. the Mexican border patrol

6. By looking at the pie charts on page 29, we can conclude that, to many Americans,
   □ a. life in Asia is preferable to life in America.
   □ b. life in Asia leaves something to be desired.
   □ c. immigrating to Europe is more practical than immigrating to America.

☆　☆　☆

The immigration story is interesting in regard to the news value of recency, since the main story is actually an old one: decade upon decade, people from all over the world have been immigrating to the United States.

As it happens, the story of the flow of immigrants has been thrown into the spotlight cast on the Liberty celebration. The hot story on the birthday of the symbol of freedom leads naturally into an examination of what that freedom means to Americans who journeyed here long ago and those who arrived lately. What is actually recent, or new, is the *story's treatment of the events*—the events it reports have been going on all along.

The editorial on the "Liberty Hoopla," as the USA TODAY headline has it, was in the newspaper as the hoopla was happening, making it timely indeed. Read on to see what the editorial writer has to say about a news story in progress.

OPINION

The Debate: LIBERTY HOOPLA

Commercialism isn't ruining Miss Liberty

Her figure isn't fashionable—she measures 35 feet around the waist. Her dress would never be found in a fine boutique—not in *that* shade of green. And her face, with its refrigerator-sized nose, is one that only her children could love.

And love her we do.

We love the Statue of Liberty so much that to celebrate her 100th birthday, we have given her a $70 million face lift, invited the USA to a massive gala at her New York Harbor home this weekend, and printed her image everywhere.

Turn on the television, and there's the Statue of Liberty in commercials, logos, and news stories. Drive down the street, and there's Lady Liberty on billboards, placards, and storefronts. Flip through the newspaper, and there's Miss Liberty on posters, ads, and cartoons.

Go picnicking, and she's on the paper plates. Go downtown, and she's on shopping bags. Climb into the tub, and—yoo-hoo—there's Lady Liberty on the shower curtain.

Some critics think this sort of thing is too, too tacky. They complain that commercializing the USA's symbol of freedom is an insult to her citizens; that it makes our land of opportunity seem more like a land of opportunists.

Of course people who buy Liberty souvenirs should realize that many enrich the promoter, not the lady.

But bad taste in the celebration of liberty is no vice.

What the elitists forget is that there is a patriotic impulse behind people's purchase of Liberty goodies. They forget that commercialism is a by-product of the free market that makes the USA the land of opportunity that it is. And they forget that it's a great U.S. tradition to enlist the Statue of Liberty's help in commercial ventures.

In 1876, Frederic Bartholdi, French designer of the statue, held a fund-raiser in Liberty's knee. In 1885, Joseph Pulitzer

Continued on following page

Continued from preceding page
raised the $100,000 for her pedestal by printing donors' names in his New York *World*.

Now, as then, the sponsors got the job done.

Nearly half the $252 million raised to restore Liberty and neighboring Ellis Island came from official sponsors—USA TODAY is one—and the sale of official statue products, stamps, coins, and books.

The money bought her a new stainless steel skeleton, a beautiful new golden torch, and a nice nose job. Thanks to these efforts, Liberty will have the vitality to welcome immigrants to our shores for another 100 years—or more.

Liberty's torch will shine then, as always, for all.

It shines for the poets, the philosophers—and makers of Spirit of America air fresheners. It shines for the tired, the poor—and celebrants wearing Statue of Liberty crowns made of green foam. It shines for the huddled masses—and those wearing Tiffany's $650 Statue of Liberty watches.

It's too bad that some people are weary of the commercialization. It's too bad that some people think Liberty's birthday hoopla is in bad taste.

But Liberty doesn't mind. She lifts her lamp beside the golden door to welcome *all* her children. Even them.

Checking Your Comprehension

Read the following questions. Put an *x* in the box beside the answer that best completes each one.

1. Some critics, the editorial writer explains, feel that the commercialism makes "our land of opportunity seem more like a land of opportunists." An *opportunist* is
   - ☐ a. one who makes jobs available to a number of people.
   - ☐ b. a political activist.
   - ☐ c. one who takes advantage of circumstances.

2. The writer says the "elitists forget . . . that there is a patriotic impulse behind people's purchase of Liberty goodies." By *elitists,* he means people who
   - ☐ a. identify themselves with the masses.
   - ☐ b. are or consider themselves socially superior.
   - ☐ c. hate commercialism in all its forms.

3. All of the following are examples of fund-raising efforts to build or restore the Statue of Liberty except the
   - ☐ a. 1876 fund-raiser in the statue's knee.
   - ☐ b. 1885 printing of donors' names in the New York *World.*
   - ☐ c. 1986 sale of $650 Statue of Liberty watches.

4. The writer believes that commercialism
   - ☐ a. is a by-product of the free market in the United States.
   - ☐ b. will ruin the spirit of freedom represented by the Statue of Liberty.
   - ☐ c. is a necessary part of raising large sums of money.

5. Evidently, the most recent fund-raising efforts to restore the Statue of Liberty were
   - ☐ a. a dismal failure.
   - ☐ b. successful.
   - ☐ c. misguided.

6. In the last paragraph the editorialist writes, "She lifts her lamp beside the golden door to welcome *all* children. Even them." By *them,* he means
   - ☐ a. recent immigrants.
   - ☐ b. the promoters and sponsors of Lady Liberty products and ads.
   - ☐ c. the critics and opponents of bad taste and tackiness.

☆ ☆ ☆

Immigration to the United States is both a part of the country's history and a daily occurrence. And as the first story in the lesson illustrates, all immigrants share some common experiences, even as each immigrant has a perspective unique to himself or herself.

In any event, all immigrants to the United States, be they legal or illegal, recent or not-so-recent, share one thing: a relationship to the ideas of freedom and equality represented by the Statue of Liberty. The one-hundredth birthday of the statue caused many people, immigrants *and* non-immigrants, to think about those ideas and that relationship. The editorial in *USA TODAY* shows that some thought the birthday bash tarnished the dignity of those concepts through commercialism. Others thought commercialism to be as American as apple pie, and therefore appropriate.

☆ ☆ ☆

Linking Facts from a Feature Story to Charts and Graphs

The immigration story is in part made up of other stories, stories of people who have emigrated from their homelands to live in the United States.

Accompanying the immigration story are a bar graph and a pie chart. The bar graph shows the number of immigrants to the United States from 1900 to 1980 by decade. Capsule accounts of major events are included for each decade. The pie chart shows the breakdown by percentage of the continents, countries, and territories that people emigrated from in the years 1901 to 1980.

Look again at the immigration story and find nine stories that tell you each immigrant's name, the country he or she

emigrated from, and the year in which he or she emigrated.

For each person, write the name, country and year in the spaces provided in the chart below. Then consult the bar graph to see what major event was taking place in the year he or she came to America (use the closest year if the actual year is not given). Write that event in the space provided in the chart. Add the year if you must use the closest year.

After you have finished, consult the pie chart to find the percentage figure of immigrants from the person's continent, country, or territory during that time in which the person came to the United States. Do you see any immigration trends?

The first of the nine stories is done for you.

	Name	Country Emigrated From	Year of Immigration	Major Event of that Year or Closest Year
1	Dino Hirsch	Germany	1941	U.S. enters World War II after Japanese bomb Pearl Harbor
2				not shown
3				
4				
5				not shown
6			not shown	not shown
7				
8				
9				

Using Your Newspaper

The opinion piece from USA TODAY was one of many in newspapers across the country commenting on a major news event. The event, of course, was the birthday celebration of the Statue of Liberty.

Over the next week, look in your newspaper for straight news stories or feature stories on major news events. At the same time, look for opinion pieces that interpret those events. Save the stories and editorials you consider most important. At the end of the week, survey the stories you

have saved. Select the news story that generated the most editorials or that interests you most.

Write two or three paragraphs about the news story and the editorials. Tell whether the story was a straight news story or a feature, account for the newsworthiness of the event, and describe how much space it was granted in the paper. Then describe the editorial responses to the story. Tell how you agree or disagree with the opinions expressed.

It is not uncommon to find a front page news story devoted to the events surrounding an invention or a discovery. For example, stories that report on possible breakthroughs in the search for an AIDS cure regularly make the front page. Some daily newspapers even devote an entire section to discovery and invention—the *Boston Globe*'s Monday Sci-Tech Section covers such diverse topics as health care and medicine, space research, and archaeology.

As readers, we are intrigued by the new and exciting things inventors and discoverers are creating or finding. There is always the possibility that one of their inventions or discoveries could affect our own lives. The fascination we feel is what reporters and feature writers play on in writing their stories.

The story from the *Houston Post* below offers a look at some inventors and their inventions.

Invention alive and swell in Houston

Necessity is still its mother, but money is relative

John Patterson says his 1,212-dimple ball is the most accurate ball in the world.

Pete Markos and his lighted plumb bob have taken the guesswork out of judging if walls are completely vertical.

No one questions the workability of Dale Fortenberry's knife sharpener as he demonstrates its use—with his cut hand wrapped in bandages.

Tina Hinds hugs her Hug Doll—despite having an apartment full of them.

Jim Harness, above, once fought off alligators in the murky waters of Bolivia before the idea of this rotary steam engine popped into his head. The foggy mirror is a thing of the past, as Robert Gottlieb demonstrates at left.

Post photos by Manuel Chavez

Continued on following page

Continued from preceding page

By ERIKA FISKE
Post Reporter

They don't like to be laughed at. And who can blame them? Inventors have given us all the conveniences of modern living—electricity, running water, cars, lava lamps.

Lava lamps? OK, so not all inventions are created equal . . . But all inventors share the same drive, the same curiosity about life. And there are a lot of them around. About 200 belong to the Houston Inventors Association and Houston's National Association of Inventors and Entrepreneurs alone.

It was an inventor, remember, who designed the carpet sweeper in 1875. M. R. Bissell became allergic to the dust in his china shop, so he devised a roller brush that swept dust into a box.

New York socialite Mary Phelps Jacob and her maid constructed the first brassiere from two handkerchiefs and pink ribbon, and Jacob was granted a patent in 1914. Before there's any chuckling, note that the patent was eventually worth $15 million.

"Inventors aren't eccentric. That's a misnomer," said Jack Kinsler of Seabrook, a member of the Houston Inventors Association. "Inventors are extremely anxious to produce something usable. They can't resist making things better. In general, they're pretty bright—better than average in intelligence. And sometimes they're so dedicated that they give 100 percent of their time to inventing and drop out of society. That's just being dedicated, I think."

Although Kinsler's been inventing for decades, he also windsurfs, snow-skis, bowls and plays softball.

"I'm not too eccentric," he said.

So inventors are just like everyone else, except maybe a little smarter, a little more creative, and . . . well, just a tiny bit "different"—as seen by Kinsler's colleagues in the local inventor's association.

How many people walk around holding a tin bucket fitted with a shower head and mirror, for instance? Robert Gottlieb, 39, of Clear Lake does. That's his invention, or at least it demonstrates his invention. Gottlieb fills the tub with hot water and turns on the shower head to prove that his mirror won't fog.

Now if he could just find a way to get his creation out before the public eye so all those people suffering with foggy mirrors in the morning could buy one.

Start chatting with Gottlieb about this, and he'll probably pull out his wrench. Don't jump, it's just another invention. This crescent wrench locks, so its grip won't slip. How many times have mechanics growled over a slipping wrench?

Gottlieb could reach into his bag of inventions and pull out many that have withered and died before his very eyes—like that special sled he invented in Kansas with runners made of skis. The neighborhood kids loved it. But it didn't bring in any money.

Gottlieb's motivation for inventing is simple: He wanted these items and couldn't find them in a store.

Inventors are driven by different reasons. Pete Markos of Houston knew the plumb bob could be better, even though it had been around forever. So he made a lighted plumb bob which more accurately determines whether a wall is perfectly vertical.

Landscaper Odell Pointer invented a better way of watering hanging plants after listening to customers complain about having to drag plants outside to water them. Pointer's cone-shaped device attaches above the pot and allows water to drip slowly onto the plant.

Tina Hinds invented a Hug Doll when she moved to Houston because she was lonely. Now her dolls, which can be wrapped around one's neck, are used by a couple of Houston psychologists and have been sold to 400 "lonely people," she said.

David Hayles, a former boiler maker, invented a way to take multiple pictures—putting more than one photo on a negative—because he was bored. He quit working after breaking his back and feet and developing arthritis, so he took up photography as a hobby.

But what better reason for inventing something than to make a lot of money—to hit the jackpot. That's what Dale Fortenberry has in mind. "I've got two businesses, one related to construction and another related to the oil industry. If I had to depend on those, I'd starve to death," said the 48-year-old Friendswood inventor. So he made a tungsten carbide-bladed knife and scissor sharpener.

"I've probably sold close to 100,000 knife sharpeners," he said.

Kinsler began inventing when he worked for NASA. The retired chief of the technical services division at NASA holds four NASA patents and once designed a space umbrella that saved the Skylab space station when its heat shield tore away during launching. The parasol had to be completed and deployed as quickly as possible in order to save the space station from extreme temperatures. Kinsler invented the parasol and sent it off within a week, winning him the distinguished service medal, NASA's highest award.

"It was a very pressure thing. I stayed at work the whole week, catching a couple of hours of sleep now and then," he said.

Another of his brainstorms, however, might bring a chuckle from his buddies at NASA. Kinsler designed the Apollo moon flag so that it would look as though it were blowing in the wind.

"There's a pole along the top to suspend the flag. Since there's no atmosphere on the moon—no wind—you pull the curtain rod out and it looks like there's a bit of a breeze," he said.

Today Kinsler operates a motorcycle machine shop, but he hasn't stopped inventing. Most recently he devised a new method of rethreading damaged threads. "A thread that might take 15 minutes to prepare, I could rethread in 30 seconds with my die nut, so it's a great time saver."

Jim Harness, 58, of southwest Houston, is an inventor with a somewhat different background. He likes to talk about his days of eating monkeys, parrots and alligators as a Catholic missionary in the jungles of Bolivia.

"I was a mechanic down there. I was trying to maintain internal combustion engines with no spare parts, and it was almost impossible to keep them running," he said. So Harness came up with a rotary steam engine in 1971, which he's still perfecting in his apartment.

"It looks like a cyclone hit. There are engineering books, tools, motors and catalogs all over, and we store household goods there, too, " he said. "You'd think it was complete chaos, but that's what an inventor does, brings chaos into order."

Out of that mess came Harness' motor, which he says could run off the raw sewage in Lake Houston if the sewage were converted into methane gas, as well

Continued on following page

Continued from preceding page
as several other inventions, including an all-terrain vehicle that moves like a worm. Unfortunately, none of them has gotten past the prototype stage. Harness doesn't have the money.

Charles Mullen of Clear Lake has been luckier. The experienced inventor, who also works as an advertising sales manager, has sold 14 inventions so far, including the first hamburger cooker, marketed in 1974. If the company had taken his advice and made it a single instead of a triple cooker, Mullen says, he might have made millions of dollars instead of just $300,000.

There's a secret to selling inventions. "You have to get to the top guys in the company," Mullen said. "If you go the regular way, you've got to go through 10 people, and if an idea is any good, it'll never get through. If those people were capable of spotting new products, they wouldn't be at the bottom."

One of Mullen's biggest problems has been the theft of his ideas, he said. "You present your ideas to someone, they say they're not interested, and a few years later you see a variation of what you invented, or the same thing, on the market."

John Patterson, 40, of the Walnut Bend area, took someone else's successful invention and made it much better—he invented the 1,212-dimple ball. Patterson calls it the most accurate ball in the world—the ball of the future.

"It has to do with the size of the dimple," he said. "Smaller dimples eliminate equipment error. So no matter how you strike this ball, you can't strike it on the edge of a dimple."

These inventions are downright practical compared to what inventors in other parts of the country have been doing. Harold W. Dahly of Chicago made a hat with a solar-powered fan, for instance. John D. Wise of Paterson, N.J., invented an automatic house-painting machine. And James M. Stubbs, a dentist in Rockingham, N.C., designed a Weight Repulsing and Cigarette Reneging Appliance— an adult pacifier to help people lose weight and stop smoking. None of these inventions made its creator rich.

And so it is with inventing.

"Inventing is sort of like panning for gold," said Gottlieb, the inventor of the fog-free mirror. "You go out, risk a lot and hope to discover something someone will want."

Checking Your Comprehension

Read the following questions. Put an *x* in the box beside the answer that best completes each one.

1. The story says that "all inventors share the same drive, the same curiosity about life." As it is used here, *drive* means
   - ☐ a. speediness.
   - ☐ b. motivation.
   - ☐ c. a desire to use high-tech gadgetry.

2. Jack Kinsler says, "Inventors aren't eccentric. That's a misnomer." A *misnomer* is a
   - ☐ a. wrong name or designation.
   - ☐ b. lie.
   - ☐ c. misconception or misunderstanding.

3. Inventors share some common characteristics. The one characteristic below not specifically mentioned in the story is the
   - ☐ a. desire to make things better.
   - ☐ b. curiosity about life.
   - ☐ c. difficulty getting patents.

4. Robert Gottlieb, a member of the Houston Inventors Association, is responsible for all of the following inventions except
   - ☐ a. a sled with runners made of skis.
   - ☐ b. a cone-shaped device to water plants.
   - ☐ c. a fog-free mirror.

5. Inventor Charles Mullen suggests that when a person has an idea to sell he should go to the "top guys" in a company because
   - ☐ a. they are the smartest and most capable of spotting a new product.
   - ☐ b. other people will steal your ideas.
   - ☐ c. they are the people who can help you get a patent.

6. This quote, "Necessity is still its mother, but money is relative," emphasizes the point made in the article that
   - ☐ a. inventors all hope to hit the jackpot.
   - ☐ b. inventors work hardest and most quickly when they are being paid a lot.
   - ☐ c. inventors want most to make something usable, but money helps.

☆ ☆ ☆

Newspaper stories about inventors and their inventions are of interest to a wide readership. Readers like to learn about new products, from the whimsical to the truly useful, and they like to read about the people who spend their time creating those products.

In contrast to the survey of inventors that you have just read, the following story concerns just one inventor and his invention. As you read, see what characteristics he shares with the inventors described in the first story.

Company boasts it has a better mousetrap

Plaistow man's invention features sanitary, safe way of catching rodents

"If a man can write a better book, preach a better sermon, or make a better mouse-trap than his neighbor, though he builds his house in the woods, the world will make a beaten path to his door."
— Ralph Waldo Emerson

By MARY BETH LAPIN
Contributing Reporter

PLAISTOW—After months of tinkering with live mice and plastic in his cluttered tool shop, a 59-year-old man may have achieved what many felt was impossible. He has brought a cliché to life and invented what he feels is "a better mousetrap."

The world has yet to make "a beaten path" to the door of Pied Piper International. But with orders in hand for 65,000 traps and nibbles coming from big businesses, Ken Bernard has to consider the possibility of making his first million at an age when many men are considering retirement.

Bernard's partner, Tom Eifler, the self-proclaimed spokesman of Pied Piper International, encourages Bernard to think big. As far as he's concerned, Eifler said, the bigger the company gets, the better.

The cause of all this excitement is the "Mice Cube," a 5-inch-long Lucite rectangle with a one-way door. The mouse, attracted by the odor of a peanut butter-smeared cracker, pushes open the door to get inside, then is unable to get out unless set free by the trap-setter. Mouse hunters may set the trap on end, blocking the air holes in the door, and the mouse will suffocate in a matter of minutes.

It is simple, Bernard admitted, so simple he wonders why no one thought of it before. It is also effective, Eifler pointed out, as two field mice squeezed through the door of the one-mouse trap, not once, but three times in succession.

When he first heard rumors about a local man and his "better mousetrap," Eifler said, "I just groaned. The same thing has been said a thousand times." But Eifler, who in 1986 was "drumming

Ken Bernard shows off his Mice Cube.

up business" as a self-employed publicist, visited Bernard's unassuming workroom at the A-Z Tool Co. for a demonstration.

The demonstration impressed him, Eifler said, but only mildly. Then he asked Bernard where he had bought the 18 brown mice. "I didn't buy them," Bernard said. "I caught them."

And that was when Eifler realized the little plastic rectangle could potentially make Bernard, and his partners, very wealthy.

Bernard had applied for patents and was trying to market the product by mailing out letters to prospective customers, Eifler said. The fledgling company was in dire need of organization. "Their methods honestly made me nauseous," said Eifler, who had worked for big businesses like Wang and Honeywell. "They had a high-school girl typing these letters. But they had sent out 21, and already had six replies. I couldn't believe they were getting replies."

TV breakthrough

So Eifler and Bernard struck a deal and sealed it with a handshake. Eifler agreed

to work free of charge until the business got off the ground, when he would receive an unspecified percentage of the company. Pied Piper was incorporated last December. Eifler now owns 20 percent, Bernard owns 50 percent and two other partners own 20 and 10 percent respectively.

Their big breakthrough came in the form of a phone call from Channel 11 in Durham last year, a phone call that Bernard was ready to ignore, Eifler said.

"He told me Channel 11 had called him and wanted to do a television spot on the business, but he was too shy." Eifler recalled. "He asked if I would mind doing it. Me mind? I was practically jumping for joy, this was finally it."

Since then Pied Piper International has been featured on CBS-TV's "Today's Business," and on two Canadian and three US radio stations. But Eifler said he knew they were really onto something when Bernard's patent attorney called and wanted to buy a piece of the company.

The traps, which have been in production for just over a month, have been packaged and are already selling in stores
Continued on following page

Continued from preceding page
such as Shaws Supermarkets for $2.89 to $3.00 each. Although the company has no full-time employees, there are several private distributors in New England.

Humane way

The "Mice Cubes" are manufactured in Hamden, Conn., at the rate of 25,000 per week and are available in clear or opaque Lucite. Eifler said soon they will add colors like red and blue. Apparently the mice don't care what color the cube is, "They'll even go into a black one," Eifler said.

This is the only trap on the market with a one-way door, Eifler said, it may be the only trap that lets a person choose between killing the mouse or setting it free. Eifler said the Animal Rights League has requested permission to use the trap in commercials as an example of a humane way to dispose of mice.

Bernard said mice used to make him "nervous."

Bernard crafts measuring instruments for his A-Z Tool Co. The company was successful when Bernard started out in 1956 "with a file and a vise," but had been in a slump since the 1970s. A friend jokingly advised Bernard to build a better mousetrap. Bernard took the advice literally and headed off to the local library to research the problem.

From his reading, Bernard learned that mice hate to back up. Therefore any trap he built needed a one-way door. With that in mind, he proceeded to reinvent the mousetrap. And when he set the model in his backyard, he caught 16 mice in 18 nights.

Noiseless trap

Bernard has also designed a "Condomicium" that can catch up to 16 mice at a time and has nearly completed a

prototype "Eraticator" that Eifler thinks may be the answer to the city of Boston's rodent problem.

Unlike the original mouse trap, the "Mice Cube" is completely noiseless. "You don't hear a 'snap,' " Eifler said. The trap is washable and reusable. And at less than $4 per cube, squeamish consumers can throw the whole device away after each capture.

The trap is safe, even in households with dogs, cats and toddlers. "You could put it in a baby's crib," Eifler said. "It's very sanitary."

Speaking of cats, Eifler said, the cube may well put mousers out of business. Bernard, who keeps a cat himself, said he still caught several mice in his house with the "Mice Cube," as did their two other partners. "They were furious at their cats," Eifler said, because the "Mice Cube" did a better job and cost less to maintain.

Checking Your Comprehension

Read the following questions. Put an x in the box beside the answer that best completes each one.

1. The reporter says that Ken Bernard, in inventing a better mousetrap, "has brought a cliché to life." A cliché is
   □ a. an overworked expression.
   □ b. an old story passed from generation to generation.
   □ c. a calamity.

2. The Animal Rights League considers the trap a "humane way to dispose of mice." Humane means
   □ a. hostile.
   □ b. easy.
   □ c. kind.

3. The inventor of the Mice Cube, Ken Bernard, has not done which of the following to promote his mousetrap?
   □ a. He has applied for a patent.
   □ b. He appeared on the CBS TV show "Today's Business."
   □ c. He mailed out letters to prospective customers.

4. An example of the mousetrap's safety mentioned in the article is that it
   □ a. could be put in a baby's crib.
   □ b. passed a test by the Food and Drug Administration.
   □ c. did a better job than Bernard's cat.

5. When Eifler says that Mice Cubes could put mousers out of business he means
   □ a. other mousetraps won't be used anymore.
   □ b. people won't need cats to catch rodents anymore.
   □ c. other companies will go bankrupt.

6. The story begins with this quote by Emerson: "If a man . . . can make a better mousetrap than his neighbor . . . the world will make a beaten path to his door." The quote means
   □ a. an inventor tries to find an easier way.
   □ b. people are interested in inventors, especially those who come up with crackpot inventions that are absurd failures.
   □ c. if an inventor comes up with something really useful, people will want it and be willing to buy it.

☆ ☆ ☆

An invention or discovery is most newsworthy when it is brand new. People like to read about a discovery while it is fresh and exciting, but for the general reader, that freshness wears off after the initial burst of information has ended. As for inventions, many people are eager to learn all about "the latest thing." They may even be moved to buy and use what they have read about. But they will not pay much attention to newspaper stories on inventions after those inventions have become not

just household words but also household products. Who wants to read about a CD player when they can listen to one?

This has a lot to do with what you read about recency in the last lesson. Stories on inventions and discovery follow guidelines similar to those that govern straight news stories. If a story is fresh and delivers information that people do not already possess, they will want to read the story. If a story is full of old news, it will go unread.

Drawing Conclusions from Feature Stories

Inventions, as the two stories point out, are almost always the result of some need that the inventor identifies. But sometimes that perceived need is not great enough, and the invention does not catch on. When an invention does catch on, the inventor stands to make some money. When an invention is not a success, the inventor takes a loss on the time and money he or she has invested.

In the stories, the writers clearly identify some inventions as successes or failures. About other inventions they are not so clear—they leave you to your own conclusions. As you read the following statements be on the lookout for words on which you can base a conclusion. Then, in the space provided, write *successful* if the statement describes what would seem to be a successful invention or *unsuccessful* if the statement describes what sounds like an unsuccessful invention.

_____ 1. fog-free mirror: Now if he could just figure out a way to get his creation out before the public eye. . . .

_____ 2. sled with ski runners: Gottlieb could . . . pull out many that have withered and died before his very eyes. . . .

_____ 3. Hug Doll: Now her dolls . . . have been sold to 400 "lonely people," she said.

_____ 4. Mice Cube: But with orders in hand for 65,000 traps and nibbles coming from big business . . . Ken Bernard has to consider . . . making his first million. . . .

_____ 5. space umbrella: The retired chief . . . designed a space umbrella that saved the Skylab space station. . . .

_____ 6. rotary steam engine: So Harness came up with a rotary steam engine in 1971, which he's still perfecting in his apartment.

_____ 7. hamburger cooker: The experienced inventor . . . has sold 14 inventions so far, including the first hamburger cooker. . . .

_____ 8. solar-powered fan: These inventions are downright practical compared to what inventors in other parts of the country have been doing. Harold W. Dahly . . . made a hat with a solar-powered fan, for instance.

Using Your Newspaper

Over the next three days, look at the advertisements for popular, modern products. Concentrate on those products that are intended to make life more liveable or pleasure more pleasurable: home computers, electric toothbrushes, portable cassette players of the Walkman variety, and so on.

Pick one of the products. Write a brief essay that deals with these questions:

- What was the need perceived by the inventor that caused him to invent this product?

- Has the invention been a successful one for the inventor?

- How long ago was the product invented?

- Who uses the product?

- What did people do before the product was invented? Did they perform the activity connected to the product in a different way, or was the activity connected to the product simply not done before the product was in existence?

- Is the product necessary? Could people get along without it just as well as with it? Is the world a better place thanks to the invention of this product?

Practicing Newspaper Skills

Write a feature story on a new product. Many high-tech products are available for personal use, especially in the fields of sight and sound and home computers. There are video cassette recorders with numerous options and capabilities, and big-screen, stereo-sound televisions. People can listen to music in a variety of formats, from Walkmans to compact disc players. And computing in the home has become a fact of modern life. One can choose from an array of terminals, printers, programs, and disk drives.

To get information on such a product, interview someone who sells it for a living. Stop in at a store that sells the product most interesting to you and arrange to interview the store manager or a knowledgeable salesperson. State the purpose of the interview to make sure the person can tell you what you need to know.

As always, go to the interview prepared, with a list of questions, and paper and pen or a tape recorder. Focus the interview on the latest things, the most up-to-date devices that people are buying. Determine what the hottest-selling new item is. Then find out who is buying it and why. What need does the product meet—does it save time or labor, does it offer the best picture, the brightest sound, or is it simply a status item that people want because it can be had? Try to establish also what product the new item has improved on, and what the difference between old and new is. Ask the store person to give you, if possible, a forecast of the item's selling power. Will it be a hot product for only a short time, or will it sell well on its own merit for years and years?

Use your notes as the basis for a feature story on the product discussed in your interview.

Many newspapers include an entire section devoted to lifestyle topics. Often given a name like "Living," or "Lifestyle," such a section contains mainly feature stories, many of which report on trends in pleasure, recreation, and people's lifestyles.

The first story in this lesson is a lifestyle piece about men's sweaters, a clothing item in vogue in the 1980s. The second story deals with an ever-popular American fashion accessory, sunglasses. Obviously, these two subjects are relatively light compared to straight news and other serious reportage. Each story boasts a catchy headline and a bold graphic reflecting that absence of seriousness, and each is written in a witty, informal tone conveying a sense of fun and enjoyment.

The writers of both stories want to engage and entertain their readers as well as inform them. Read carefully to see how each writer creates a tone that suits the information being presented.

THE SWEATER REVOLUTION

NIFTY KNITS: Color and design combine in Saratoga's pullover, left, while the Resilio sweater, at right, uses bold stripes. And even women might be tempted by Robert Stock's golf sweater.

COVER STORY

Man's new uniform: Bold, bright knits

Fashion trend-setter Cosby leads the charge against plain old pullovers

By ELIZABETH SPORKIN
USA TODAY

Bill Cosby may not know it, but he promotes more than Puddin' Pops, E.F. Hutton and fatherhood. Every Thursday night, he gives a prime-time boost to what has become the fastest growing category in men's clothing: sweaters.

Thanks in part to the Cos—who favors colorful, patterned pullovers—sweaters in all shapes and shades have become fashion heavyweights.

"People are more likely to get their ideas of what to wear from pop-culture figures than from fashion magazines," says fashion psychologist Michael Solomon of New York University. "Bill Cosby has been a tremendous positive for the sweater industry."

Sweater sales rose by 40 percent between 1981 and 1985, according to MRCA Information Services, a Connecticut-based firm that tracks consumer clothing purchases. By comparison, the entire men's apparel market grew by only 17 percent.

In 1985 alone (the last year for which figures are available), almost 100 million men's sweaters—about $2 billion worth —were sold in the USA.

Cotton sweaters, especially, have been firing up sales recently. (Production is up 33 percent over last year, says the National

Continued on following page

Continued from preceding page

Knitwear and Sportswear Association.) These lightweight knits are taking center stage today through Sunday as the Men's Fashion Association meets in Atlanta to preview spring clothes for fashion editors.

"Nowadays, men are wearing sweaters all year round," says Chip Tolbert, the association's fashion director. For spring, designers are showing loose-fitting cotton pullovers with punchy sports motifs, nautical designs, geometric patterns and wide stripes.

In embracing these spiffy Cosby-era styles, USA men have raised their fashion-consciousness to new heights. "In the past, we wore solid color cashmere or shetland sweaters with V-necks or crew necks," Tolbert says. "Men would never be caught dead in anything else."

Indeed, men's sweaters used to be strictly homey or preppy—images represented by pre-Cosby sweater men Fred Rogers and Dan Rather.

Rogers has been wearing zip-front, solid color cardigans for almost 20 years on *Mister Rogers' Neighborhood* "as a symbol for getting into play clothes," says his publicist David Newell. Rogers' late mother, Nancy, knit most of the 20 comfy cardigans in her son's TV repertoire.

Rather has attracted attention since 1981 by sporting V-neck sweater vests with jackets and ties on the air.

Other Hollywood hotshots are also into sweaters. "Sweaters are the hottest thing right now," says Rick Pallack, a Los Angeles menswear designer and retailer whose customers include scores of television and film personalities. "We're doing double the sales of a year ago."

Pallack recently sold a season's worth of colorful sweater vests to Michael J. Fox's *Family Ties* wardrobe. Billy Dee Williams came into Pallack's shop not long ago for three Italian-made pullovers trimmed in leather and suede. Mitch Gaylord bought a half-dozen cotton crew necks in bright solid colors. Lorenzo Lamas purchased 40 oversize, high-fashion sweaters in wild patterns.

But it is still Cosby who gets the credit for introducing USA men to stylish sweaters by demystifying a high-fashion look.

Cliff Huxtable's passion for sweaters mirrors Cosby's own taste, says Sarah Lemire, the show's costume designer. As a bonus, the colorful sweaters play well on television, compared to other men's clothes that look drab.

Although Cosby sports styles by a variety of designers and manufacturers, one of his favorite labels is Koos van den Akker. The Dutch-born designer creates hand-made patchwork sweaters featuring as many as 15 fabrics. Cosby owns about 25, Koos guesses. "This man buys at retail, no discounts, no nothing. He is a wonderful customer."

Koos' business, however, has not boomed since *The Cosby Show* premiered in September 1984. "We get lots of cute mail addressed to 'The Man Who Makes Bill Cosby's Sweaters,' " he says. "But the problem is, my sweaters cost $750 apiece and the people who watch *The Cosby Show* can afford $60. I'm waiting for a manufacturer to come to me to license an inexpensive Bill Cosby line."

In the meantime, men are finding plenty of snazzy alternatives.

"We're doing a huge business in fancy sweaters," says Therese Oniskin, a buyer at Marshall Field's in Chicago. "We don't sell too many solid, flat sweaters in plain knits."

At Britches of Georgetowne, a chain of upscale stores based in Washington, D.C., sweater sales made up 30 percent of all clothing sales at Christmas. The top seller: a $69.50 cotton crew neck in turquoise or pink.

"Men consider what they wear to the office a statement of their authority," says Linda Lee, vice president of Macy's by Appointment, the New York department store's fashion and gift consulting service. "But when they choose sweaters for recreation, they choose whatever fantasy they might want."

Although most of her clients go for traditional shapes, they are adventuresome when it comes to patterns and colors, Lee says. Cotton or cashmere sweaters in ice cream colors and jewel tones are current big sellers.

"Color sells sweaters," says Jerry Lauren, vice president of men's design for Polo Ralph Lauren. "We don't have just one orange. We have two oranges. We have two shades of purple. Men come into our Madison Avenue store and say, 'I can't decide which to buy. Let's buy them all.' "

If this infectiousness continues, men's sweaters eventually may outgrow their storage space. It seems men have a quirk when it comes to sweaters: They'll keep buying more, but they won't part with their old ones. Patched sleeves or faded colors become badges of honor rather than reasons to give a sweater away.

"It's a comfort kind of thing, a modern-day security blanket," fashion psychologist Solomon says. "The older a sweater gets, the better. It can remind a man of his college days and break up the frustration and despair that comes with middle age.

"Men pretend they're not so attached to an old sweater," he says. "But the real litmus test is to gauge their reaction when their wife throws it out."

To cope with the loss of an old sweater or prevent an overcrowded chest of drawers, men can, once again, buck up and take their cues from Cosby.

Says designer Koos: "Bill Cosby wears my sweaters, gets tired of them, gives them away to friends and comes in for more. I'm telling you, he's great."

Checking Your Comprehension

Read the following questions. Put an x in the box beside the answer that best completes each one.

1. The story asserts that it is "Cosby who gets the credit for introducing USA men to stylish sweaters by demystifying a high-fashion look." *Demystifying* means making something
   ☐ a. easier to understand.
   ☐ b. more exciting.
   ☐ c. more of a mystery.

2. The writer observes that, "if this infectiousness continues, men's sweaters eventually may outgrow their storage space." *Infectiousness* means
   ☐ a. unhealthiness.
   ☐ b. rapid spread.
   ☐ c. contaminating effect.

3. MRCA Information Services, a firm that tracks consumer clothing purchases, found that from 1981 to 1985
   ☐ a. sweater sales rose 40 percent.
   ☐ b. men bought more sweaters than women.
   ☐ c. Dan Rather often wore V-neck sweater vests on the air.

4. The big increase in cotton sweaters is *not* caused by which of the following?
   ☐ a. Men are wearing sweaters all year.
   ☐ b. Cotton sweaters are cheaper than wool.
   ☐ c. Cotton sweaters are loose-fitting and lightweight.

5. A man who is fond of an old sweater will probably *not*
   ☐ a. get upset if his wife throws an old sweater away.
   ☐ b. see patched sleeves or faded colors as a badge of honor or reminder of the past.
   ☐ c. give the old sweater to a friend.

6. Koos van den Akker's business has not boomed despite Cosby's influence because
   ☐ a. the sweaters cost too much for most viewers of the show.
   ☐ b. Bill Cosby won't allow the styles he wears to be copied.
   ☐ c. he is so busy answering his mail.

☆ ☆ ☆

There is one key term in the blurb under the headline of the USA TODAY story. The term is *trend-setter.* It seems plain that the story is aimed directly at those people who read the life-style section of a newspaper because they are interested in trends. Of course, using the name *Cosby* in the blurb is no accident, either. We learned in Lesson 2, Unit One, that famous names attract readers. And the name of a famous person who is riding the crest of a trend is doubly potent. Such a person is Bill Cosby, who at the time of this story's publication was starring in one of the top-rated TV shows in the country.

The following story is all about sunglasses. As you will see, it also begins with a burst of celebrity power.

Saying it with sunglasses

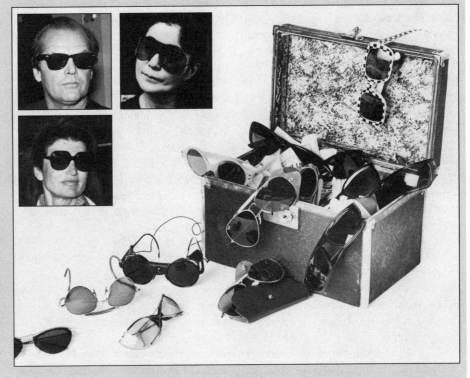

AMERICAN POP

By Nathan Cobb

A few words about sunglasses.

Sunglasses are American Cool. Europeans may influence them, Asians may manufacture them, but Americans wear them. They are the great democratizer of Cool: They make everyone Cool. You're Cool. Don Johnson is Cool. I'm Cool. Jacqueline Onassis is Cool. Remember that rock lyric? *"I want to be like Jackie Onassis, I want to wear a pair of dark sunglasses."* Why, just slip into a pair of Jackie O. wraparounds. That's Cool.

Who's that behind those Foster Grants? (Or Ray-Bans? Or Vaurnets? Or Gargoyles?) Jack Nicholson, Lolita, Michael Jackson, Gen. Douglas MacArthur, Moammar Khadafy, Annie Hall, Roy Orbison, Greta Garbo, Yasser Arafat, James Bond, Jean-Claude Killy, Daniel Ortega, Lester Maddox, Yoko Ono, Vito Genovese. The rest of us simply ape them. Everybody wants to be a movie star, a rock star, a mobster, a dictator, a hipster, a spy.

In this, the 50th anniversary year of classic aviator shades, there is a "sunglass boom." But that is not the point. Sunglasses are something more than optical necessities or even fashion accessories. They are Cool. Further proof of their American Coolness lies in the fact that the United States now represents about half of the worldwide over-the-counter, non-prescription sunglass market. That is the claim of the Sunglass Association of America, a trade group of about 75 manufacturers and importers, both domestic and foreign. America, SAA reasons, has an abundance of the two items most required for high sunglass consumption: sun and money. (Although the true sunglass aficionado might ask, "Who needs sunlight?")

Styles come, but styles seldom go. Heed the words of Mauri Edwards, public relations counsel to SAA: "Everything that ever happened in sunglasses is still out there someplace." Meaning—to paraphrase

Continued on following page

Continued from preceding page

Gen. MacArthur, who paraded through World War II as a sunglass billboard—that old sunglasses never die.

Americans have been wearing sunglasses since the 1920s, but it wasn't until the '50s that shades turned Cool. We have since endured such gimmicks as rhinestone-studded harlequins, mood frames, granny glasses, mirrored lenses and designer signatures. But there have been classics, too. Let us examine seven important moments in sunglass history:

1936: The Aviator. The commercial version of the Bausch & Lomb Anti-Glare Goggle drops into the marketplace, priced at $3.75. Pilots have been wearing them since 1932, after they were requested by the U.S. Army Air Corps. Soon named Ray-Ban, they eventually become the eyewear equivalent of the Eisenhower jacket. War is Cool.

1952: The Wayfarer. Ray-Ban's clunky '50s stereotype arrives, yours in '52 for about $6. A classic story ensues: Dying a natural death, the Wayfarer is resurrected amid some shrewd 1980s promotion (as we shall see). Today's price is around $50, but there are dozens of inexpensive knockoffs. Nerdy is Cool.

1956: The Skilynx Acier. The original glacier glasses for the common man: plastic frames, small round lenses, leather side guards. The maker is Sporoptic Pouilloux, of France, which today manufactures Vaurnets. The current version, with a nylon frame, sells for about $60, but there are several imitations on the market. Mountains are Cool.

1962: The Balorama. Introduced at a retail price of about $8, the narrow, curved Baloramas become the standard shades of be-boppers, finger-poppers and even international crime-stoppers. (Say, aren't those Baloramas on "The Man From U.N.C.L.E.?") In 1986 they're still hanging in: Bausch & Lomb expects to sell about 55,000 pairs this year. Jazz is Cool.

1968: The Vaurnet Cat-Eye: Jean-Claude Killy wins three Olympic medals at Grenoble, France, and is photographed in his $15 Vaurnets. Sales soar. (Ironically, Vaurnets are named for Jean Vaurnet, the 1960 Olympic downhill winner.) Still big among the California surfing set, the various Vaurnet Cat-Eye offspring now fetch between $55 and $75. Skiing is Cool.

1978: The Carrera Porsche. What kind of man reads Playboy? The kind who pays $85 for a famous automotive name, changeable aviator lenses, gold plating and a registration number. More than one million Austrian-made Carrera Porsches have been sold in the U.S. There's now a complete line, topping off at $2900 for a pair in 14-karat gold. Cars are Cool.

1982: The Gargoyle. You saw them on Clint Eastwood in "Sudden Impact" in 1983, on Arnold Schwarzenegger in "The Terminator" in 1984. OK, so they are not classics. But these American-made, frameless, rectangular bugeyes—priced from $54 to $75—are so far the 1980s' principal contribution to sunglass culture. Tough is Cool.

Such pricey icons stand foresquare among the trend-setters. But it is well to remember that the average pair of sunglasses bought in America last year cost $6.85, according to SAA. So meet Robert Shelton, director of product design and development at the Foster Grant Corp., which is headquartered in Leominster and has been making sunglasses for 54 years. The 1987 Foster Grant catalog pictures 164 different pairs of sunglasses, all of them priced at $20 and under. "Glasses for the masses," is how one executive describes the product. The same official estimates that the firm will produce in excess of 15 million pairs this year.

Foster Grant is the major purveyor of low-end American Cool, albeit Mexican-assembled. "We try to be all things to all people," explains Shelton, who is currently overseeing the design of the company's 1988 line. Drawings must be turned out, prototypes developed, engineering models made, injection molds created. Between 30 and 40 percent of the 1988 line will represent new styling, Shelton estimates. But he also speaks of "updating" and "retro," and as he thumbs through Foster Grant's current catalog he points out several styles that are clearly culled from the classics. Item 18166 represents the Vaurnet look. Item 15160 is your basic aviator. Item 9124 is a variation of the Wayfarer.

"We're well aware that fashion doesn't happen here in Leominster," the designer says. "We go to fashion shows, we go to trade shows, we read a lot of magazines. We watch every end of the marketplace, from our own competitors to people who make $300 sunglasses. And there are always celebrities that are influencing the fashion scene. We've had to react to the Wayfarer thing."

Ah, the Wayfarer thing. It is a story that proves that Cool is made, not born. Here it is:

By the early 1980s, the bulky '50s Wayfarer was all but dead. "We used to make plans to attend its funeral every two weeks," Norman Salik, a Bausch & Lomb, Inc. vice president, likes to say. Only 18,000 Wayfarers were sold in 1981, even after the glasses were worn by John Belushi and Dan Aykroyd in the movie "The Blues Brothers." But a fashion layout in the May 1982 issue of Gentleman's Quarterly magazine lifted that year's sales to 110,000. And another movie appearance—this time on Tom Cruise in "Risky Business"—helped push 360,000 units over the counter in 1983. The curve has continued to rise. This year, Salik says, Bausch & Lomb expects to peddle 1.5 million Wayfarers—representing nearly 30 percent of the company's sunglass sales—at approximately double the 1982 retail price.

A lesson was learned. In 1982, Bausch & Lomb signed a contract, at approximately $30,000 per year, with a company that places products in movies. "They originally guaranteed me 30 movies," Salik explains. "But last year our sunglasses were in 79 movies and television shows. Sales of our classic aviator had been flat until May of this year when Tom Cruise wore them in 'Top Gun,' which is basically a two-hour sunglass commercial. Within two weeks we were up 20 percent over the year before. It's gotten to the point where everyone in this business is after movie placements. It works better than advertising."

Muses SAA's Edwards: "If somebody appears on MTV tonight wearing a certain type of sunglasses, I can guarantee there will be a run on them tomorrow."

Meanwhile, Vaurnet-France, the American distributor of Vaurnet sunglasses, has learned the value of a logotype. The company's tri-color signature now appears on so many promotional items—T-shirts, beach chairs, hats, etc.—that U.S. sales of such items are expected to equal nearly *half* of those garnered by the firm's sunglasses themselves in America in 1987.

Domestic retail sales of sunglasses are expected to jump 16 percent this year, to $1.2 billion, according to SAA. Unit sales are again likely to be split fairly evenly between men and women. We could all just squint, of course, but that wouldn't work at all. Squinting's not American Cool.

Checking Your Comprehension

Read the following questions. Put an *x* in the box beside the answer that best completes each one.

1. The story names some famous sunglass wearers, then says that the rest of us "ape them." As it is used here, *ape* means to
   - ☐ a. make fun of.
   - ☐ b. copy.
   - ☐ c. act foolish.

2. The writer says that sunglasses are "the great democratizer of Cool." A *democratizer*
   - ☐ a. makes one a Democrat.
   - ☐ b. appeals to the masses.
   - ☐ c. makes everyone equal.

3. According to the Sunglass Association of America, the two items required for high sunglass consumption are
   - ☐ a. styles and prices.
   - ☐ b. sun and money.
   - ☐ c. gimmicky styles and classic styles.

4. The paraphrase of General MacArthur, "old sunglasses never die," means that
   - ☐ a. sunglasses cannot be destroyed.
   - ☐ b. the best sunglass ads are the people wearing sunglasses.
   - ☐ c. old sunglass styles may still be considered cool in the future.

5. According to the article, people in the 1980s choose the Gargoyle model sunglasses because they
   - ☐ a. want to look tough like Clint Eastwood and Arnold Schwarzenegger.
   - ☐ b. like American-made products.
   - ☐ c. know they are durable.

6. People seem most likely to buy sunglasses they see
   - ☐ a. in TV commercials.
   - ☐ b. on stars in current movies.
   - ☐ c. in attractive ads and displays at the stores.

☆ ☆ ☆

The stories in this lesson deal with trends as news. It is news of a sort that sweaters are popular, and that sunglasses are more popular than ever. The fame aspect of the subject matter is helpful, of course, in making the stories attractive to readers, but it is not an aspect the writer exploits purely for its celebrity appeal. On the contrary, the famous people named in the stories truly have contributed to the popularity of sweaters and sunglasses. Without their high-profile movie and television work, the trends would not have happened as they did. Thus, reporting on the trend includes evaluating that part of the trend that is directly caused by people who are famous.

☆ ☆ ☆

Recognizing Signal Words and Phrases in Feature Stories

The main idea in the first story is that men's sweaters are as popular as they have ever been. In the second story the main idea is that sunglasses are more popular than ever. Both stories emphasize the idea that the items are popular *now*—these are stories on trends, after all, and old trends are no more interesting than old news.

Both stories quote sales figures as evidence of a positive trend. But each writer also employs signal words and phrases throughout the story to reinforce the idea of current popularity. For instance, near the beginning of the *USA TODAY* story, the writer says that sweaters "*have become* fashion heavy-weights." Likewise, the writer of the sunglasses story states that "*today's* price" for a pair of Wayfarers is fifty dollars. The more you look, the more the signal words and phrases surface—*right now, so far, recent,* and so on.

Reread the stories. In each one, find five statements that contain signal words or phrases. In the spaces that follow, write the statements and underline the specific words that make up the signal phrase. An example from each story is done for you.

Sweaters

ice cream colors and jewel tones <u>are current</u> big sellers

1. _____

2. _____

Sunglasses

But these . . . <u>are so far</u> the 1980s principal contribution

1. _____

2. _____

3. _____   3. _____

4. _____   4. _____

5. _____   5. _____

Using Your Newspaper

Make a collage of pictures of people wearing a popular fashion item. Look in your newspaper or in special interest magazines for pictures of famous people wearing articles of clothing that have caught on with the general public or with a segment of the general public. The pictures might be of actors, musicians, political figures—anyone who is well known.

Pick at least five people from different walks of public life whose pictures clearly show that they make a particular fashion statement, be it with a suit, a hat, glasses, even a haircut. Make these pictures the foundation of your collage. Then place pictures of nonfamous people who embrace the same fashions near the pictures of the celebrities. You might find photos of fashion models, of course, but you might also come across pictures of people on the street in crowded cities or in other public places.

After you have finished putting together your collage, display it. Be prepared to discuss each fashion shown. What influence has the famous person had on the particular fashion? Which came first, to your knowledge, the celebrity or the fashion? What group of people would be most likely to copy the fashion—teenagers, parents, teachers, or other celebrities?

Practicing Newspaper Skills

Write a feature story on a fashion trend that is popular at your school.

There is probably, right now, a fashion trend that a large segment of the student body embraces. To write about the trend, you will have to research its history, evaluate how widespread the trend is currently, and make a guess as to how long-lived the trend will be.

First, the history. Can you trace the particular fashion to a rock star, an actor, a sports star, a politician, an influential student? If you can't trace the trend back to a specific person or persons, can you at least discover when the fashion first started showing up on people around school? This step may require you to interview some students who follow the trend. You might also have to look at back issues of magazines to track the trend down. Of course, you might remember when the trend started, or it might be common knowledge.

Next, look around at lunch or between classes and see how many people actually follow the trend. You may want to count how many trendy people out of twenty, fifty, or one hundred you can spot at any given time.

Finally, now that you are a qualified trend spotter, how long is the thing going to last? This will most likely have to be a guess on your part.

Use the three steps above as the basis for your feature story. In an introduction, identify the trend. Then give its history in as much detail as possible. Include any quotes that your interviews have produced. The end of the history section should move smoothly into an account of how widespread the trend is. In this section, you might want to describe how you came by your figures. Wrap up with your prediction on the trend's future. Watch in the months (years?) to come to see if you were right.

This lesson presents two news stories on the boys' high school basketball championship game in Illinois. The East St. Louis Lincoln High School Tigers came out on top in the contest, handing the Chicago King High School Jaguars a 79-to-62 defeat.

But we are not interested in just the score. We want to look at the ways the game is described by two reporters, one writing for the *St. Louis Post-Dispatch* and the other for the *Chicago Tribune.*

Both reporters worked from the same facts. Both presumably saw the same game. Yet the two stories do not offer similar descriptions, as you might think, because they are written to appeal to different readerships in different places. In other words, where the people who read a newspaper live affects how the news is shaped by the reporter.

With that in mind, read "Red-hot Lincoln dethrones King," the account of the matchup in the *St. Louis Post-Dispatch.* Notice how many paragraphs are about Lincoln, the home team.

Illinois AA Boys

Red-hot Lincoln dethrones King

By DAN O'NEILL
Of the Post-Dispatch Staff

CHAMPAIGN, ILL.—The match that many anticipated at the start of the prep basketball season finally materialized Saturday night at Assembly Hall.

It turned out to be a match made in heaven for East St. Louis Lincoln High.

With their running game going full throttle, Lincoln (28–1) jumped all over Chicago King (28–5) and never let up as they defeated the Jaguars 79–62 to win the Illinois Class AA state title.

"We've been waiting for this matchup for a long time," said Lincoln 6-foot-7 forward Chris Rodgers. "We felt we could beat them, but not by this much. It's a great feeling."

The game featured two of the state's premier players in Lincoln's 6-9 LaPhonso Ellis and King's 6-8 Marcus Liberty. Each was spectacular. Liberty scored 41 points and grabbed 15 rebounds, while Ellis poured in 27 points and grabbed 10 rebounds. But Ellis enjoyed the better supporting cast.

"We can keep coming at you one after another," said Lincoln's 6-7 forward James Harris, who finished with 23 points. "That's the way we played all year.

"Everyone had been slowing it down against us and it took some of the spark out of us. We didn't look like the Lincoln that everyone knows. When you make it to this game, you better play your best. I think we played it tonight."

Unlike its performance in recent games,

Defensive rebounds sparked the Lincoln running game.

Continued on following page

Continued from preceding page

Lincoln got off to a fast start against King. The game opened with a bang when Harris broke loose for a slam dunk off the opening tip. Rodgers, who had 13 points, then added a three-point play and Ellis scored inside to give Lincoln a 9-0 edge.

After a basket by Liberty, Ellis came back with a basket and a three-point play that stretched the margin to 14-2 with less than four minutes left in the opening period.

The quick start by Ellis was a good omen for the Tigers. The standout junior had struggled with just two points in Lincoln's semifinal victory over Quincy.

"It was the last game of the year and the state championship," said Ellis. "People were playing it up big. And on the television, every time they mentioned Lincoln they mentioned my name. That kind of hurt me because I didn't feel like

I was giving them enough. Now, I feel like I gave them a good game. Now I can feel good when they talk about Lincoln and LaPhonso Ellis."

King's only real threat came midway through the first half. Three consecutive turnovers by the Tigers helped the Jaguars reel off seven consecutive points and trim the Lincoln lead to 15-11 at the end of the first quarter.

King carried the momentum into the early moments of the second quarter. A breakaway basket by Carl Stanley and two free throws by Liberty tied the score at 15-15. But Lincoln kicked its running game into high gear and burst ahead to stay.

Two consecutive dunks by Ellis gave the Tigers a 25-21 edge. Harris slammed home a lob from Rodney Chavis and added a layin to increase the margin to 29-21. Rodgers then scored inside and

Mark Chambers finished off a fast break to make it 33-21 with 2:25 left in the half. The Tigers poured it on with two consecutive baskets from Lawrence Bradford, and Ellis then hit an 18-foot jumper at the halftime buzzer to send the Tigers to the locker room with a 41-24 lead.

"You have to be mighty tough to run up and down the court with us," said Lincoln coach Bennie Lewis, whose team also won a state title in 1982.

"We'd seen them play and we knew that they didn't really get back on defense real fast. So every time we got the ball, we would run it, run it, run it."

With Liberty scoring 12 consecutive points on an array of shots, the Jaguars cut the lead to 55-46 with 1:29 left in the third quarter. But Lincoln put together another spurt that increased the margin to 65-48 early in the fourth quarter, and the Tigers coasted.

Checking Your Comprehension

Read the following questions. Put an x in the box beside the answer that best completes each one.

1. The story's lead, or first paragraph, is: "The match that many anticipated at the start of the prep basketball season finally materialized Saturday night at Assembly Hall." By *materialized,* the reporter means that the
   - ☐ a. uniform material was delivered.
   - ☐ b. game happened.
   - ☐ c. teams scored.

2. The reporter calls Ellis and Liberty "two of the state's premier players." *Premier* means
   - ☐ a. first ranked.
   - ☐ b. most well-known.
   - ☐ c. tallest and fastest.

3. Lincoln was able to push the score to 14-2 in the first period because
   - ☐ a. Liberty hit a slam dunk for the first play.
   - ☐ b. Rodgers and Ellis were making three-point plays and inside baskets.
   - ☐ c. they played a slow, control-style game.

4. When did King's only challenge to Lincoln occur?
   - ☐ a. midway through the first half
   - ☐ b. when Liberty scored twelve consecutive points
   - ☐ c. early in the fourth quarter

5. In order to make their game strategy work, the Lincoln players had to
   - ☐ a. rely on Ellis' shooting and rebounding.
   - ☐ b. keep running and shooting well.
   - ☐ c. get a big lead in the first quarter and coast for the rest of the game.

6. Although both Ellis and Liberty were spectacular, why did Ellis have an easier game?
   - ☐ a. He wanted to play better because he felt he hadn't given enough in the earlier games.
   - ☐ b. He got off to a quick start, scoring early in the game.
   - ☐ c. He was not the only scorer, since other Lincoln players were hitting baskets, too.

☆ ☆ ☆

Look back at the *St. Louis Post-Dispatch* story. In which paragraph is Chicago star Marcus Liberty mentioned? Now look ahead to the *Chicago Tribune* story. In which paragraph does Marcus Liberty's name first appear?

Each reporter shows bias toward his hometown team. The East St. Louis reporter concentrates on how well Lincoln High played, not even mentioning Marcus Liberty until well into the story. In contrast, the reporter from the *Chicago*

Tribune immediately tells his readers how well Liberty played. Each article, in effect, supports the local team. The reporters write with the idea in mind that the hometown fans want to read about their boys, their team—win or lose—not a group of strangers from another school in a distant city.

As you continue reading the story from the Chicago paper, notice how the reporter expresses his support for the King High School basketball team.

Lincoln rocks King for Class AA title

By JERRY SHNAY
Chicago Tribune

CHAMPAIGN—Not even a record-setting effort by the best high school player in the nation could keep East St. Louis Lincoln from winning the Class AA state basketball championship Saturday night.

Marcus Liberty, the 6-foot-8-inch senior with silky moves who has been named the Player of the Year by Parade magazine, scored a title-game record 41 points for King [28-5], but that was almost all of the Jaguars' offense as East St. Louis Lincoln [28-1] stunned the defending state champions 79-62 in the Assembly Hall in front of a crowd of 10,280.

It was an impressive calling card for Liberty's future fans, who are anxious to see him play at Illinois next season [pending results of an April ACT test]. And as he left the court, Liberty whispered something to Lincoln's awesome 6-9½ junior, LaPhonso Ellis, who led the winners with 27 points.

"He wished me luck and asked me to consider going to Illinois," said Ellis with a smile. "I told him he was a great player."

Liberty's one-man show smashed the title-game mark of 37 set by Thornridge's Boyd Batts in 1972. He also established a AA record of 143 points in four games, surpassing the 115 by Effingham's Mitch Arnold in 1980. He finished 14 points shy of the tourney record for any class, 157 by Lawrenceville's Jay Shidler in 1976.

And Liberty accomplished his scoring feat despite constant pressure from Lincoln's massive front line of Ellis, 6-8 James Harris and 6-7 Chris Rodgers.

The victory plan was simple, said Lincoln coach Bennie Lewis, savoring his second big-school state title in five years.

" 'Run it, run it, run it!' I told the team," said Lewis. "I didn't think they could stay with us. So when the numbers were on our side, when we had the break, we ran."

It was a strategy made to order for the bigger, stronger Tigers, who blew a 9-0 lead in the first quarter but outscored King 18-3 in the last four minutes of the first half to take control of the game.

Ellis and Harris rattled the backboards with some power slams and kept King on its heels all night. For his first three tournament games, Ellis, a member of The Tribune's all-state first team with Liberty, scored only 22 points.

"I was disappointed in my play earlier," he said. "I wanted to show what I could do tonight. I concentrated on my shots. I wanted them to be perfect, and they were."

Ellis was 12-for-18 from the field with 10 rebounds, four blocked shots and two steals. Not only did he score inside, but he climaxed his team's first-half outburst by hitting a 22-footer at the buzzer.

Harris added 23 points on 11-for-13 shooting, and Rodgers had 13 points and 13 rebounds. Guard Rodney Chavis helped everything happen with 11 assists, some on crisp half-court passes.

This was the first time in seven tries that a team from the Public League has not won a state title after getting to the championship game. The loss prevented the Jaguars from becoming the first back-to-back titleholder among big schools since Thornridge did it in 1971–72.

King coach Landon Cox said he was dismayed by the "let-'em-play" attitude of the officials. "We didn't get a call all night." He acknowledged that Lincoln "was a well-coached, tough team," but said he thought Collins, which beat King once this year and took the Jaguars into overtime in the city playoffs, was every bit the equal of the Tigers.

Maybe so, but the only thing Lincoln couldn't do was stop Liberty. Swooping from end to end, or slithering through defenders like a shark, the King star put on a last, great show in defeat, going 16-for-33 from the field despite a poor start. He was 2-for-10 in the first quarter.

"There were so many trees out there, even I had to change my shot," said Liberty. "That just doesn't happen. And at the start, I think I was too pumped up to play well."

Checking Your Comprehension

Read the following questions. Put an *x* in the box beside the answer that best completes each one.

1. The reporter characterizes Marcus Liberty's point total as a "scoring feat." By *feat,* he means
   ☐ a. career record.
   ☐ b. a disappointment.
   ☐ c. an accomplishment.

2. The account has Lincoln coach Benny Lewis "savoring his second big-school state title in five years." As it is used here, *savoring* means
   ☐ a. smelling or tasting.
   ☐ b. enjoying, delighting in.
   ☐ c. winning.

3. Which record did Liberty *not* break during the championship series?
   ☐ a. title game scoring record
   ☐ b. Class AA scoring record
   ☐ c. tournament record for any class

4. Who won the state championship last year?
   ☐ a. Chicago's King High School
   ☐ b. East St. Louis Lincoln High School
   ☐ c. Thornridge High School

5. Which of the following best summarizes Lincoln's strategy for the championship game?
   ☐ a. The "let-'em-play" attitude of the officials.
   ☐ b. Liberty was to score a record number of points.
   ☐ c. "Run it, run it, run it."

6. Lincoln's massive front line of Ellis, Harris, and Rodgers forced Liberty to do which of the following?
   ☐ a. change his shot
   ☐ b. not achieve any scoring records
   ☐ c. rattle the backboards

☆ ☆ ☆

We learned in Lesson 1, Unit One how a news event's proximity to a readership influences what information is reported and how it is reported. Locality affects the news in much the same way. As we have seen, each of our two reporters knows local fans will be reading his story. Consequently, each chooses different facts to include. The *Chicago Tribune* reporter tells more about Marcus Liberty's outstanding records and efforts than the *St. Louis Post-Dispatch* reporter does. In turn, the St. Louis reporter includes more about the contributions of Ellis and the other top players to the Lincoln win. We can see, then, that where the paper and its readers are from influences how the news is shaped. Stories are slanted or biased because they are written to appeal to that local fan's point of view. Thus, what a person reads in the newspaper depends to some extent on where that person lives.

☆ ☆ ☆

Detecting Bias in Sports Writing

As you can tell from the two headlines "Red-hot Lincoln dethrones King" and " Lincoln rocks King for Class AA title," both stories express the main idea that Lincoln beat King for the state championship.

But as we have noted, the two reporters are writing for their local fans. As a result, the East St. Louis reporter focuses on how Lincoln won the game, and the Chicago reporter emphasizes Marcus Liberty's outstanding play. As readers of both articles, we can see how each reporter's story is designed to satisfy the needs of a partisan, home-town readership.

As you read each statement below, decide if the statement shows bias and, if it does, which locality it is biased toward. In the space provided before each statement, write *E* if the statement is biased toward East St. Louis or *C* if the statement is biased toward Chicago. Write *NB* if the statement shows no bias.

_____ 1. With their running game going full throttle, the Tigers jumped all over Chicago King and never let up as they defeated the Jaguars 79-62 to win the Illinois Class AA state title.

_____ 2. Not even a record-setting effort by the best high school player in the nation could keep East St. Louis Lincoln from winning the Class AA state basketball championship Saturday night.

_____ 3. Marcus Liberty, the 6-foot-8-inch senior with silky moves who has been named the Player of the Year by Parade magazine, scored a title-game record 41 points for King, but that was almost all of the Jaguars' offense as East St. Louis Lincoln stunned the defending state champions 79-62. . . .

_____ 4. Unlike its performance in recent games, Lincoln got off to a fast start against King.

_____ 5. After a basket by Liberty, Ellis came back with a basket and a three-point play that stretched the margin to 14-2 with less than four minutes left in the opening period.

_____ 6. And Liberty accomplished his scoring feat despite constant pressure from Lincoln's massive front line of Ellis, 6-8 James Harris and 6-7 Chris Rodgers.

_____ 7. The match that many anticipated at the start of the prep basketball season finally materialized last night at Assembly Hall.

_____ 8. "You have to be mighty tough to run up and down a court with us," said Lincoln coach Bennie Lewis, whose team also won a state title in 1982.

Using Your Newspaper

Look in your newspaper for an account of a sports event and examine that story for bias. You may use a story on a professional, college, or high school team sport.

First try to determine if the story seems balanced. Count the paragraphs that deal with one team and those that deal with the other. Is it an equal number? Then see if the story quotes both coaches or just the hometown coach. If the opposing coach is quoted, is he or she quoted fully, or are selected phrases dropped into new contexts that might give the quoted material altered meanings? Does the piece recount the exploits of the opposing star athletes as well as those of the hometown stars?

Next, check the language. Did the hometown players "pump in points" while the opponents "scored"? Did the hometown "hurling ace" or "fireballing moundsman" duel someone known simply as the "opposing pitcher"? Of course, those examples are extreme—biased language is usually more subtle, so read carefully.

Finally, does the story seem to accurately represent what happened? In other words, does the account match the score? Does what is described as being the tone and tenor of the game seem likely given the raw data contained in the box score?

After you have analyzed the story, write a paragraph or two explaining why you think it is or is not biased.

Practicing Newspaper Skills

Attend a team sports event, take notes on the entire game or match, and write a newspaper-style account of it.

In writing your story, be evenhanded—devote equal space to both teams, the stars for both teams, and the important plays made by both teams. In other words, create a sports report that would give someone who was not there an accurate picture of the contest.

Once your story is finished, pick a favorite of the two teams and exercise your bias: turn your story into one that the hometown fans would love.

Start by deleting whole sentences, even paragraphs, that discuss the opposing players. Don't allow their personalities to emerge. Also downplay the other team's scoring efforts—mention them almost in passing.

Next go over the writing in which you describe the exploits of your team. Punch up the verbs and nouns the way sportswriters do, making the plays sound exciting and the players real and interesting. Include (or, for the purposes of this exercise, make up) some quotes from stars or coaches.

Finally, compare the two versions of the story. One is obviously more accurate than the other—is one more interesting? How do you feel about this kind of newspaper writing? How would you feel about front-page major news stories written this way?

Jane Goodall is renowned in certain circles yet does not boast broad fame. Dr. Vicky Neave is even less well known than Goodall. We can't really measure the "celebrity" status of these women against that of Tempestt Bledsoe or Senator Edward Kennedy and his son, whose stories we read in Unit One, Lesson 2. Goodall and Neave claim a more subdued type of recognition. Still, both women are names in the news.

Jane Goodall is a pioneer in scientific research who, by living with champanzees in the jungle, has discovered much about the way they live. When she published a book covering her twenty-five years of experience, the wheels of book promotion began to turn and articles about her (and her book) began to appear in newspapers. Our story comes from a national newspaper, *USA TODAY.*

Only a few doctors and neurosurgeons would recognize Dr. Vicky Neave's name, but she is an important person to the people in North Carolina, her recently adopted home. The *High Point Enterprise* story in this lesson informs readers about the contributions Neave will no doubt make to medical care in North Carolina.

The writers of the two feature articles meant to inform and entertain readers by reporting on people who are making news because of their work. As you read the stories, concentrate on the accomplishments that have made the two women newsworthy.

JANE GOODALL

The best chum a chimp ever had, she leads fight to save the species

CHAMPION OF CHIMPANZEES: Goodall, in front of a Mexican statue at the National Geographic building in Washington, D.C. The chimps she has studied for 25 years 'are so like us,' she says. They experience 'joy, rage, sorrow, fear, excitement, a sense of fun.'

Continued on following page

Continued from preceding page
By DEIRDRE DONAHUE
USA TODAY

"Errch, errch." With a friendly chimpanzee grunt, Jane Goodall strides into an office at *National Geographic* headquarters.

Immediately recognizable from TV documentaries and magazine articles, Goodall is that slender Englishwoman who has spent decades in Africa amid the furry species humans most resemble.

At 52, she finds that her eyes tire easily. "I work in the jungle where it's dark and gloomy," says Goodall, requesting that the lights be turned off.

But she still pursues her passion with gusto. Goodall remains as transfixed by animals as she was a quarter of a century ago when, as an untrained secretary, she headed off to Africa. The harvest of 25 years is collected in her new, 673-page study, *The Chimpanzees of Gombe: Patterns of Behavior* (Belknap/Harvard University Press, $30).

Goodall's natural volubility has not been stifled by years spent on the isolated shores of Lake Tanganyika in Gombe, Tanzania. She pours forth a torrent of words describing the findings of a recent chimpanzee conservation conference.

"We're going to end up with practically no chimps at all in the next 100 years," says Goodall, blaming deforestation, agriculture, infants being sold for research and the fact that people eat chimps.

Chimpanzee conservation is not antithetical to the needs of hungry Africans, she maintains. "If we destroy all the forests, then we create deserts." Among her many projects is getting the chimpanzee changed from a threatened to an endangered species.

Chimpanzees have much to teach us, she believes, particularly in the area of mother-child relationships. Her next scholarly book will be about that topic. "Chimps are so like us" she says. They experience "joy, rage, sorrow, fear, excitement, a sense of fun, probably even embarrassment." She has observed that chimps who have poor relationships with their mothers carry those problems to the next generation.

With her oval face and calm hazel eyes, Goodall resembles a Jane Austen heroine; her voice has a schoolgirlish pipe to it. "My major goals," she says, "other than

☐ Bio

■ **Born:** April 3, 1934, one of two daughters of a business executive and a writer. Raised in London and in Bournemouth, England.

■ **Education:** Received Ph.D. from Cambridge University in ethology after submitting thesis "Behavior of the Free-Ranging Chimpanzee," in 1965. She was the eighth person in the history of the university to study for a Ph.D. without first earning a B.A.

■ **Career:** On July 14, 1960, Goodall set up camp at Gombe to observe the chimpanzees with binoculars. She established the longest continuous field study of a living creature. In 1976, she founded the Jane Goodall Institute for Wildlife Research, Education, and Conservation. Observed and named the chimpanzees she studied: one of them, Flo, earned an obituary in the *London Times.*

■ **Books:** *In the Shadow of Man* (1971); its forthcoming sequel, *Through a Window; The Chimpanzees of Gombe* (1986).

■ **Awards:** The Netherlands' Order of the Golden Ark, the San Diego Zoological Society's Golden Medal of Conservation, and the J. Paul Getty Wildlife Conservation Prize.

■ **Personal:** Married in 1964 to photographer Baron Hugo van Lawick. Son Hugo now lives in Tanzania; will attend university in England. Divorced in 1972. Remarried in 1975 to Derek Bryceson, Tanzania's park director, who died of cancer in 1980.

keeping Gombe going, are chimp conservation and welfare and the raising of human children."

Motherhood is a subject Goodall knows intimately. Her marriage to Dutch photographer Baron Hugo van Lawick produced a son named Hugo, born in 1967, nicknamed Grub. (Divorced in 1972, they still collaborate; many of the book's photos are his.) In 1975, Goodall married Derek Bryceson, Tanzania's park director. In 1980, he died of cancer.

Goodall raised Grub in a fashion similar to the way a chimp would: constant attention and physical affection. "He came first in my life," she says. "For the first three years, I wasn't away from him for a single day. I did administration with him running around my legs. Every afternoon was his. I gave up what I like best, which is following chimps." At 9, he went to live with her mother in England but spent vacations and summers with Goodall.

Devoted to her mother, Goodall dedicated the book to her. At 82, "Mum" came on this trip. Goodall credits her with fostering the love of animals she was born with. "As a teeny toddler, I would collect worms and take them to bed."

"Always encouraged" by her mother, Goodall continued to watch and read about animals. After high school, Goodall visited Africa, where she met paleontologist Louis Leakey and began working for him as a secretary. Her energy and

interest in animals spurred Leakey to choose Goodall as the one to observe the chimps at Gombe. "What a far-sighted genius *he* was," she says. "When he was trying to get money to send me out, people thought he was immoral."

Indeed, the British authorities insisted that Goodall have a chaperone. Goodall's mum came along as her daughter embarked on what has become the longest continuous field study of any creature.

Although her gender worried the authorities, Goodall believes it has aided her. "It's helped me, certainly in Africa. I'm much less of a threat there than if I were a man. The human female is much less threatening to the chimps. I've not found a single solitary drawback except one. Some of the adolescent males, when they go through their bit of wanting to dominate females, include me."

Before Goodall, chimps were believed to be gentle vegetarians. She discovered that chimps make tools and eat meat. "For the first 10 years, I thought they were very much like us but much nicer, and then I learned . . ."

She revealed that chimps practice warfare and even cannibalism. It's "heartbreaking," she says, "but it does make them more human."

Human cruelty has also touched Goodall. Four of her students were kidnapped by rebels from Zaire for several months
Continued on following page

Continued from preceding page
in 1975. Since then, Goodall has trained a group of "absolutely fabulous" Tanzanians to observe the chimps. "The Tanzanians are like me. They're always there. They're not just coming in for a bit of data and hopping out again." Goodall spends five or six weeks at a time at Gombe (where her house has neither electricity nor running water) and the rest of the time either in Dar es Salaam or fund-raising abroad.

Although she has spent her life in close quarters with chimpanzees, each encounter remains remarkable. "The fact that an animal born in the wild will approach, lie down and sleep near my foot, that they have that much trust in an animal of another species, that means more to me than anything else."

The mysterious death of the gorillas' guardian

Louis Leakey sent another young woman off to Africa to study apes. Dian Fossey spent her life observing gorillas in Rwanda, until she was murdered with a machete last Christmas in her hut. A fellow researcher, Wayne McGuire, was charged in August with the crime, but mystery surrounds the case.

Of Fossey, Goodall says, "Dian was a very good friend of mine. But we had a lot of arguments. I didn't approve of the way she would sit in (the apes') laps.

I had done this in the beginning and then realized this could affect their behavior.

"Dian was faced with this horrifying situation where her gorillas were being poached. I haven't had to face this situation. I wouldn't be brave enough to carry on a vendetta (against poachers) on a personal level the way she did. I think it was a mistake but I think it was incredibly brave—and I can sympathize with her absolutely."

Checking Your Comprehension

Read the following questions. Put an *x* in the box beside the answer that best completes each one.

1. The reporter observes that "Goodall's natural volubility has not been stifled" by the many years she has worked in isolated Gombe, Tanzania. *Volubility* means
   - ☐ a. changeability.
   - ☐ b. curiosity.
   - ☐ c. talkativeness.

2. Goodall maintains that chimpanzee conservation "is not antithetical to the needs of hungry Africans." By *antithetical*, she means
   - ☐ a. in opposition to.
   - ☐ b. immoral.
   - ☐ c. antisocial.

3. Why does Goodall think there may be no chimps at all in one hundred years?
   - ☐ a. The forests are disappearing and chimps are sold for research or eaten.
   - ☐ b. Chimps are classified as a threatened species.
   - ☐ c. People don't recognize how chimps are really like humans.

4. Goodall changed our perception of chimpanzees when she discovered that chimps
   - ☐ a. are vegetarians and are gentle.
   - ☐ b. make tools, eat meat, and practice warfare.
   - ☐ c. will lie down and sleep at her feet.

5. Why did Goodall dedicate her new book to her "Mum"?
   - ☐ a. Goodall's mother is now eighty-two years old.
   - ☐ b. Goodall's mother has sponsored conservation projects both in Africa and in England.
   - ☐ c. Her mother fostered Goodall's childhood interest in animals.

6. Why does Goodall continue to study chimpanzees?
   - ☐ a. She wants to learn about how the mother-child relationships of chimps can be applied to human relationships.
   - ☐ b. She wants to apply the warfare tactics of chimps to human relationships because they are similar in their cruelty.
   - ☐ c. Both answers above are correct.

☆ ☆ ☆

After reading the Goodall story, it should be plain that Goodall is a name in the news for (1) her twenty-five years of ground-breaking work with chimpanzees, and (2) her book *about* that work.

Vicky Neave is newsworthy because of her work as a neurosurgeon, but there is more to it than that. Look at the headline of the second feature story. The word *atypical* should give you a clue as to why young (another clue) Dr. Neave merits a feature story.

Atypical neurosurgeon beats odds—her way

By CINDE STEPHENS
Staff Writer

Each time she lifts the skull, Vicky Neave stops and admires the glistening golden brain underneath.

At times, she races against a throbbing aneurysm that threatens to rupture spontaneously, much like an elaborate ticking bomb. At other times, she is more free to manipulate the interwoven threads of red and blue vessels.

For Dr. Neave, operating is a thrill just above a skydiving free fall and the galloping, jumping excitement of riding horses cross-country, which helped attract her to High Point.

There are about 3,265 neurosurgeons practicing in the United States. Approximately 36 are women.

It's an understatement to point out that Dr. Neave, 31, is High Point's first woman neurosurgeon. Maybe it's of greater significance to mention that she's one of the youngest practicing neurosurgeons in the nation, or that next month she's scheduled to receive the Congress of Neurological Surgery's Resident of the Year award.

She finished her residency training this summer at age 30. "That's about the earliest that it can possibly be done," said Dr. James Johnson. "I think it's safe to say she is one of the youngest neurosurgeons in the country."

Johnson used the words intelligent, professional, competent and superbly trained to describe his new partner. But her most outstanding quality is her vivaciousness, he said. "That's what's unique about her. She's just great fun. She does add a new dimension" to Johnson Neurological Clinic, on Elm Street, he said.

She brings with her some techniques that are relatively new to the state, including stereotactic and pediatric neurosurgery. The stereotactic procedure—which uses a computed axial tomographer or CAT scanner to ease diagnosis by obtaining biopsies and implanting radioactive particles—is an important advance, Johnson said.

Her skills also include new techniques for operating on certain tumors going through the nose rather than through the skull. Pediatric surgery is especially rewarding because of the amazing recovery abilities of young patients, she said.

The freshness of the idea of a young woman neurosurgeon is not lost on the clinic's patients in High Point, Thomasville, Asheboro and Lexington. Almost without fail, when Dr. Johnson introduces Dr. Neave, the patient looks at a physician's assistant and nods.

While Dr. Neave is modest when asked about her own accomplishments, she needs no prompting to talk about surgery.

In surgery, the brain and the inside of the skull are a golden color, not the white cauliflower-like substance floating in formaldehyde exhibits. "Every time we take the bone off and open up the covering of the brain, every time it still gets to me," she said. "You just sort of stop for a moment and look at it. It's beautiful. It's just beautiful."

"I've been doing it for six years and I'll be, hopefully, doing it for the rest of my professional life, and there's not one time I don't uncover the brain and not just stop for a moment to admire it before getting into whatever I'm supposed to be doing. And some of what I do isn't all that pretty."

Aneurysm surgery isn't pretty, but makes up for it with the excitement and frustration it causes, she said.

Aneurysms are "little balloons off of blood vessel walls inside the brain and they rupture spontaneously," she explained. "Operating on those can be a real challenge because you never know. From the moment you make your skin incision until you finally get the clip on the aneurysm, that thing could rupture at any time.

"We use the microscope for it and... you're lifting up the brain to see the arteries down at the base of it and you have to dissect around this big, red thing that's pulsating in your face. I hold my breath. You forget to breathe. You go in with the clip and you sort of take a deep breath, you send up a couple of prayers.

"There's a lot that's interesting and challenging, but that's the most exciting. You're literally sitting there with bated breath, hoping this thing isn't going to rupture before you get to it."

Surgery for aneurysms may be the most exciting, but the condition is also among the most frustrating because it is potentially preventable, she said.

Continued on following page

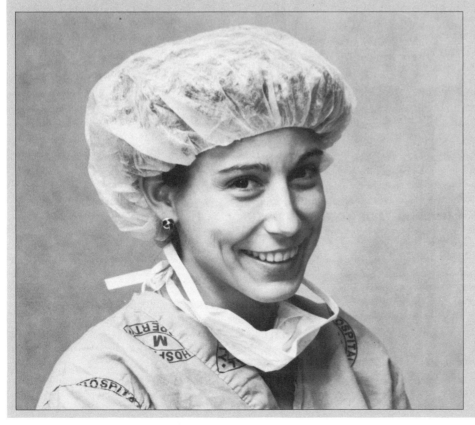

Continued from preceding page

Occasionally we operate on people whose aneurysms haven't ruptured and those people uniformly do well. That's one of those areas where there is so much yet to do, to develop screening tools and try to pick them up before they rupture.

"Cancer is very difficult to deal with, but you sort of accept it as something that there's not much you can do about," she said. "I think that the most frustrating and challenging things are the non-malignant either tumors or congenital malformations that aren't cancers but end up causing incredible deficits anyway.

"They can make people paralyzed, they can make people blind, and it's so frustrating to know that this thing is potentially curable and yet not be able to cure it, usually because of the location.

"Even though we go in knowing a lot of times that we're not going to be able to cure things, the intent is one of helping. A lot of what we do is palliative, in that it gives people time," she said.

Dr. Neave comes by her love of surgery naturally. Her mother's father was a neurosurgeon and her mother was a doctor. Friends of the family still like to recall that as a child she often said she wanted to be a neurosurgeon like other children sometimes say they want to be a firefighter or a police officer. She says now she's sure she simply liked the sound of the word.

Born in New York, she lived in Greensboro until she was 6. Then her family moved to Jamaica because of her father's work in the State Department's foreign service branch.

While attending school predominately in Southeast Asia, she found that overseas school systems were attuned to the individual's pace. She combined the fourth and fifth grades and skipped the eleventh grade.

Because of that early advancement and "knowing very early what I wanted to do and how long it was going to take, I sort of went straight through," she recalled. "I didn't stop and particularly play like a lot of people do either between college and med school or med school and residency."

She was essentially two years ahead when she entered Johns Hopkins University, where she majored in biophysics to avoid the "crazy, cut-throat intense" pre-med students.

"Organic chemistry was like the cut-throat class of the century," she recalled with an easy laugh. "You'd be in this room with 240 people, each hoping everyone else in the class fails or does poorly. You're in lab with them and they're glaring at your laboratory experiment, hoping it turns into some green rock or something and you'll get an F."

She had been warned about the pre-medical school atmosphere, so she took her advisor's advice about majoring in biophysics and went through the program "underneath the table," she said. "It was the best advice anyone ever gave me."

While at Johns Hopkins, she took several neurophysiology courses and "fell in love with the nervous system," she recalled.

"It fascinated me and there was so much that wasn't known. It was just like a frontier that hadn't been crossed yet. A lot of the other organ systems have been fairly well standardized, but there's so much about neuro that you just shrug your shoulders and say, 'I don't know, that's just the way it is.'

"That continued in medical school. My very favorite courses and clinical rotations were always in neuro. Then I stepped foot in the O.R. and that was it.

I was immediately at home. I watched people operate and I just wanted to dive in myself," she said with a laugh.

"It was sort of an inexplicable feeling, but I knew that was exactly what I was supposed to do and what I would have fun doing. It talks to me. There's no other good way to explain it."

After graduating from Johns Hopkins, she went to medical school at the Medical College of Virginia, then to Los Angeles for her residency.

The 2,000-bed Los Angeles County Hospital, connected with the University of Southern California, is one of the prime spots in the country to train because "you see every kind of pathology numerous times over," she said. "I will do those kinds of cases, but never in that quantity again. You come out of residency feeling comfortable doing anything."

It was during those years of residency that she found another activity she felt comfortable with: cross-country horseback riding. She calls it her "sanity saver."

"There's nothing like racing through the woods and jumping over anything that happens to be in front of you," she said.

The cross-country style of riding is largely what attracted her to the North Carolina-Virginia area, and she's now looking for an Irish Hunter gelding to complete her dream.

Her six years in Los Angeles and her early years in Greensboro are the longest stints she's lived anywhere, she said. "I don't really have a home, but Greensboro feels as close as anything does."

Even during her years in Los Angeles, her life was geared toward North Carolina's style, she said. "I was still doing the outdoorsy things that I like to do and I was always dreaming of green and hills and places to ride."

Checking Your Comprehension

Read the following questions. Put an *x* in the box beside the answer that best completes each one.

1. Dr. Neave says she is most frustrated by "non-malignant ...tumors or congenital malformations." Something that is *congenital*
   □ a. is congested.
   □ b. is cancerous.
   □ c. exists from birth.

2. On being able to help but not cure, Neave says: "A lot of what we do is palliative in that it gives people time." Something that is *palliative*
   □ a. moderates the intensity of something, an illness, for example.
   □ b. gives apologies for negative behavior or attitudes.
   □ c. is inoperable.

3. What is Neave's first reaction every time she opens up a skull and sees the brain?
   □ a. She thinks of a white cauliflower-like substance.
   □ b. She admires its golden beauty.
   □ c. She becomes excited and frustrated by surgery.

4. Neave finds aneurysm surgery frustrating because
   □ a. an aneurysm could explode anytime.
   □ b. there is a need for a screening tool that would discover aneurysms before they rupture.
   □ c. people recover well from surgery when the aneurysm hasn't ruptured.

5. Neave is valuable to the medical profession in the North Carolina area in that she
   □ a. is the youngest neurosurgeon in the nation.
   □ b. is one of only thirty-six surgeons in the country.
   □ c. brings techniques for neurosurgery that are new to the community.

6. Which event was most influential in Neave's decision to become a neurosurgeon?
   □ a. Her grandfather and her mother were doctors.
   □ b. She entered medical school two years earlier because she skipped some grades.
   □ c. In her neurophysiology courses, she became intrigued because so little is known about the nervous system.

☆ ☆ ☆

Each of the feature stories you have just read focuses on a woman who is considered newsworthy. Goodall stands at the apogee of an impressive and meaningful scientific career. That and the publication of her book prompted USA TODAY to run an article on her. In contrast, Neave is not well known, though the people in her community will surely know her in the years to come. As a young neurosurgeon, Neave can claim recent accomplishments, but more important to readers are her future contributions. That is why Neave is a name in the news, even if it is the local news.

☆ ☆ ☆

Examining Sequence in Feature Story Biographies

In writing the feature stories about Goodall and Neave, the reporters have actually written biographies. Both stories tell how the women became fascinated with their work, how their childhood experiences influenced them, and what their early accomplishments were. But the reporters do not write these biographies in strict chronological sequence. Instead, the reporters arrange the events in order of importance.

Both reporters begin by telling why the subject of the story is a name in the news. Next they outline future goals. Then they relate important events from the past. Still, even though the reporters do not arrange the events in chronological order, they give us clues about when the events occurred. Such clues include phrases like "after high school" or "as a child," which indicate when the events happened.

Listed below and on the next page are sets of statements about Goodall and Neave. The statements in each set are listed in the order in which they appeared in the articles. Read the statements, then number them in chronological order. Look for words and phrases that act as clues indicating the chronological sequence in which the events happened.

Jane Goodall

_____ 1. The harvest of 25 years is collected in her new, 673-page study, *The Chimpanzees of Gombe: Patterns of Behavior.* . . .

_____ 2. Her next scholarly book will be about chimpanzee mother-child relationships. Her major goals, other than keeping Gombe going, are chimp conservation and welfare and the raising of human children.

_____ 3. "Always encouraged" by her mother, Goodall continued to watch and read about animals.

_____ 4. After high school, Goodall visited Africa, where she met Paleontologist Louis Leakey and began working for him as a secretary. Her energy and interest in animals spurred Leakey to choose Goodall as the one to observe the chimps at Gombe.

_____ 5. "For the first 10 years, I thought they were very much like us but much nicer, and then I learned . . . that chimps practice warfare and even cannibalism."

Vicky Neave

_____ 1. It is an understatement to point out that Dr. Neave, 31, is High Point's first woman neurosurgeon. Maybe it's of greater significance to mention that she's one of the youngest practicing neuro-surgeons in the nation, or that next month she's scheduled to receive the Congress of Neurological Surgery's Resident of the Year award.

_____ 2. Her grandfather was a neurosurgeon and her mother was a doctor. As a child she often said she wanted to be a neurosurgeon, though she says now she just liked the sound of the word.

_____ 3. While at Johns Hopkins, she fell in love with the nervous system because so much was unknown. That continued in medical school. "Then, I watched people operate and I just wanted to dive in myself. It was an inexplicable feeling, but I knew that was exactly what I was supposed to do and what I would have fun doing. It talks to me. There's no other good way to explain it."

_____ 4. She combined the fourth and fifth grades and skipped the eleventh grade.

Using Your Newspaper

In your newspaper, find a feature story about a name in the news. You might find an article about a politician, an enter-tainer, an educator, a sports figure, an author—there will be no shortage of stories on public people.

Think back to the stories on Jane Goodall and Vicky Neave. We have identified reasons for their appearing in the newspaper; we know what made them newsworthy. To do this exercise, you will want to look at the subjects of your selected feature stories in the same way we looked at Goodall and Neave.

In a written analysis of three or four paragraphs, answer these questions: Why is the person in the newspaper—what is the accomplishment or activity that is meant to interest readers? Is that accomplishment or activity unique, as was the case with Vicky Neave, or just timely? Is the accomplish-ment itself the reason for the news story, or is the accom-plishment related to another event, a seasonal theme, or even a book promotion, in the manner of Jane Goodall?

At the end of your analysis state whether you think the person is a good subject for a story. In other words, just how newsworthy is the person? Is he or she important enough to a wide range of people to justify being in the newspaper?

Practicing Newspaper Skills

Act as a feature reporter and interview someone in your school or community who you think deserves recognition. You might choose a senior citizen with years and years of experience and living to discuss, or you might choose a person with an unusual job, hobby, or skill. Perhaps you can find a person who is trying to discover or invent something.

Arrange for an interview. Go to the interview prepared to take notes or to tape record the conversation. Also, well before the appointed time, write out a list of questions. Here are some areas you might want to cover with your subject (let's say she's a woman):

- How did she become interested and involved in her work?
- Who influenced her childhood?
- Was there a particular event that inspired her to go into her work?
- What changes has she seen in her work over the years?
- What are her future goals? How would she like to see her job develop?

For your article, select the most important facts gathered in the interview. Pick the item that would seem to be the natural main idea of the story. Make that main idea your story's angle. Many of the lesser facts can function as details supporting the main idea. Some other items will provide bits of interesting color and background.

Since this is a feature, you might want to work gradually into the story by starting with a paragraph that sets the tone or is designed to grab the reader's interest. (Look back at the open-ing paragraphs in the Goodall and Neave pieces—both are "grabbers.") You can follow such an opening with a paragraph introducing the angle. In subsequent paragraphs you can flesh out the story with what your subject had to say in response to the interview questions. Use some direct quotes, as well—that adds a human touch.

When you have finished the story, compose a headline that expresses in typical headline shorthand the main idea of the story. The headline should hint at the reason for the person's newsworthiness.

Recency is an important news quality. There is nothing as vibrant as a fresh story—and nothing as deadly as old news. Some events take place and make news for a day, then disappear. Other events sustain over a number of days. Then there are events or issues that are important and complicated that appear in newspapers on a continual basis over an extended period. Such events are often covered in various sections of the paper by a variety of writers—reporters, columnists, editors, cartoonists—who come to the topic with facts, questions, answers, and opinions that they feel will interest their readers.

The spread of AIDS is an important, complicated topic. It is receiving wide coverage by the press. Almost daily, a reader can find articles on the need for increased funding for AIDS research, or on proposed methods to halt the spread of the disease. Editorials appear and people write letters to the editor. Local newspapers may publish articles about the legal issues surrounding school attendance of a child with AIDS, or about the controversy surrounding a community educational or testing program. AIDS is even an occasional topic in such sections of the newspaper as the travel and entertainment pages. Thus, as it deals with recent events and issues, the newspaper serves as a major source of information and education for people who are trying to be informed about AIDS.

Read the two articles in this lesson, one a special feature, the other an advice column. Decide what readership or audience each article was written for. Finally, think about any new information that has surfaced since these articles were written in the late spring of 1987 that would have to be added to make them more current.

Q & A

By JUDY FOREMAN
Globe Staff

*T*he AIDS epidemic is now in its seventh year, a plague caused by a deadly virus that has already killed 20,557 Americans and is believed to have infected at least 1.5 million more.

It is beginning to fill our hospitals and empty our coffers. It has jet-propelled basic science and revolutionized the language of everyday conversation.

In the hysteria surrounding it, however, a number of misconceptions remain. Many people do not realize, for instance, that AIDS is actually not easy to "catch." The following are some of the most frequently asked questions about AIDS, and answers.

Q. What is AIDS? What is ARC?
A. AIDS stands for Acquired Immune Deficiency Syndrome. It's caused by a special virus called a retrovirus that invades important immune cells and kills them. Without a healthy immune system, the body can't fight off infections and some cancers.

ARC stands for AIDS-Related Complex, a milder form of AIDS, though it, too, can be fatal.

Q. What fluids in the body is the AIDS virus found in?
A. Mainly in semen, vaginal fluid and blood and to a lesser extent, saliva, tears, sweat, urine, vomit and feces.

Q. How do you get AIDS?
A. Chiefly by contact with the virus in blood, semen and vaginal fluid. The AIDS virus is not spread casually, for instance, by shaking hands, sharing toilet seats or being sneezed upon. People get AIDS from unprotected sex with an infected person; from blood or blood products or from sharing drug needles with an infected abuser. Babies get AIDS by exposure to the virus from contact with the mother's blood in pregnancy or childbirth.

Just sharing a household with an infected person is not risky, nor are working or going to school with a person with AIDS. Even health workers who accidentally stick themselves with AIDS-contaminated needles rarely become infected.

Q. How do you know if you have been exposed? What are the symptoms?
A. There is absolutely no way to tell just by looking at someone whether he or she carries the AIDS virus. Only blood tests can reveal the presence of antibodies to the virus, a sign of exposure to the virus itself. But it takes two weeks to six months after infection to build up detectable antibodies.

Q. If you get infected, do you automatically get AIDS or ARC?
A. No one knows because the disease has not been studied long enough. But it appears that over time, progression from infection to AIDS is likely. The National Academy of Sciences estimates that five to 10 years after infection, at least 50 percent of those infected will come down with AIDS. The average incubation period, once believed to be two to five years, is now believed to be much longer, suggesting that infected people should be given AIDS drugs long before they get sick.

Q. Once you get AIDS, is it inevitable that you will die?
A. No one knows, though the US Surgeon General has said that AIDS is "100 percent fatal." So far, only one AIDS drug (AZT) has been approved by the US Food and Drug Administration.

Q. Who is most at risk for AIDS?
A. The short answer is gay and bisexual men and intravenous drug users. But the real answer is anyone, gay or straight, who engages in high risk behavior, chiefly sex with an infected person, especially without a condom, and sharing IV drug needles. Since 1981 when the AIDS epidemic began, the proportions of adult cases have held steady: gay and bisexual men, 66 percent; IV drug abusers, 17 percent; gay/bisexual men who are also IV drug abusers, 8 percent. Only 1 percent of cases are in hemophiliacs, who received contaminated blood products, and 2 percent in people who have received contaminated blood transfusions. So far,

Continued on following page

Continued from preceding page
only 4 percent of AIDS cases involve heterosexual transmission. Mode of transmission is unknown in 3 percent of cases.

Even though AIDS is not yet rampant in the American heterosexual community, it could be. In Africa, heterosexual transmission is the main mode of viral spread, and men and women have the disease in equal numbers.

Another way of looking at risk is sociological. Probably because of higher IV drug abuse, blacks, though only 11 percent of the population, account for 25 percent of AIDS cases and Hispanics, only 8 percent of the population, account for 14 percent of AIDS cases. So far, women account for only 7 percent of adult AIDS cases.

Q. If the virus is still mainly in special groups, how would it get into the heterosexual population?
A. The "bridges" are bisexual men, intravenous drug users and people who have sex with infected prostitutes, male and female. About 11 percent of prostitutes now carry the AIDS virus and in the New York/New Jersey area, more than half the prostitutes are infected.

Q. Can you get AIDS from mosquitoes or other insects?
A. Probably not, though the virus has been found in insects from Africa. The reason scientists think insects probably aren't spreading AIDS is that, if they did, people at all ages, especially in Africa where the disease is rampant, would have AIDS, because bugs bite everyone. In fact, primarily young children (exposed in utero and during birth) and sexually active teenagers and adults get AIDS.

Q. Can you get AIDS from kissing? From oral sex?
A. Deep kissing with an exchange of saliva is risky because the virus exists in saliva, though at low concentrations, and could enter the body through minute cuts in the mouth, even cuts caused by dental flossing or tooth brushing. Oral sex without a condom is even more risky because semen contains more virus than saliva.

Q. Can you get AIDS from saunas, swimming pools, hot tubs, sweaty gym equipment?
A. No, no, no and no. Saunas, swimming pools and hot tubs are chlorinated and heated. Chlorine kills the AIDS virus, as does heat. Though tiny amounts of virus exist in sweat, no one has ever been known to get AIDS from another person's sweat.

Q. Can you get AIDS in just one sexual encounter or just one IV drug injection?
A. Yes. It's like roulette—one unlucky encounter can do it, but of course, the more partners one has and the more often one "shoots up" with contaminated drug needles, the more likely one is to acquire the virus. On the other hand, the virus is not always transmitted in every sexual encounter with an infected person.

Q. Can you get AIDS from your dentist?
A. Again, theoretically, yes, and he/she could get it from you. But if this were a major mode of transmission, far more people would already be infected. Even so, dentists should wear protective gloves and masks, for their sake, and yours.

Q. If you can't stop using IV drugs, is there anything you can do to protect yourself?
A. Yes. Don't share needles—use your own. If you must share, soak your entire "works" (needle, syringe and bottlecap "cooker") in a solution of 2 tablespoons of bleach and 1 cup of water for 10 minutes to kill the virus. Then wash "works" thoroughly in water because bleach is poisonous if injected. Alternately, soak your "works" for 10 minutes in 1 cup of rubbing alcohol, then rinse.

Q. Can you get AIDS from giving blood?
A. No; this is one of the worst misconceptions about AIDS. Donating blood is safe.

Q. Can you get the AIDS virus from blood transfusions? What should you do if you are worried about a past transfusion?
A. Yes, but since the spring of 1985, hospitals have tested blood. Before 1985, donated blood was not tested and an estimated 12,000 people may have been exposed to AIDS. The only way to tell if you are infected is through the blood test.

Q. In a nutshell, what is safe sex, or "safer sex"?
A. Using a condom throughout the entire sex act so that even small amounts of fluid emitted before ejaculation cannot enter your partner. No deep kissing of an infected person.

Q. Do spermicides, especially those containing nonoxynol-9, kill the AIDS virus?
A. In test tubes, there's some evidence they do. But no one should rely on them for protection.

Q. Will AIDS ever be curable? Will there be a vaccine?
A. Maybe, to both questions. Scientists now understand more about the AIDS virus than about many other disease agents. Many pharmaceutical companies, universities and government labs are working feverishly on both drugs and vaccines. But how well they will work is still undetermined.

Checking Your Comprehension

Read the following questions. Put an x in the box beside the answer that best completes each one.

1. The introduction states that in the hysteria over AIDS, a "number of misconceptions remain." *Misconceptions* are
   ☐ a. misunderstandings.
   ☐ b. miscalculations.
   ☐ c. mysteries.

2. One of the answers in the column says that "AIDS is not yet rampant in the American heterosexual community." *Rampant* means
   ☐ a. dominant.
   ☐ b. widespread.
   ☐ c. reputable.

3. The article states that the following are included in the highest risk groups for contracting AIDS except
   □ a. intravenous drug users.
   □ b. gay and bisexual men.
   □ c. hemophiliacs.

4. All of the ways below are among the known ways people get AIDS except
   □ a. from unprotected sex with an infected person.
   □ b. by shaking hands or being sneezed upon by an infected person.
   □ c. from blood or blood products.

5. In the introduction to this article, Globe staff writer Judy Foreman refers to AIDS as an epidemic and a plague. It seems justified for her to do this because
   □ a. it was first identified seven years ago.
   □ b. its victims are beginning to fill hospitals.
   □ c. it is actually not easy to "catch."

6. Certain new information makes AIDS seem even more frightening than was originally believed. An example of such a recent finding reported in the article is
   □ a. AIDS is caused by a virus that invades immune cells so that one can't fight off infection and some cancers.
   □ b. the National Academy of Sciences now estimates that five to ten years after exposure, at least 50 percent of exposed individuals will come down with AIDS.
   □ c. only blood tests can clearly reveal the presence of antibodies to the virus and it takes from two weeks to six months after infection to build up detectable amounts of these antibodies.

☆ ☆ ☆

The feature article you just read was part of an in-depth special section of the *Boston Globe* called "Living with AIDS." The reporter's introduction (the first three paragraphs, in italics), clearly shows that AIDS is a current threat, a modern-day epidemic arousing greater and greater concern. Reporter Judy Foreman is aware of that concern, and she realizes that many people have questions about the disease. The question-and-answer format of her article is meant to answer those questions and clear up misinformation for a wide readership.

In the following article, *Ask Beth,* the question-and-answer format is geared to teenagers and their concerns. Read the letters in the advice column to see if you think the format invites the reader's participation. Notice how the questions asked and the facts presented are similar to those in the first article.

ASK BETH

Sex too soon

Having sex before you're ready brings more problems than pleasure

Sexual activity among teenagers is suddenly in all the headlines. Changing moral values and the proliferation of explicit and illicit sex in the media and advertising are largely reponsible. Another major problem is the sense of hopelessness that afflicts many kids today. If your future doesn't look bright, why bother to resist temptation? What are you saving yourself for? Until this social and economic problem can be addressed, information is the only remedy we have.

Dear Beth:
I have a son, 17. He knows all the facts, but I never delve into his personal affairs. I suppose that he has been intimate with girls, but I don't really know. Now that AIDS is getting to be a problem for heterosexuals, I am really worried. What should I say to him?

Parent of Teen

Make sure he has accurate information about this infection. Ask him how it is transmitted and what are the greatest risks. Talk to him about what it means to practice "safe sex"; always using spermicidal latex condoms and using them correctly; not practicing oral or anal intercourse; not being promiscuous; not going to prostitutes.

AIDS must be explained to every child, but we mustn't make this the only formula for giving information about sex. Despite the seriousness of AIDS, sex is not just bad and dangerous. It is still a wonderful expression of love between loving and responsible adults.

Only 20 percent of sexually active adolescents now practice "safe sex." *Continued on following page*

Continued from preceding page

Teenagers know quite a bit about AIDS and how dangerous it is, but they ignore this information. This proves, once again, that this age group simply isn't mature enough to take responsibility for its sexual behavior.

While we hope young people will wait until they are mature before they become sexually active, we also hope they will grow up to have happy and fulfilling sex lives. We just don't want them to spoil things before they are ready.

Dear Beth:

I'm 16 and Paul is 20. He took me out and we had a really long talk, discussing everything, including our ages. He told me that didn't matter. I thought he really loved me, and we almost made love that night.

Now he's avoiding me. I found out he has a girlfriend he's supposed to be marrying because she's pregnant. I also heard he is gay, and that there are at least 10 girls pregnant by him. Now I'm worried I could have AIDS. But remember, I still love him.

Used and Abused in New Haven

If you were used, you cooperated, didn't you? If you didn't have intercourse, your chances of having AIDS are negligible. The rumors sound contradictory anyway, but it's clear he's no boyfriend for you.

Think this over carefully. Can you really love someone you've just met? If it's just infatuation, it won't last. So why make love?

Dear Beth:

I have contracted a sexually transmitted disease. I can neither tell my parents, nor pay for treatment. Are there any free clinics in New York?

T.Y.

Yes, several, and none of them notify your parents. Look under the city listings (or county or state where appropriate) under the heading "Health" for Venereal Disease (VD) Control or Sexually Transmitted Disease (STD) Control or Communicable Disease. Call and ask for the nearest clinic, and whether you need an appointment or can just walk in.

Checking Your Comprehension

Read the following questions. Put an *x* in the box beside the answer that best completes each one.

1. The first parent writes about her son: "He knows all the facts, but I never delve into his personal affairs. The word *delve* means
   - ☐ a. search for information.
   - ☐ b. make a dent.
   - ☐ c. jump.

2. Beth tells the girl in New Haven that "the rumors sound contradictory anyway, but it's clear he's no boyfriend for you." *Contradictory* means
   - ☐ a. negative.
   - ☐ b. contrived.
   - ☐ c. conflicting.

3. In Beth's reply to the Parent of Teen, she suggests that the parent talk to her son about "safe sex." Her definition includes all of the following except
   - ☐ a. using spermicidal latex condoms correctly.
   - ☐ b. not going to prostitutes.
   - ☐ c. having sex only with females.

4. The parent who wrote to Beth is worried because
   - ☐ a. someone has said their seventeen-year-old son is promiscuous.
   - ☐ b. AIDS is getting to be a problem for heterosexuals.
   - ☐ c. only 20 percent of the sexually active teenage population practices safe sex.

5. When Beth responds in the second letter to Used and Abused in New Haven, Beth suggests the girl not make love because
   - ☐ a. Paul is too old for her.
   - ☐ b. When you have just met someone, you can't be sure if you love them and want to have a close relationship.
   - ☐ c. Paul probably has AIDS.

6. In her first response, Beth seems concerned that if the only information teens get from their parents about sex is information related to AIDS
   - ☐ a. the teens will see sex as bad and dangerous, rather than an expression of mature love.
   - ☐ b. they will ignore the information they are given because it's too depressing.
   - ☐ c. they will frighten younger children with the information.

☆ ☆ ☆

Most people have a need to be informed and up-to-date on current events. That is one reason newspapers sell, and it is one of the reasons for the recent surge in popularity of television news shows.

The phrase *up-to-date,* of course, connects directly to the idea of recency. "New" news is the lifeblood of the newspaper industry; recency is of paramount importance. This is in part caused by competition among news purveyors: newspaper editors rush major stories into print because they know other editors on other papers are doing the same. Given that situation and the constant presence of television news, we as readers are concerned with, and feel we are most affected by, up-to-date information.

☆ ☆ ☆

Fact and Opinion in the Question-and-Answer Format

In her introduction to her question-and-answer piece, reporter Judy Foreman points out that many people harbor misconceptions about AIDS. Some of the questions *Ask Beth* handles bear that notion out. Even researchers searching for a cure have only a few facts and a great many theories, theories further research will prove or disprove. At present, the disease occupies the center of a swirling storm of fact and opinion.

Below are statements from the two articles. Some are fact statements and some are opinion statements. You will also find opinions embodied in some of the fact statements. In the space provided, write *fact* if the statement gives information that is accepted as being factual. Write *opinion* if the statement expresses an opinion. Write *both* if the statement contains elements of both fact and opinion. Refer to the statements in context as necessary.

_____ 1. The AIDS epidemic is now in its seventh year. . . .

_____ 2. ARC stands for AIDS-Related Complex, a milder form of AIDS. . . .

_____ 3. The average incubation period, once believed to be two to five years, is now believed to be much longer, suggesting that people should be given AIDS drugs long before they get sick.

_____ 4. Even though AIDS is not yet rampant in the heterosexual community, it could be.

_____ 5. Even so, dentists should wear protective gloves and masks, for their sake, and yours.

_____ 6. Donating blood is safe.

_____ 7. Until this social and economic problem can be addressed, information is the only remedy we have.

_____ 8. Teenagers know quite a bit about AIDS and how dangerous it is, but they ignore this information. This proves . . . that this age group simply isn't mature enough to take responsibility for its sexual behavior.

Using Your Newspaper

Scan your newspaper over several days for stories about AIDS. Collect front-page news reports, columns like *Ask Beth,* special features, and editorials.

Distill the information from your collected articles into three categories: facts, opinions, and mixtures of fact and opinion. On a sheet of paper, make a *Fact* heading, an *Opinion* heading, and a *Both Fact and Opinion* heading. Then list relevant information under each heading. Under the Fact heading you would list a fact such as this: 20,557 Americans have died of the disease. Under the Opinion heading you would list this statement: One in every ninety-three persons between the ages of twenty and fifty-nine may carry the virus.

As you can see, the opinion given is a medical estimate, a kind of theory. For your purposes, scientific theories that contain no facts must be classed as opinions. But as we have seen, speculation on medical matters is often based in fact. Many statements that you collect from researchers may contain factual information as well as thoughts, beliefs, guesses, and hunches. If you feel that a statement contains elements of fact and opinion, list that statement under the Both Fact and Opinion heading.

Who Reports the News

UNIT OVERVIEW

In Unit One you read front page news reports, sports stories, feature stories, an editorial, and a question-and-answer column. In Unit Two we will look at the journalists who write these and other types of stories.

First we will look at the role of the *reporter.* Reporters write news stories about important events of the day. Many reporters specialize in the news they report. This is called *covering a beat.* A beat can be a subject, such as science, education, business or sports. A beat can also be a particular building or organization, such as city hall, police headquarters, or the courthouse. In covering a particular beat, a reporter uses research, interviews, and investigative techniques to collect facts for stories. For example, to gather information at a sports event, a sports reporter takes notes on important plays and interviews key players. Either before or after the event the reporter researches any needed facts. Likewise, a city hall reporter attending a press conference by the mayor would take notes and try to interview the mayor and other key people as well as doing "homework" on relevant political issues. After the note-taking and reporting is done, a reporter writes up the story, beginning with a *lead,* or opening paragraph, that answers the questions *Who? What? When? Where? Why?* and *How?* In the subsequent paragraphs, the reporter elaborates on the lead paragraph, stating the most important facts first and working down to the least important by the end of the story.

Unit Two also contains stories by *feature writers.* Feature writers report on a variety of topics that appeal to readers. Typical feature stories include interviews with famous entertainers, stories on upcoming events, and accounts of unusual places to visit. Like reporters, feature writers collect data by researching facts, attending events, and interviewing people. Feature stories are often entertaining and informative biographies of noteworthy people.

In Unit Two we will also read the work of *editorial writers.* These writers give opinions and interpret news events for readers. Each day, the editorial writers on a newspaper's staff meet to pick the topics that they will write about. They also decide what stance to assume in the editorials. Their articles, which appear on a newspaper's editorial pages, are statements of opinion that seek to persuade readers to adopt the newspaper's view of events. The ultimate goal of an editorial is to move someone to act on the problem under discussion. The editorial writer may offer a solution, make a plea that someone find a solution, or voice an emphatic demand that someone find a solution.

Many readers value the opinions of newspaper *critics,* whose contributions to the paper appear mainly in the lifestyle, arts, and entertainment sections. Newspaper critics offer their opinions about movies, theatrical performances, musical events, books, restaurants, and so on. In the case of a performance, a critic gathers information by attending the event and taking notes on the performance and, perhaps, the audience's reaction to the performance. Then the critic sorts out his or her impressions and writes a review that tells readers about the event and whether it is worth attending. Likewise, a critic reads a book before writing about it or listens to an album before describing it to readers. Newspaper critics, then, review events or products with an expression of personal opinion drawn from experience.

News *columnists* express their personal opinions of news events, not the newspaper's official opinion, as do staff editorial writers. Many such columnists are *syndicated,* which means that their columns appear in many newspapers. Their columns can be found in virtually every section of the newspaper, from the sports pages to the lifestyle section to the editorial page. The news columnist voices his or her opinion, trying to persuade readers to adopt that personal view. Like editorial writers, columnists form and express opinions on current news events. Also like editorial writers, their opinions may embody proposed solutions or include a plea or a demand for a solution. News columnists sometimes simply comment on the news, expressing a reaction to current events. This unit features two columns by a syndicated columnist.

Also in this unit is an example of a type of article meant to inform readers and to assist them in their daily lives, namely, the how-to column. *How-to columnists* frequently use a step-by-step direction format that is both easy to read and to apply. Some how-to columnists are experts in a particular field such as cooking, medicine, or chess. When the columnist is not an expert, he or she will consult with someone who is before writing the column. Whether they are experts or not, all columnists collect factual information by reading articles, by interviewing people, and, sometimes, by experimenting for themselves. Then when the columnists write their columns, they report not only the factual information but also their opinions on how best to do something. Through their blend of fact and opinions, how-to writers inform and aid readers.

Because "a picture is worth a thousand words," as the saying goes, most newspapers employ photographers, artists, and cartoonists. Unit Two offers a look at the types of photos, artists' renderings, and cartoons commonly found in newspapers.

Photographers often cover stories alongside reporters

or feature writers. Taking many shots during an event, photographers try to capture interesting people, expressions of emotion on faces, the climax of an event, or the height of the action. From the many shots, photographers and editors select the best picture. The right photograph does double duty, not only drawing a reader into the story, but also providing visual information that complements the story.

To help readers comprehend information quickly and easily, *artists* draw charts, tables, maps, and diagrams to accompany stories. Weather maps, TV listing charts, clothes in ads or in fashion articles—all are from the drawing boards of newspaper artists. This unit contains a drawing intended to help readers understand in step-by-step detail how a tragic accident occurred.

If you are a reader of the comics, you recognize the role of the *cartoonist*. There are, of course, serious cartoonists whose political and cultural observations can be found in many sections of the newspaper. In this unit, however, we will concentrate on two cartoonists from the comics pages, one a pioneering innovator and one a relative newcomer. No look at the newspaper would be complete without an examination of the role of entertainment, and no section of the newspaper better represents entertainment than the comics.

While you read Unit Two, try to imagine the activities of the writers responsible for the stories. If you were to go into journalism, which job role would you most like to fill?

According to the Neilsen ratings, a record seventy million people watched TV to see the seventh game of the 1986 World Series between the New York Mets and the Boston Red Sox. In this lesson are stories on that game from the *New York Post*. If you recall Lesson 6, Unit One, which deals with hometown bias in sports reporting, you will know not to expect objective, neutral treatments of the Mets-Sox series in a New York paper.

The story below is a straight-news sports story. As you can see, the lead paragraph (which in this case is the second paragraph, following a colorful, tone-setting first paragraph) answers the questions *Who? What? When? Where? Why?* and *How?* For the rest of the story the reporter, Bob Klapisch, recounts the major events that produced the final score. To add human interest, Klapisch intersperses comments from the players on big plays and how they are feeling.

Ray Knight, the Most Valuable Player of the series, is the subject of the second story, which is a feature story with a narrower, more limited angle.

WE'RE #1

Amazin's rally past Red Sox to win Series

By BOB KLAPISCH

They spoke thousands of words—but in reality they were speechless. The Mets were too numb to make sense. They chugged champagne. They hugged each other. They wept. They exchanged looks that said: *The world is ours.*

It took seven exhausting games, but the World Series ended last night at 11:26. It was the Mets who outlasted the Red Sox, 8-5. It was the Mets who scored eight runs in the final three innings—capturing their first World Championship since 1969. It is the Mets who can now shake their fists at the National League.

Finally? Yes. Finally.

"Regardless of the jealousy, the envy, the hatred that exists for us, we have to be considered a great team now. We have to," Gary Carter said. "We showed our own true character in this Series. This team is... I don't know. I really don't know what to say."

Carter—like every other champagne-drenched body in the Met clubhouse will be emotionally spent for weeks. The post-game riot in the locker room was more relief than celebration.

* * *

It was Wally Backman high-fiving Howard Johnson, saying only: "We did it, didn't we." It was Keith Hernandez-to-Jesse Orosco: "You're a man, Jess." It was Darryl Strawberry-to-Ray Knight: "I love you."

* * *

How many times had we seen it? What

Continued on following page

Series MVP Ray Knight celebrates 7th-inning homer that gave Mets 4–3 lead last night at Shea.

Continued from preceding page

did we learn from Game 6 in Houston? Character. And Game 6 at Shea? Character. The Mets used the word in every breath. And who can argue?

* * *

Bruce Hurst owned them for five innings with a 3-0 lead—but Strawberry said, "We were sitting in the dugout telling ourselves, 'We can get this guy. He's not sharp.' No one on this team thought he was going to beat us again."

* * *

And then came the sixth-, seventh- and eighth-inning explosions that left the Red Sox crushed. John McNamara went through six pitchers, looking for a way to contain the Mets. There were no answers. Not last night. Not in 1986.

* * *

Destiny? "Yeah, we were destined to win this," said Ron Darling—who lasted only 3½ innings and admitted, "I had nothing."

* * *

"We didn't even play well and we won. We may not have even deserved to win—and we did. Yeah, I'd call it destiny."

* * *

Destiny: Sid Fernandez bailed out Darling, threw zeroes until the sixth and fanned four Red Sox hitters. Boston's offense vanished.

* * *

Destiny: Hurst simply lost his stuff in the sixth. With one out, Lee Mazzilli singled, Mookie Wilson singled, Tim Teufel walked and Hernandez came to the plate.

* * *

Hernandez was hitting .251 in the postseason. He'd heard grumblings about only four RBIs in 13 games. But the bases were loaded now. His chance was in front of him.

* * *

"I told my brother in the morning, 'Gary, if there is any justice in the world, I'll get up in a tight situation and get a big hit.'" Hernandez said, "I've hit so many balls right at people...I looked at it this way: I knew Hurst was going on three days' rest, and he wasn't as sharp as Game 5. He was pitching me the way he did in Game One (also on three days' rest). Mostly fastballs. I figured on the same pattern."

* * *

Hernandez smiled. "That was a big, big hit."

* * *

This big: a fastball. A two-run single, roped up the gap in left-center. It brought the Mets within 3-2, and told them: Hurst is mortal tonight.

* * *

Why? How? Wasn't this the same Hurst who'd ruled the Mets like house pets for 17 innings? Yes, it was. But this time, Hurst was working on just three days' rest—McNamara's gamble in passing over Oil Can Boyd.

* * *

To a man, the Mets said Hurst's fastball was a little fatter than Games 1 and 5. His corner-strikes were a little too good. His time was coming.

* * *

"I just wasn't conditioned to pitch on three days' rest," Hurst admitted in a very quiet Red Sox locker room. "I hadn't done it all season. I knew I couldn't go the whole way. But I wanted to hold the lead."

* * *

He was through now. Carter lifted a bloop to right—caught and bobbled by a diving Dwight Evans, who nailed Hernandez at second. No matter. Wally Backman, pinch-running for Teufel, scored with the tying run.

* * *

Hurst was gone. Replaced by Calvin Schiraldi. Schiraldi? "We know about Schiraldi," one Met said. "We knew he didn't have any guts. We remembered him. Believe me. Guys don't change overnight."

* * *

The Mets scored three times on Schiraldi in the seventh. For all that happened afterward—Orosco's heroics in the eighth, two more Met runs in the bottom of that inning—it was Ray Knight's leadoff home run that told the Mets: *The world is ours.*

Knight—voted the Series MVP—said diplomatically, "Once we got into the Sox' bullpen, I knew we were in good shape. They didn't have any lefthanders. They were playing right into our strength...and they all throw hard."

Hard throwers. The Mets dine on them. When Schiraldi went 2-1 on Knight, the Mets' third baseman stepped out of the box, took a deep breath and told himself, "A fastball is coming. It's his best pitch."

It came. Knight crushed it. And in the instant the ball sailed over the left-field wall, the world *did* belong to the Mets. The rest was moot: Two more hits, Rafael Santana's RBI single, Hernandez' sacrifice fly.

Three runs—all of which gave Orosco the cushion to bail out Roger McDowell. Evans' two-run double in the eighth made it 6-5. Orosco arrived, and admitted so much nervousness, "that I was looking for the bathroom. I just told myself, 'This is no time to fold, Jesse.'"

He didn't. Rich Gedman lined out to Backman. Dave Henderson swung over four sliders. And Don Baylor bounced to short. The rally had evaporated, and so had the Red Sox.

Imagine how they felt watching Strawberry's solo homer off Al Nipper in the eighth? And Orosco's RBI single over a bunt-poised infield? The World Series was slipping away in Boston.

Schiraldi quietly called it, "a very weird game. I thought we would get some good after the bad (in Game 6). We didn't. Who can explain it? It just didn't work out for us."

Who *can* explain it? The Mets lost two straight at home, then took 4-of-5 from the best the American League had to offer. Champions. Say it. Champions.

METS 8, RED SOX 5

BOSTON	ab	r	h	bi	METS	ab	r	h	bi
Boggs 3b	4	0	1	1	Wilson cf	3	1	1	0
Barrett 2b	5	0	1	0	Teufel 2b	2	0	0	0
Bucknr 1b	4	1	2	0	Bckmn 2b	1	1	0	0
Rice lf	4	1	2	0	Hrnndz 1b	4	0	1	3
Evans rf	4	1	2	3	Carter c	4	0	0	1
Gedman c	4	1	1	1	Strwbry rf	4	1	1	1
Hendrsn cf	2	1	0	0	Knight 3b	4	2	3	1
Owen ss	3	0	0	0	Mitchell lf	2	0	0	0
Baylor ph	1	0	0	0	Dykstra cf	2	1	1	0
Nipper p	0	0	0	0	Santana ss	3	1	1	1
Crawfrd p	0	0	0	0	Darling p	1	0	0	0
Hurst p	0	0	0	0	Fernndz p	0	0	0	0
Armas ph	1	0	0	0	Mazzilli ph	1	1	1	0
Schiraldi p	0	0	0	0	McDowl p	0	0	0	0
Sambito p	0	0	0	0	Orosco p	1	0	1	1
Stanley p	0	0	0	0					
Romero ss	1	0	0	0					
Totals:	33	5	9	5	Totals:	32	8	10	8

Boston ....030 000 020 — 5
Mets ....000 003 32x — 8

Game-Winning RBI—Knight (1).
LOB— Boston 6, Mets 7. 2B— Evans. HR— Evans (2), Gedman (1), Knight (1), Strawberry (1). S— Hurst 2, McDowell. SF— Hernandez.

	IP	H	R	ER	BB	SO
Boston						
Hurst	6	4	3	3	1	3
Schiraldi L, 0-2	⅓	3	3	3	0	0
Sambito	⅓	0	0	0	2	0
Stanley	⅓	0	0	0	0	0
Nipper	⅓	3	2	2	1	0
Crawford	⅔	0	0	0	0	0
Mets						
Darling	3⅔	6	3	3	1	0
Fernandez	2⅓	0	0	0	1	4
McDowll W, 1-0	1	3	2	2	0	1
Orosco S, 2	2	0	0	0	0	2

McDowell pitched to 3 batters in the 8th.
HBP— Henderson by Darling. Wilson by Crawford.
WP—Schiraldi. T—3:11. A—55,032.
Umpires—Home, Kibler (NL); First, Evans (AL); Second, Wendelstedt (NL); Third, Brinkman (AL); Left, Montague (NL); Right, Ford (AL).

Checking Your Comprehension

Read the following questions. Put an x in the box beside the answer that best completes each one.

1. The single by Hernandez "brought the Mets within 3-2 and told them: Hurst is mortal tonight." *Mortal* means
   - ☐ a. deadly.
   - ☐ b. subject to death; human.
   - ☐ c. invincible; possessed of supernatural strength.

2. After Knight's homer, the "rest was moot: two more hits, Rafael Santana's single, Hernandez' sacrifice fly." To be *moot* means to be
   - ☐ a. surprising.
   - ☐ b. of no consequence.
   - ☐ c. hotly disputed.

3. In which innings did the Mets score their winning eight runs?
   - ☐ a. the sixth, seventh, and eighth
   - ☐ b. the second and eighth
   - ☐ c. the second, seventh and eighth

4. Have the Mets ever won the World Series before?
   - ☐ a. Yes, they won in 11:26.
   - ☐ b. No, they finally won the series last night.
   - ☐ c. Yes, they won in 1969.

5. When Knight hit a home run, why did the Mets feel that the world belonged to them?
   - ☐ a. The tie was broken with the winning run.
   - ☐ b. The Boston Red Sox rally evaporated.
   - ☐ c. Knight had hit Schiraldi's pitch, a fastball.

6. The Mets were described as being "destined" to win the seventh game in the World Series. Which statement below would support that description?
   - ☐ a. The Mets played well and were winning early in the game.
   - ☐ b. The Mets won despite the fact that they did not play their best.
   - ☐ c. The Mets had the Most Valuable Player on their team.

☆ ☆ ☆

As we have seen, the lead paragraph in "WE'RE #1" answers the questions *Who? What? When? Where? Why?* and *How?* Now look at the lead paragraph of the feature story that follows. Is the writer concerned with answering those questions immediately, or is he more concerned with stating a general theme for the rest of the story?

A sports feature writer may not discuss all the big plays of a game nor ask players and coaches to comment on them. Rather, he may choose a theme and write a story in support of it. In this case, the theme is that Ray Knight of the Mets went from being a player with uncertain career prospects to MVP of the World Series in one season. As you read, notice what information the feature writer includes in support of the theme.

MVP Knight becomes King of the Series

By STEVE WILDER

In spring training, Ray Knight was the Mets' Most Unwanted Player. Last night, after the Red Sox were dispatched to Boston as losers once again, Knight was named the World Series Most Valuable Player.

Mr. Intensity, whose future with the Mets is uncertain since his contract expired last night, concluded a storybook campaign with three hits in four at-bats in the Mets' 8-5 victory. He had nine hits for a .391 Series average with five RBIs and four runs scored. His lead-off homer to left off Calvin Schiraldi in the seventh broke a 3-3 tie and put the Mets ahead for good.

"I was just looking for a fastball and trying to be very, very aggressive," said Knight, an almost sure bet to be named the National League's Comeback Player of the Year.

"Every hit I got this year was a big hit for me because I felt I was under great scrutiny to hit and produce," he said. "Maybe it was of my own accord, but I felt if I didn't produce, someone else would play.

"I don't have any speed and I've had three shoulder operations, but I've always prided myself as being a winner. What hurt me the most the last couple of years was that people lost faith in me."

One person who didn't was Davey Johnson, who convinced his bosses last spring that Knight could help the Mets.

"It wasn't just in spring training. It was also the year before," Johnson said. "He was always in my ear. Always telling me how good he was. He came to spring training this year in great shape. He had lost weight and worked hard. You can tell a guy with tremendous desire and tremendous fight."

Added Keith Hernandez: "Ray is our unsung hero. He's the No. 2 or maybe even the No. 1 leader on this team. He is a very

Continued on following page

Continued from preceding page
giving person. My giving is forced. I have a somewhat selfish nature. It was something I felt I had to do. He does it naturally. Of the 24 players on this team, he's one of the top five most important."

Knight seemingly has earned a return engagement by virtue of his consistent bat, steady glove and high-octane intensity.

But with Howard Johnson, Kevin Mitchell and Dave Magadan lurking in the shadows, Knight's future remains cloudy. His age (34 next month) and his salary ($600,000 this season) are certain to come under intense scrutiny by Met management.

"Of course, I'd like to be back," Knight said. "And if they want me back and they're fair to me, I will be back.

"But if it becomes a push-and-shove situation, I'll exercise my option and see if anyone else is interested."

For now, though, he can bask in his '86 dream-come-true.

"It was trying for me the last couple of years," Knight said. "But now that's all behind me."

Checking Your Comprehension

Read the following questions. Put an *x* in the box beside the answer that best completes each one.

1. According to the reporter, "Knight seemingly has earned a return engagement by virtue of his consistent bat, steady glove, and high-octane intensity." By *intensity,* the reporter means
   □ a. nervousness or tenseness.
   □ b. desire.
   □ c. energy or force.

2. Says Knight, "Every hit I got this year was a big hit for me because I felt I was under great scrutiny to hit and produce." As used in that statement, *scrutiny* means
   □ a. scruples.
   □ b. examination.
   □ c. selfishness.

3. Which statement below would *not* be evidence for Knight's being named the Most Valuable Player for the World Series?
   □ a. He had nine hits for .391 series average with five RBIs and four runs scored.
   □ b. He worked hard in training and produced big hits all season long.
   □ c. He had three hits in four at-bats and his lead-off homer broke the tie score.

4. Which of the following problems worried Knight the most during the last couple of years?
   □ a. If he didn't produce hits, someone else would play.
   □ b. He didn't have great speed and had had three shoulder operations.
   □ c. He felt that people in management had lost faith in him.

5. If the Mets want Knight back next year, it will be because
   □ a. he is thirty-four and earns $600,000.
   □ b. he is an unselfish leader and his play on the field and at bat is consistent.
   □ c. he went from the most unwanted player to the most valuable player.

6. Why can Knight bask in his "dream-come-true"?
   □ a. He has proved he has the ability and the desire to play good baseball, especially by helping win the World Series.
   □ b. The Red Sox lost the World Series.
   □ c. The Mets management will surely renew his contract.

☆   ☆   ☆

The writer of the first Mets-Sox story concentrates on imparting basic baseball information, some of it broad, some of it detailed. For example, the reader learns not only who hit the winning homer—Ray Knight—but also that the pitch Knight belted out of the park was a fastball, and that he was expecting it. The reporter, then, goes beyond the most important facts—who won and by what score. Quotes from players and coaches are included to shed light on the mechanics of winning, and every added detail serves to make a Mets

fan feel more exhilarated by the victory.

On the other hand, feature writer Steve Wilder focuses solely on Ray Knight. He includes facts that pertain to Knight's baseball past, present, and future. Interviews with players and coaches are all intended to reveal Knight's personality and his attitude toward the game. The format and approach of this story could be used on any person, not just a baseball player.

Interpreting Colorful Language in Sports Stories

Sports writing is known for its colorful language. Feature writer Wilder, for instance, writes that Knight's World Series heroics concluded a "storybook campaign." What he means is that Knight had a good season with a happy ending. That type of language makes reading the sports more enjoyable, especially since many fans know who has won before they look in the paper.

Below are colorful statements from both stories. In the space provided under each statement, write a plain-language "translation" of the colorful statement. Refer to the stories for the statements in context as necessary.

1. Then came the sixth-, seventh- and eighth-inning explosions that left the Red Sox crushed.

_____

_____

_____

2. Sid Fernandez bailed out Darling, threw zeroes until the sixth, and fanned four Red Sox hitters.

_____

_____

_____

3. A two-run single, roped up the gap in left-center.

_____

_____

_____

4. Wasn't this the same Hurst who'd ruled the Mets like house pets for 17 innings?

_____

_____

_____

5. [A fastball] came. Knight crushed it.

_____

_____

_____

6. In spring training, Ray Knight was the Met's Most Unwanted Player.

_____

_____

_____

7. Knight seemingly has earned a return engagement by virtue of his consistent bat, steady glove and high-octane intensity.

_____

_____

_____

8. For now, though, he can bask in his '86 dream-come-true.

_____

_____

_____

Using Your Newspaper

In your newspaper's sports section, find a story that uses colorful language. Circle five sentences that you find especially colorful.

On a separate sheet of paper, write the sentences you have picked. Leave plenty of space between each sentence and the one that follows it.

In the space under each sentence write a plain-language "translation." But do not stop there. After examining the colorful sentences and writing the translations, you should understand the meanings of the sentences pretty well. In fact, you should be able to translate the plain-language statements back into colorful language of your own. Use a thesaurus, if necessary, to come up with vivid synonyms for the verbs, nouns, and adjectives. After you have finished, compare all three versions of each sentence. Which do you like the best?

Practicing Newspaper Skills

Write a news report or a feature story about a sports event of your choice—a baseball game, a tennis match, a gymnastics meet, a synchronized swimming event—whatever you like.

Before you attend the sports event, you will need to prepare. You will want to take notes on the event, as sportswriters do, so bring along paper and pencil. If you prefer, you may use a tape recorder, especially for interviews. As for the interviews, two things: you may need to contact the team or athlete to arrange for the interview before you attend the contest; also, go to the interview prepared, with some background questions already in mind, if not written out. Of course, you will want to deviate from your prepared questions to ask about important plays from the game.

If you are conducting an interview, some of the notes you take during the event should be taken in anticipation of asking questions of a player or coach. If you are not interviewing anyone, you should take notes with an eye toward turning the notes into the body of your story.

If you are writing a news story, your purpose is to inform your readers about the major plays and turning points of the game. You will interview players and coaches for their thoughts about those important plays and turning points. And you must provide the information fans want: who won, by how much, how they did it, and so on.

If you are writing a feature article, your purpose is to entertain as well as inform readers. Accordingly, you will want to pick an interesting topic. You could write about the most valuable player of the game or about a player trying to make a comeback after being sidelined for a while with an injury. You could write about the player who hustles the most or shows the most team spirit (or individual courage). You could write about the fans or the business organization behind the team or athlete. If you conduct interviews, ask questions that will lead players or coaches to provide insights into the game or the players that fans would not otherwise know.

Do many teenagers in your school have jobs? Do you think that if teenagers don't have summer jobs they will get into trouble? Do you think having an after-school job interferes with a student's schoolwork?

Those questions are not easily answered, but the article below tells how some people feel about them. The reporter has attended Boston's Fourth Annual Leadership Breakfast and interviewed the participants. The reporter's role, in this case, is to tell readers what took place and to report the opinions of those interviewed.

He does not offer his own opinions.

The second article, on the other hand, is an editorial, which serves as a vehicle for the opinions of a staff editorial writer. The writer offers facts gleaned from two surveys, but his main purpose is to give his opinion. He wants to persuade readers to share his view of the problem and to act to remedy it in the way he suggests.

As you read the articles, consider your opinions about teenagers and jobs.

Teenagers emphasize need for jobs, antidrug messages

By MICHAEL K. FRISBY
Globe Staff

Two months ago, Frank Whitney was a troubled teenager spending much of his time "hanging out on street corners" in Roxbury and playing Russian roulette with his life.

But yesterday Whitney told guests at Mayor Flynn's Fourth Annual Leadership Breakfast that his life changed after he joined the Citywide Youth Congress, an organization of about 300 city youths working on issues that affect teenagers.

"I didn't want to die just yet," Whitney told the business, civic and clergy leaders gathered at the Parkman House to discuss youth issues. "I was bad and everything. If I had kept going, I'd be going to Walpole or in jail...but I started going to programs like the Youth Congress and changed."

In an interview, Whitney, 17, said that instead of "hanging out on street corners, I think about going to college. I used to beat up a lot of people, but I started thinking that some of those people might see me some day and kill me. I know a lot of kids that have gotten killed. I don't want to be one of them."

Whitney and other Youth Congress leaders yesterday advised the civic and public leaders on ways to help troubled youths and encourage them into positive activities. Among the recommendations were that the media not glamorize negative activities involving youths and pay more attention to positive stories, and that more youths be recruited to give antidrug

messages to their peers.

The teenagers also asked for more jobs, but while many of their suggestions were well received, they got some bad news on summer jobs.

Robert Coard, the director of Action for Boston Community Development, told the group that due to cuts in federal funds, his agency will have 12,875 fewer summer jobs for teenagers this year. Coard said he will receive only $1.7 million this year— a $1 million decrease—and will only be able to provide 1,425 summer jobs compared with 3,300 last year.

"It is mindboggling," said Coard, who said that in 1976 he received $6 million for 10,000 summer jobs. "These are positions in summer camps and day-care facilities. There will be a ripple effect. The kids won't have jobs and some services won't be there either.

"What this means," he said, "is that there will be more kids on the street corners. These jobs kept kids out of trouble."

James Daar, executive director of the Boston Private Industry Council, said the council hopes to provide 2,800 summer jobs this year, up 200 over last year. But he said the private industry cannot make up for the cut in public sector summer jobs.

Flynn, in his opening remarks to the group, noted that summer is always an anxious time in American cities "because kids are out of school with free time and idle time on their hands." He said that with the decrease in summer jobs, city officials and business leaders will have to work harder to keep the city peaceful this year.

The mayor received some advice yesterday from some teenagers.

"Kids don't have anywhere to go on weekends or after school," complained Warren Chase, 19, of Roxbury. "That's why they are turning to violence. It is very important for gyms and pools to be open so there is something to do."

Walter Applerwhite, 17, of Dorchester, described teenage life as "a constant struggle for survival," and said the media should not make heroes out of criminals. "If you shoot someone, the media plays it up and you become a superstar. All your friends write on walls that they know you. It encourages kids to do bad things and nothing is written when we do good things."

Bernadette Merullo, 17, of Charlestown, offered her views on the city's racial problems.

"People should be exposed to people who are different from them," she said.

"I don't think of people as being black or Hispanic. I think of them as my friends. More people should be exposed to other people around the city."

Some adults agreed with the teenagers.

Cardinal Bernard Law, who attended part of the session, said that adults must give attention to positive youth activities and not be "narrowly focused on problem areas."

And Flynn said: "These young people say they are tired of being surrounded by negative images of youth. They say that teenagers are often looked at as problems, while the good they do is often ignored... They are tired of hearing discouraging comments about their future. They want to hear us telling them what they can do."

Checking Your Comprehension

Read the following questions. Put an x in the box beside the answer that best completes each one.

1. The young people spoke to "civic and public leaders on ways to help troubled youths." A *civic* leader might also be called a
   - ☐ a. businessman.
   - ☐ b. citizen who is a community leader.
   - ☐ c. politician.

2. It was suggested that the media should not "glamorize negative activities." To *glamorize* means to
   - ☐ a. pay attention.
   - ☐ b. put on makeup.
   - ☐ c. make attractive.

3. One recommendation that the teenagers gave to the adults was to have
   - ☐ a. less media coverage of positive teenage activities.
   - ☐ b. more antidrug messages and more jobs.
   - ☐ c. peer leaders on street corners.

4. According to Robert Coard and James Daar, how many jobs will be available for teenagers during the summer?
   - ☐ a. 1,875
   - ☐ b. 4,225
   - ☐ c. 3,300

5. What does Mr. Coard, Director of Action for Boston Community Development, mean when he says there will be a "ripple effect"?
   - ☐ a. Teenagers won't have work, and the community won't benefit from the services provided by their work.
   - ☐ b. Only kids in camp or day-care services will be hurt by the cutbacks.
   - ☐ c. Private industry will not enlist the services of teenagers.

6. Why does Coard predict that more teenagers will be in trouble on street corners?
   - ☐ a. The federal government has cut the funds for jobs for teenagers.
   - ☐ b. Private industry does not employ teenagers.
   - ☐ c. The police arrest teenagers loitering in streets.

☆　☆　☆

The headline "Teenagers emphasize need for jobs, antidrug messages" is a fact statement that reports the opinions of a group of people. The reporter must objectively gather and present the facts, even when reporting on emotional, contested issues.

Look at the headline that follows. Even if the piece were not on the opinion pages of the newspaper, a reader might reasonably expect an opinion to follow that headline. The headline is, after all, not like an active, news-story headline: no one is doing anything or having anything happen to them. This headline practically says, "Limiting after-school work—do you want to talk about that?" Of course, the editorial writer is going to do all the talking.

Limiting after-school work

When high school students themselves come to realize that long hours of after-school work too often mean low grades, it is time for parents and school officials—and anyone else who cares about the importance of education—to set some reasonable limits.

At Hingham High School, students helped conduct a survey aimed at finding out how much of a link there was between after-school work and low grades. The results indicate that anything over 15 hours a week is cause for concern.

The findings are similar to those in Walpole, where teachers conducted a survey after the school nurse reported that many students asked to leave school early because they were tired from after-school work.

Seventy percent of Hingham's high school students work—a figure that surprised school officials in that relatively affluent community. About a third work more than 15 hours a week—and half of that group recorded the worst grades. Teacher Steve Herrmann, who worked on the survey with the students, agreed there was a correlation, but said it was possible some students doing poorly in school turned to outside work for "enjoyment or success."

There has long been a myth that work is good for adolescents, a myth that is only slowly being debunked. Ellen Greenberger and Laurence Steinberg, in summarizing their study "When Teen-agers Work," note that "extensive part-time employment during the school year may undermine youngsters' education" by leading to luxury consumer spending, increased drug and alcohol use, anti-social behavior, and "increased cynicism about the pleasures of productive work."

If it were not that the service economy—everything from fast-food outlets to nursing homes—depended on the unskilled and underpaid services of young people, some control would have been placed on after-school working hours a long time ago.

The evidence is increasing that such controls are necessary. Political leaders who talk about the value of a skilled and educated work force should be the first to insist on them.

Checking Your Comprehension

Read the following questions. Put an *x* in the box beside the answer that best completes each one.

1. Greenberger and Steinberg believe that "extensive part-time employment during the school year may undermine youngsters' education." To *undermine* is to
   - ☐ a. contribute.
   - ☐ b. reinforce.
   - ☐ c. weaken.

2. The two researchers also feel that "increased cynicism about the pleasures of productive work" may result from too heavy a workload. *Cynicism* means
   - ☐ a. a spendthrift approach.
   - ☐ b. an affluent lifestyle.
   - ☐ c. a distrustful attitude.

3. Which students received the worst grades, according to the survey in Hingham High School?
   - ☐ a. 70 percent of the high school students
   - ☐ b. half of the 70 percent who work
   - ☐ c. half of the students who work more than fifteen hours a week

4. What do Greenberger and Steinberg *not* suggest may result from extensive part-time employment?
   - ☐ a. Teenagers have more money for luxuries, drugs, and alcohol.
   - ☐ b. Teenagers contribute to their families' budgets.
   - ☐ c. Teenagers become anti-social and anti-work.

5. What is teacher Steve Herrmann's opinion about extensive part-time work automatically resulting in poor grades?
   - ☐ a. He thinks all of the students who work more than fifteen hours a week have poor grades.
   - ☐ b. He thinks some poor students may get jobs in order to experience success in some area of their lives.
   - ☐ c. He thinks work is not related at all to grades.

6. Who does the editor think will argue for *not* limiting after-school work hours?
   - ☐ a. owners of service businesses
   - ☐ b. parents and teachers
   - ☐ c. politicians

☆ ☆ ☆

Reporters and editorial writers perform different roles. The reporter covers the scene of news-making events and writes stories that keep readers informed of the facts (and sometimes those facts include the opinions of witnesses or people involved in the events).

The editorial writer's task is to present a problem, persuade readers to share his view of the problem, and move readers to act to solve the problem. Although the editorial writer deals in opinion, he often makes use of facts. In the editorial you just read, the editor used the facts of the survey taken at Hingham High School to support his opinions.

A reporter could write a news report about the Hingham

High survey. But in doing so, the reporter would not try to persuade us to act to set guidelines for the number of hours teenagers should work after school. Instead, the reporter would tell readers how the survey was conducted, and when, and where, and why, and by whom. As readers we would learn more details about the survey than from the editorial, but we would not be purposely stimulated by the writer to form opinions. We would have to draw our own conclusions based on the facts. The different roles, then, produce different types of news articles that call for different responses from the reader.

☆ ☆ ☆

Recognizing Fact and Opinion in News Stories and Editorials

The first story in the lesson is a factual, informative piece of news reporting. The second article is an opinion piece. As we have said, however, both stories use a mixture of facts and opinions.

The statements that follow are taken from the stories.

Some are fact statements and some are opinion statements. Read the statements. In the space provided before each one, write *fact* if the statement expresses a fact or *opinion* if the statement expresses an opinion. Refer to the stories as often as necessary.

News Story

_____ 1. Whitney and other Youth Congress leaders yesterday advised the civic and public leaders on ways to help troubled youths.

_____ 2. "If you shoot someone, the media plays it up and you become a superstar. . . . It encourages kids to do bad things and nothing is written when we do good things."

_____ 3. Coard said he will receive only $1.7 million this year . . . and will only be able to provide 1,425 summer jobs.

_____ 4. "It is mindboggling. . . . What this means is that there will be more kids on the street corners."

_____ 5. The teenagers also asked for more jobs, but . . . they got some bad news on summer jobs.

_____ 6. "People should be exposed to people who are different from them."

Editorial

_____ 1. . . . it is time for parents and school officials—and anyone else who cares about the importance of education—to set some reasonable limits.

_____ 2. At Hingham High School, students helped conduct a survey aimed at finding out how much of a link there was between after-school work and low grades.

_____ 3. Seventy percent of Hingham's high school students work. . . . About a third work more than 15 hours a week—and half of that group recorded the worst grades.

_____ 4. . . . it was possible some students doing poorly in school turned to outside work for "enjoyment or success."

_____ 5. If it were not that the service economy . . . depended on the unskilled and underpaid services of young people, some control would have been placed on after-school work hours a long time ago.

_____ 6. The evidence is increasing that such controls are necessary.

Using Your Newspaper

Survey your newspaper for about two weeks for news reports and editorials on teenagers. You may find stories about changes in laws that affect teens or stories reporting developments in education. You may find stories having to do with teen activities, or fashion trends, or entertainers and sports figures popular with teenagers.

The purpose of your survey is to arrive at an idea of how teenagers are presented in the newspaper and, as a result, how they are perceived by newspaper readers. In other words, which dominates the news—a positive or a negative image of teenagers?

Make a list of the stories you collect under two headings, _Positive_ and _Negative._ Which list is longer? Is the overriding image a fair one, in your opinion?

To add to your survey, consider your list again. Do the positive stories tend to appear on the straight news pages and the negative stories in editorials? Is the opposite the case? Is there no such identifiable trend? In your future reading of the newspaper, look at stories on teens in this critical fashion. Perhaps you will be able to see each story as part of a general treatment of teen-related topics.

Practicing Newspaper Skills

Conduct a survey in your high school on a topic or issue you and other students find interesting. You may choose to gather facts and opinions on teenage employment, teenage crime, teenage consumer problems, teenage achievements, or teenage hobbies and other non-school interests.

Decide what questions you will ask on your survey. You will find it easier to count the results if you ask multiple choice questions. If, for example, you were to ask students how many hours they work after school, you would give them three choices: (a) 0–5 hours, (b) 6–15 hours, (c) 15 or more hours.

After you have tabulated the results of your survey, state the results in either a news report or an editorial. If you choose to do a news report, remember that you must tell how, when, where, and why you conducted your survey. Tell also who answered the survey questions. Of course, you will present the results of the survey in your report.

If you choose to write an editorial, you may present the results of the survey, but you will need to concentrate on your opinion of the results. Based on your results, what in your opinion is the nature of the problem, and what course should be taken to remedy the problem?

Make photocopies of your news story or editorial and distribute the copies to the class.

When entertainers like Madonna bring their tours to town, newspapers often run feature stories on them. Ads have no doubt been in the papers earlier, so the purpose of the story is not to sell tickets. Rather, it is to sell papers—readers gobble up timely stories on famous people.

Before Madonna performed in the Boston area, feature writer Brett Milano wrote the story below for the *Boston Globe*. His feature story provides background information on Madonna's career and what she has planned for the current tour. In addition, he includes comments from critics who have already seen the show. He is not reviewing Madonna's show himself but offering the opinions of these critics for all readers who might find them valuable.

Actually attending Madonna's concert at Sullivan Stadium was critic Steve Morse. His review is the second story in this lesson.

In general, any performance critic's task is twofold. He or she must state the facts about what took place—how long the show was, what songs were performed, what the performer wore, and so on. Then the critic must tell readers the opinions he or she formed watching the show—the show was exciting (or dull), the backup band was tight and solid (or loose and sloppy), the costumes were a delight (or an abomination). Many people decide whether they want to spend money on tickets to a performance based on a reviewer's piece in the paper.

As you read the story below, look for information about the changes in Madonna's act. Read the opinions of the two critics quoted. Are they in agreement?

MADONNA
More Than A Material Girl

By BRETT MILANO

Once it was easy to be a "Madonna wanna-be." All you needed was a halter top, a few gold crosses, a bottle of blonde hair dye, and a well-worn copy of the "Like a Virgin" album. But that was two years ago, when her trashy-classy persona got as much notice as her music, and there were doubts about how long she'd last.

But as time goes on, Madonna pulls new tricks from her sleeve: a successful film career, an ever-changing image and a stack of hit singles that hasn't let up. So nowadays, if you really want to be like Madonna, you have more of a challenge. You'll need to keep changing your style, from flashy pinup, to elegant film star, to dance-club queen, to serious songwriter. You'll need an album ("True Blue") on the charts, a film (the gangster comedy "Who's That Girl") on the way, and a recent Latin-flavored hit ("La Isla Bonita"). You'll need 375 tons of equipment to carry around the world on a record-breaking tour. And you'll need to be one of pop's most recognizable faces while you're still only 28.

When Madonna hits Sullivan Stadium tonight, she'll bring one of the splashiest shows in pop history. Instead of a conventional pop concert, it's designed as a moveable Broadway show—carried by a whopping 25 semi-trucks. (David Lee Roth, on one of last year's bigger tours, used only eight.)

Continued on following page

Continued from preceding page

Here's what's planned:

- Seven costume changes, ranging from formal gowns, to a "Material Girl" mink, to lingerie from "Virgin" days.
- Two giant video screens.
- An array of props and production numbers—including a Spanish fantasy for "Isla Bonita" and a gangster takeoff on "White Heat."
- A troupe of six dancers.
- A band of studio aces, led by her keyboardist and co-writer Pat Leonard.
- A musical set heavy on greatest hits, including the movie themes ("Into the Groove" from "Desperately Seeking Susan"), the dance club faves ("Holiday"), and, most likely, next month's hit (the new "Causing a Commotion").

"She wanted a visual impact that would knock people out," says Madonna's publicist Liz Rosenberg. "She was very determined about this. And she's the type that makes a lot of decisions quickly: If something doesn't work, she starts over. One day she might get sick of her bracelets and rip them all off. You'll see a different look this year but it's still Madonna, still bigger than life."

"It's the largest show we've ever seen go on the road," says Neil Jacobsen, vice president of Tea Party Concerts, the promoter of tonight's show. "There's an aura of excitement there, because this is only her second tour. You can tell she has her heart set on doing a real production."

The show, he said, was simply too big and costly to fit into Great Woods in Mansfield or in the Worcester Centrum—which brings Madonna to the largest venue in town, a site usually reserved for the Dylans and the Bowies, the long-established stars. "Sure, there's always a risk," Jacobsen says. "But we're looking at someone who's sold a serious amount of records and had 12 consecutive Top Five singles, so those are pretty good numbers. Remember that the Police have sold out here, and they had a lot less stage presence." (At this writing, all but 1500 of a possible 48,000 tickets have been sold.)

The big question is whether Madonna's show can carry to such large audiences. Two years ago, Bruce Springsteen drew criticism for moving from concert halls to football stadiums; this year U2 also moved to bigger-than-ever venues. But both had come up through the clubs and theaters and built a solid bond with their

fans. For Madonna, this is only the second tour.

Her initial fame came from records and video, not concerts and club gigs. Her debut LP, with the hits "Holiday" and "Borderline," created the initial buzz; 1984's "Like a Virgin" album took her to No. 1. Fans saw her on film ("Desperately Seeking Susan"), in magazines and on video; but they never saw her live, until 1985's "Virgin" tour.

Was the real Madonna as exciting as the media image? Audiences weren't sure. With its glossy lighting and costume changes, the show got mixed reactions when she played at the 12,700-seat Worcester Centrum; and this year's tour—dubbed the "Who's That Girl" tour, after the new movie and title song—is even larger and more ambitious. Can she handle the setting as well as the other superstars can?

The Baltimore Sun's J.D. Considine, who caught last week's opening date at Miami's 60,000-capacity Orange Bowl, thinks she can. "I've seen the Springsteen stadium tour, I've seen Dylan, and the (Grateful) Dead, and I was at Live Aid. Out of all those shows, Madonna's is the only one I'd want to see again," he told the Globe last week. "You need a larger-than-life show if you want to come off in a stadium, and Madonna does. She's not that large physically, but she holds your attention, just as Michael Jackson did in the best of the Victory tour. I was two-thirds of the way back at the Orange Bowl, which is about as distant as you can get."

"There's enough eye candy, if you will, to keep you interested. But most of the visuals are really quite intelligent, things that tie into the song and reinforce the message. For example, when she did 'Papa Don't Preach,' there was an image of John Paul II, projected in front of a Catholic church. It took two verses before it hit me: That was a pun, because in Rome, the Pope is Il Papa. You don't expect to see something that clever."

Not everyone was so impressed. Anne Ayers, the assistant entertainment editor of USA TODAY, saw the same show and found it high on glitz but low on emotional clout. "She's going for a certain kind of show: a Broadway, showbiz, song-and-dance spectacle. In that context it's hard to make a connection with the audience, and I'd have to say she didn't," said Ayers in an interview.

"I saw Springsteen in a stadium, and he was absolutely transfixing. Madonna's show was glamorous, fast-moving, at times very professional. But it didn't grab your heart. She has a problem in that a lot of people know her from video, where you can see every seam on her outfit and every expression on her face. In the show, the stage looked crowded; and the video screens weren't large enough to carry the image to the stadium. It was partly due to rainy weather, but you had to strain a lot."

There's also been talk about the "new Madonna," a stronger and more intelligent, but still sexual image. Here again, the jury is out. "The important thing Madonna does is to demonstrate how female sexuality can be a source of strength," says Considine.

"Traditionally in pop culture, there are two roles women can play—the good girl and the bad girl, and the bad girl is never taken seriously. But Madonna shows up in the trappings of a bad girl, and demands to be taken seriously because she doesn't just roll over. Lately you get more sense of the strength and power that was under her image all along."

On the other hand, Ayers thought the image wasn't strong enough. "I couldn't always tell who Madonna was trying to be. She wasn't the Marilyn Monroe vamp of 'Material Girl' at any point, or the innocent waif of other songs she's done. When she put on the black corset, some people asked me, 'What do you mean, she's not sexy?' But she looked more dancer-ly than sexual. She's got terrific moves, Bob Fosse would be glad to have her. But a real sensual quality didn't come across. It was more a safe sexuality that the 14-year-olds could relate to."

Both Considine and Ayers agree Madonna's vocals have been powerful on this tour. But other critics have charged that she isn't much of a singer, just a charismatic actress who makes records. Musical director Pat Leonard, for one, disagrees.

"I've heard the talk about how Madonna can't sing, and I can tell you that's bull," says the tour's bandleader, who co-wrote much of the "True Blue" album. "She's a natural, intuitive singer with great intonation; and she puts across a vulnerable quality that you can't copy, and I know, because I've heard people try."

For proof, Leonard gives a little-known

Continued on following page

78 UNIT TWO/LESSON 3

Continued from preceding page
story about one of her hits. "When we wrote 'Live to Tell,' she sang a rough demo version into an 8-track tape recorder. Then she listened back and heard a couple of spots where her voice went flat, so she just fixed those. And that's the vocal that went on the final record, the first time she ever sang it. The new single, 'Who's That Girl,' was done the same way. How many singers do you know who can do a rough vocal of a song they wrote two hours ago, and sell a million copies with it?"

Two more Madonna myths need to be debunked: First, that she lacks a social conscience. Two summers ago she performed at Live Aid, and sang the uplifting "Love Makes the World Go 'Round."

But she's more remembered for making the day's most irreverent comment from the stage: A week before Live Aid, Playboy magazine had published some nude photos from her days as a struggling actress. So she taunted the crowd by wearing a full-length fur coat in the summer heat. "I ain't taking (bleep) off today," she announced. "I don't want to hear about it later on."

But next Tuesday she makes a far more serious gesture, by playing an AIDS research benefit at Madison Square Garden. "Her best friend died of AIDS last year," explains publicist Rosenberg. "When he was sick, the American Foundation for AIDS Research was very helpful. She made a vow that she would do a benefit as soon

as she went on tour."

We can also discount the second myth, that Madonna appeals mainly to teenage girls. Melody Pine of Brookline's Good Vibrations store reports she saw an unusually diverse crowd when tickets went on sale there. "It wasn't just the wanna-be's that you'd expect, but a real melting pot of a crowd. She attracts an ethnically-mixed group."

"Madonna's fortunate in that the wanna-be's are growing up with her," adds Rosenberg. "She always talks about the audiences after the shows, about what each row was doing. She's always out there looking, because she wants them all to like her. She's always been happiest when she's onstage."

Checking Your Comprehension

Read the following questions. Put an *x* in the box beside the answer that best completes each one.

1. Milano refers to Madonna's "trashy-classy persona." The word *persona* means
   - ☐ a. personality.
   - ☐ b. public image.
   - ☐ c. charisma.

2. Madonna's show, Milano says, is not a "conventional pop concert." By *conventional,* he means
   - ☐ a. meeting.
   - ☐ b. usual.
   - ☐ c. original.

3. Which of the following things were *not* planned for Madonna's show?
   - ☐ a. costume changes and video screens
   - ☐ b. production numbers and musical hits
   - ☐ c. clips from her movie and Madonna alone on stage

4. Madonna's fans primarily know her because she has done
   - ☐ a. records and videos.
   - ☐ b. concerts and clubs.
   - ☐ c. films and TV shows.

5. Which question below do all the writers advise audiences to ask?
   - ☐ a. Is Madonna's show effective in a football stadium?
   - ☐ b. What kind of sexuality does Madonna communicate?
   - ☐ c. both of the questions above

6. What evidence does the feature writer use to support the view that Madonna is a powerful singer?
   - ☐ a. She sings at concerts to benefit AIDS research.
   - ☐ b. Her bandleader said Madonna's first singing of a song often is used for the final record.
   - ☐ c. Some critics think she is just a charismatic actress.

☆ ☆ ☆

Feature writer Brett Milano says the "big question is whether Madonna's show can carry to such large audiences," by which he means football-stadium crowds. One of the critics quoted, J. D. Considine, states, "you need a larger-than-life show if you want to come off in a stadium and Madonna does." But critic Anne Ayers demurs: "She's going for a certain kind of show: Broadway, showbiz, song-and-dance spectacle. In that

context it's hard to make a connection with the audience, and I'd have to say she didn't."

Critic Steve Morse, whose review follows, agrees with Ayers, as you might infer from the headline, "Madonna hidden in Hollywood." Here Morse uses *Hollywood* as a symbol for showbiz extravaganza lacking in substance, as well as a distance between star and audience. In other words, not what Steve Morse looks for in a rock 'n' roll show.

Madonna hidden in Hollywood

MADONNA—In concert with Level 42 at Sullivan Stadium Thursday night.

By STEVE MORSE
Globe Staff

FOXBOROUGH—No, the disco era didn't die in the '70s. It was alive and well in Foxborough Thursday night, as Madonna transformed Sullivan Stadium into a huge open-air, Disney-style disco complete with a mirror ball

the size of a boulder and enough lights to make Logan Airport look like a three-bulb back alley.

When the 48,000 fans weren't being blinded by lights that seemed to be borrowed from Michael Jackson's last tour, they were tracking a shimmying Madonna up and down a silver staircase and across a stage so wide you would need a megaphone to be heard on it.

This was the most lavish razzle-dazzle money could buy. It was a spectacle more than a concert: Endless costume changes and Broadway-aping production numbers with a disco beat.

It was an eye-grabbing plunge into sensation—as was always the theme of disco —though the viewer's soul and intelligence were sometimes drastically short-changed.

What would Madonna be like without the trappings? It was impossible to tell Thursday night. There was no letup in the hypercharged set pieces—and almost no attempt by Madonna to speak to the crowd between songs. About all she said was, "I hear Boston can dance. Is that right?" (Booming applause.) Or this: "Are you ready to party? So am I!" (More booming applause.)

If you were ready to join in, then you had a merrily escapist night. If you expected more from this disco diva who claims to have a more sophisticated image these days, then you were disappointed. It was hard not to veer between both extremes.

England's Level 42 opened with a serviceable dance set before the road crew came out and spotlessly vacuumed the stage to make way for Madonna. And out she came, dressed in a black Spandex corset seemingly off the racks from Frederick's of Hollywood. She pumped through "Open Your Heart," with its come-hither line of "I hold the lock and you hold the key," before the giant mirror ball made the first of its appearances on the pulse-ridden "Lucky Star."

She slowed ever so briefly for one of the night's best songs, "True Blue," the title track of her last album. She had donned a frilly white dress that made her resemble a farmer's daughter on the way to her prom. Newly slimmed down, she also engaged in some lively swing dancing with one of her three backup dancers, the famed Shabba Doo, who used to tour with Lionel Richie.

Returning to disco form, she belted out "Papa Don't Preach," a song about wanting to have a baby despite her father's advice to the contrary. To suggest father figures, the images of the pope and

Continued on following page

Continued from preceding page
Ronald Reagan were flashed overhead. An unfortunate glitch, however, was that the mirror ball hadn't been totally hoisted out of the way, so it lay between the pope's eyes—Not quite the desired effect.

Just when the 90-minute set appeared to be gaining momentum, a couple of tedious tunes snarled the pace. "White Heat," a trivialized adaptation of a James Cagney film, found Madonna skipping around in a gold lamé suit while pretending to battle 10-foot-high cardboard cutouts of gangsters with machine guns. This pointless exercise led to her supposed next hit single, "Causing a Commotion," a bump-and-grind throwaway.

Too often, Madonna, who never even introduced her seven-piece band, was guilty of narcissism. "Dress You Up" saw her wearing a red pirate's hat and preening shamelessly for the crowd, while "Material Girl" had pictures of Fred Astaire and Ginger Rogers shown above the stage, as if there could be any comparison. Madonna is a tireless dancer, but she's not in that league.

The first lady of disco, who was nowhere near as personable as during her area debut at the Worcester Centrum two years ago, finally ended with a couple of pretty Spanish-flavored songs, "La Isla Bonita" and "Who's That Girl."

But for most of the night, Madonna hid behind the Hollywood production and never really let us glimpse her soul.

Checking Your Comprehension

Read the following questions. Put an *x* in the box beside the answer that best completes each one.

1. Critic Steve Morse blames a lag in the show on "a couple of tedious tunes." By *tedious,* he means
   - ☐ a. tiresome due to length.
   - ☐ b. melodious.
   - ☐ c. short and punchy.

2. Morse also accuses the singer of being "guilty of narcissism." *Narcissism* means
   - ☐ a. generosity.
   - ☐ b. self-centeredness.
   - ☐ c. nervousness.

3. The *Globe* critic describes the show as
   - ☐ a. a lavish spectacle.
   - ☐ b. a powerful concert.
   - ☐ c. an intelligent and soulful show.

4. Who does Morse think enjoyed the show?
   - ☐ a. audiences who enjoy a sophisticated image
   - ☐ b. audiences who are ready to disco dance
   - ☐ c. audiences who attend plays on Broadway

5. Morse thought "True Blue" was the night's best song because
   - ☐ a. Madonna sang the song in disco style.
   - ☐ b. Madonna danced in front of video pictures.
   - ☐ c. Madonna's singing, costume, and dancing all fit together.

6. Finally, the critic concludes that
   - ☐ a. Madonna's performance was a glitzy production of sights and sounds.
   - ☐ b. Madonna's personality, soul, and relationship with her audience came through in her performance.
   - ☐ c. Madonna overcame the props to put on a moving, sincere performance.

☆ ☆ ☆

Newspaper critics offer a sort of consumer guide on concerts, books, movies, records—all the things they review. They tell the reader, "This movie is good, go see it," or, "Don't bother with this book, I couldn't even finish it," and so on. They also—ideally—describe the product or person objectively before offering opinions, so that the reader knows the exact nature of the thing being reviewed.

Naturally, if a product or person gets a good review, sales go up. So entertainers, book publishers, moviemakers, and others use the newspaper to promote themselves or their products.

On the other hand, newspapers use entertainers and entertainment to sell papers. When a performer who is hot comes to town, the newspaper is looking at a built-in feature story. Take Madonna. To write a feature on such a high-profile star, a reporter has only to make a few phone calls, do a minimum of research, and be reasonably up on things in the world of entertainment (which is not hard for an entertainment writer). Then when the newspaper goes on sale, the top of the front page displays a blurb to the effect that Madonna is "inside," and people who might not have bought the paper feel compelled to.

The jobs of the critic and the feature writer remain unchanged by this publicity activity. The critic writes mainly to inform, the feature writer mainly to entertain. Their stories are put to different uses by different elements of the newspaper process: the newspaper management, the readers, and in the case of publicity, the subjects of the stories themselves.

Fact and Opinion in Feature Stories and Reviews

While we get the feeling that feature writer Brett Milano enjoys the entertainer Madonna, he hasn't seen her latest tour and so does not offer his opinion about her current performances. He does report to readers what Madonna has planned for her tour, and what critics think about her show, her ability as a singer, and her career. Thus, he includes both facts and opinions as he informs readers about an upcoming event in their town.

In his review of Madonna's actual performance on Thursday night, critic Steve Morse also includes facts and opinions. In describing her performance, he tells readers the facts about what took place, and he mixes in his reactions to those facts and his overall opinions of the performance.

While the feature writer writes to entertain readers with factual information and the critic writes to give readers his opinion, both writers deal in facts and opinions. Sometimes they even slip opinions into factual sentences. Look, for example, at this phrase: "endless costume changes." The costume changes are fact—Madonna did wear numerous outfits. But to call them "endless" is to express an opinion. Such a phrase, or a sentence that contains such a phrase, mixes fact and opinion and must be considered neither a fact statement nor an opinion statement but both, a mixture of the two.

The following statements are from the feature story and the review. Read the statements. In the space provided before each one, write *fact* if the statement is a fact, *opinion* if the statement is an opinion, or *both* if the statement contains both fact and opinion.

_____ 1. But as time goes on, Madonna pulls new tricks from her sleeve: a . . . film career, an everchanging image and a stack of hit singles that hasn't let up.

_____ 2. "Instead of a conventional pop concert, it's designed as a moveable Broadway show—carried by a whopping 25 semitrucks. . . ."

_____ 3. Here's what's planned: Seven costume changes, ranging from formal gowns, to a "Material Girl" mink, to lingerie from "Virgin" days.

_____ 4. You need a larger-than-life show if you want to come off in a stadium, and Madonna does.

_____ 5. ". . . That was a pun, because in Rome, the Pope is *Il Papa.* You don't expect to see something that clever."

_____ 6. The important thing Madonna does is to demonstrate how female sexuality can be a source of strength.

_____ 7. It was an eye-grabbing plunge into sensation—as was always the theme of disco—though the viewer's soul and intelligence were sometimes drastically shortchanged.

_____ 8. There was no letup in the hyper-charged set pieces—and almost no attempt by Madonna to speak to the crowd between songs.

_____ 9. About all she said was, "I hear Boston can dance, is that right?"

_____ 10. She pumped through "Open Your Heart," with its come-hither line of "I hold the lock and you hold the key," before the giant mirror ball made the first of its appearances on the pulse-ridden "Lucky Star."

_____ 11. Just when the 90-minute set appeared to be gaining momentum, a couple of tedious tunes snarled the pace.

_____ 12. "White Heat," a trivialized adaptation of a James Cagney film, found Madonna skipping around in a gold lamé suit while pretending to battle 10-foot-high cardboard cutouts of gangsters with machine guns.

Using Your Newspaper

Find a review in your newspaper. The review might be of a record, a book, a concert, a play—you should be able to find one that interests you. Circle all statements in the review that contain *both* facts and opinions.

On a sheet of paper, make two columns, one headed *Fact* and one *Opinion.* Write the factual words and phrases from each of the circled statements in the *Fact* column. Write the words and phrases that express opinions in the *Opinion* column. Here is an example of what to look for. In the sentence "The morbid ballad brought tears to the eyes of the more sentimental fans in the front row," the words *morbid* and *sentimental* are opinions. *Ballad, brought tears to the eyes,* and *in the front row* are facts.

What do you find more of, facts or opinions? Do you find such statements complicated and tricky? Do you find them persuasive?

Practicing Newspaper Skills

Attend a performance of some kind—a play, a concert, a recital—and write either a feature story on it or a review of it.

If you choose to write a feature story, describe the event for your readers. If you attend a performance put on by local performers, you may want to interview them to find out how well they like what they are doing, how long they have been doing it, and so on. You may also want to interview a non-performer you know to be knowledgeable in the field—a teacher, a local expert, a critic for the local paper. If you attend a performance given by a famous person, you will probably not get an interview. For background you could research your subject in the *Readers' Guide to Periodical Literature* in the library.

After you have done your research and attended the performance, write a short feature story describing the event and how effective or successful it was. Incorporate background material, quotes from performers and nonperformers, and your own impressions into the story. Write an enticing headline that you feel will draw readers in.

If you choose to write a review, be sure to take notes as you witness the performance so that you can describe it fairly and accurately. Document also your impressions of the audience and your own reactions.

Once home from the event, review your notes and compose a catchy headline that expresses the main idea—your overall opinion of the performance. Write a short review that touches on the most important elements of the performance. Advise readers whether they should take in another performance, if there is one. If the event was a once-only thing that you enjoyed, don't bother telling readers they really missed a good one—they'll know. Of course, if your review is negative, they'll consider themselves lucky not to have been there. Remember to use factual details to support your opinions, but don't be shy about expressing your opinions—as a reviewer, that is your job.

Newspapers print stories about disasters, murders, or suicide because people are horrified by—yet interested in—tragic events. Opinion columnists often tackle such difficult subjects, too. Mike Royko, a columnist for the *Chicago Tribune,* wrote the column below to state his feelings about teen suicide.

A columnist's job is to express his or her opinions. It is a reader's responsibility to evaluate those opinions and agree or disagree. When Royko's column appeared, many readers were moved to write him letters, some stating their objections to his hard-nosed stance, others agreeing with it. Royko included some of the letters in the follow-up column that is the second article in this lesson.

As you read the column below, think about Royko's opinion of teen suicide. Does it make you examine your own opinion?

When a 'tragedy' is only vanity

M I K E   R O Y K O

I've received my first phone call from a teenager who indicated that she was contemplating suicide.

Actually, she didn't call to tell me that. Not at first. She opened the conversation by asking if I knew the phone number of any suicide hot lines.

I told her I didn't, but suggested she call information to see what they had listed under "suicide."

She said: "I have to talk to someone."

I said: "Why? are you thinking of killing yourself?"

She said: "I don't know. Maybe. I've been feeling depressed."

"About what?" I asked.

"Oh, things. Just things."

I said: "That's too bad. Try the information operator."

Her voice, which had sounded flat and dull, suddenly became shrill, and she said: "You don't care. You really don't care, do you?"

"If you kill yourself? Yeah, I don't think you should do it. It's kind of a dumb thing to do. But if you insist on doing it, it's not going to affect me one way or the other. That's about all I can tell you."

"Well thanks a lot," she snapped, and hung up the phone.

Now I feel bad. Not because I didn't sound deeply concerned about what she might do, because I'm not. But I should have taken the time to tell her why I wasn't deeply concerned.

There is this old man I know. When I first met him, many years ago, he was tall and handsome and proud. He worked hard in his electrician job, had a sweet and intelligent wife, a tall son and a beautiful daughter. They were a close, loving family.

When his wife was in her late 30s, she was stricken with multiple sclerosis and spent the rest of her life in a wheelchair. A tough break for both of them. But they made the best of it. I never once heard either of them complain.

I saw this man's grief when his only son, at 46, was buried after a heart attack. I was with him at the funeral of his daughter who died at only 44 of a stroke. And I was there when his wife could no longer keep up her brave fight against the ravages of her disease.

The old man suffered and wept. But he never once said pity me, oh please, feel sorry for me.

He didn't say it during those terrible times and he didn't say it when diabetes caught up with him and the doctors had to cut off one leg above the knee. Then the other leg. What he said to one of his grandsons was: "Well, now I guess you're the tallest in the family and I'm the shortest."

Now he spends his days and nights in a bed in a nursing home. And if I've ever known anyone who would be justified in taking a handful of pills and swallowing them, it's that old man.

But he hasn't done it, because if he did, he would not see his grandsons anymore. For all he's lost, he still has them. And they, as well as his courage and many wonderful memories, are enough to keep him going.

So I'm sorry, but I can't get weepy when those who are 17 and healthy say they can't go on after being jilted by a boyfriend: Life is too painful. Or they aren't popular enough in school: Life is too painful. Or their parents don't listen when they talk: Life is too painful. Or they are depressed because their best friend is depressed: Oh, life is too painful.

Don't tell me that pain is relative. Like hell it is. There's a big difference between a pinprick in the finger and a knife to the gut.

However, if someone out there insists on going into a garage, turning on the car and fading into oblivion, don't kid yourself about what you're doing.

You probably fancy yourself a tragic figure and believe that others will, too.

Forget it. Few people will care. They have their own troubles. Just check out the obit pages or the hospitals.

Oh, some strangers will glance at the TV or newspaper and wonder why you did it. A few alleged experts and TV babblers will even say we have a national crisis, which is nonsense.

But most people will give your dramatic gesture about five seconds of thought—if that much—then forget it.

Your friends at school? Sure, they'll spend a day or two striking melancholy postures. Then they'll get on with their own lives and you'll fade. Just someone they knew once. One of many kids they knew once.

And this might sound harsh, but that's really all you'll deserve because what you'll have done is nothing more than an act of vanity, selfishness and weakness. As well as stupidity.

Of course, you'll cause considerable grief for your parents, sisters and brothers, which might be your motive. But you could stick around and do that.

So that's why I didn't spend much time trying to soothe the young woman who called me. Most of us, except for saints, have only so much compassion stored away.

I prefer to dole mine out to the truly deserving.

Checking Your Comprehension

Read the following questions. Put an *x* in the box beside the answer that best completes each one.

1. Royko begins his column by saying that he's received a "call from a teenager who indicated she was contemplating suicide." *Contemplating* means
   - ☐ a. contaminating.
   - ☐ b. depressing.
   - ☐ c. considering.

2. Royko states that suicide is "nothing more than an act of vanity, selfishness, and weakness." He uses *vanity* to mean
   - ☐ a. sadness.
   - ☐ b. conceit.
   - ☐ c. value.

3. What did Royko tell the teenager to call?
   - ☐ a. 911
   - ☐ b. the information operator
   - ☐ c. a suicide hot line

4. Which tragic event below did *not* happen to the old man?
   - ☐ a. His grandsons were killed in the Vietnam war.
   - ☐ b. His son and daughter died in their forties.
   - ☐ c. His wife was confined to a wheelchair because she had multiple sclerosis.

5. Who does Royko have sympathy for?
   - ☐ a. the teenager who called him
   - ☐ b. parents of teenagers
   - ☐ c. the old man

6. What is Royko's main opinion on the issue of teen suicide?
   - ☐ a. Parents of teenagers will consider the act stupid and selfish.
   - ☐ b. Teenagers have not experienced tragic events that could justify suicide.
   - ☐ c. Teenager suicide is a national crisis.

☆   ☆   ☆

After reading Royko's column, do you agree or disagree with his opinion? What would you have said to the caller? In your notebook, write a sentence or two stating your own opinion about the problem of teenage suicide in general. Tell also what the extent of the problem seems to be in your high school or community.

As you read the second column, see if any of Royko's readers echo your thoughts and feelings.

Death wish? Then spare the self-pity

Letters, calls, complaints and great thoughts from readers:

Aaron Brooks, Highland Park: I thought you'd like to know a teenager's point of view on teenage suicides.

I'm 17 and a senior at Highland Park High School. This is an affluent suburb with a very high suicide rate. I know people who've attempted suicide. Every day I see people who are close to suicide.

The problems that the teenagers of today face are no doubt very different than the problems you faced as a teenager. I therefore feel that you are not qualified to judge how the teenager of today thinks and feels.

The pressure put on today's teenagers is unbearable. There is pressure to excel in school, to have friends, be popular and to get into a good college. Just to name a few.

Comment: Yes, earlier generations did have it easier than you overburdened North Shore teenagers. Those pampered kids who came of age in the 1930s had

M I K E   R O Y K O

nothing to worry about except surviving the Great Depression. Most didn't worry about getting into a good college. Getting a job digging ditches was challenge enough. Then they fought World War II— a lark compared with your problem of making friends and being popular. As a youth, I, too, knew many young people who were close to death. But not by their own hand. The North Koreans and Chinese were the threat. I can see how the pressures on you might be unbearable, and

I don't know how you can stand it. Does crying in your pillow help?

L.J., Chicago: I am a pre-law student and am appalled at the heartless way you treated that girl who called you for help. Your response to her was irresponsible, and so was your column. I found your column disgusting and upsetting.

Comment: Wait a minute. The girl called to ask me if I knew the phone number of a suicide hot line. I didn't and suggested she call information. What's so irresponsible about telling someone to dial 411? And if you feel disgusted and upset, I don't know what I can tell you except that if those emotions are more than your tender sensibilites can handle, you might go into your daddy's garage and start the car. I mean, it's the in thing to do.

Dr. Jonathan H. Croll, M.D., Naperville: Your thoughts about teenage suicide have prompted this note. In my practice or my relations with friends, when the bull starts to fly about how tough their life

Continued on following page

Continued from preceding page
is, I inevitably stop the conversation, offer to drive them to the nearest veterans' hospital to show them young men with no legs, arms, kidneys or what-have-you and let them measure their problems against these young men. End of troubles; end of conversation.

Comment: Are you trying to say that the loss of a few limbs in a war can compare to the terrible trauma of a suburban teenager who is trying to get good grades, be popular and get into a good college? Your heartlessness shocks me.

Pete Miller, Chicago: In the blue-collar neighborhood where I grew up on the Southwest Side, I don't remember any kids committing suicide. They were too busy hustling to get ahead and help their families make it from month to month.

When I went in the Army and ended up in Vietnam, I didn't see any suicides there, either. I think that when you get a close look at death, you appreciate life a lot more.

From what I've read, most of these teenage suicides are from well-to-do families and have luxuries that I didn't get until I grew up and went out and earned them.

What they need is a challenge. When they go to a high school counselor and say that they are thinking of killing themselves, they should be taken to a noisy factory and put on an assembly line. And after a year of that, they should be taken to the recruiting office and signed up for a couple of years in the Army. After a 10-mile hike with a sergeant yelling in their ear, they might appreciate the simpler things in life.

Comment: Not a bad idea. But do you think the sergeant might let them wear their Walkmans during the hike? Or is he

as insensitive as the rest of us?

Joanne Ekberg, Chicago: I'm a graduate student of social work and a social-work intern at Evanston Township High School. Your column on teen suicide distresses me.

Emotional pain cannot be quantified on some sort of scale. Emotional pain is uniquely the experience of an individual, whether or not you or I think it's vain or superficial, and must be dealt with, either privately or professionally.

Your attitude disappoints me. I'm just glad you're a columnist and not a social worker.

Comment: If emotional pain is uniquely the experience of an individual and can't be quantified, so is stupidity, self-pity, shallowness and the need for instant gratification. And I'm glad I'm a columnist and not a social worker, too. I've never been good at blowing somebody else's nose.

Checking Your Comprehension

Read the following questions. Put an x in the box beside the answer that best completes each one.

1. "Those pampered kids who came of age in the 1930s had nothing to worry about except surviving the Great Depression," Royko says. By *pampered,* he means
   - ☐ a. diapered.
   - ☐ b. spoiled.
   - ☐ c. rich.

2. A reader wrote: "I am a pre-law student and am appalled at the heartless way you treated that girl who called you for help." The word *appalled* means
   - ☐ a. shocked.
   - ☐ b. encouraged.
   - ☐ c. attuned.

3. Pete Miller's solutions are
   - ☐ a. visits to the Veterans' Hospital.
   - ☐ b. working on an assembly line or signing up for the Army.
   - ☐ c. moving to the Southwest side of Chicago.

4. Aaron Brooks, seventeen, thinks that the causes of teenage suicide are
   - ☐ a. the pressures of getting good grades and having friends.
   - ☐ b. the same problems their parents faced when they were teenagers.
   - ☐ c. pampering that teenagers received from their parents.

5. How many letters agree with Royko's stance on teenage suicide?
   - ☐ a. two
   - ☐ b. three
   - ☐ c. four

6. Judging by Royko's last comment, does it appear that the letters from his readers changed his opinion?
   - ☐ a. Yes, he thinks emotional pain should be treated by a counselor or social worker.
   - ☐ b. No, but he is in the process of reconsidering.
   - ☐ c. No, he thinks suicide is self-pity.

☆ ☆ ☆

A columnist's role on the newspaper is to express an opinion about the news. Columns are found not only on the editorial page, but also in the sports section or as reviews in the entertainment section.

Staff editorial columnists, who for the most part write without a byline, express the newspaper's stance on major news issues. In contrast, a columnist who has a byline expresses his or her opinion, not the paper's. Such is the case with Mike Royko.

Readers agree or disagree with columnists, critics, or editorial writers. Some of those readers decide to communicate their feelings in a letter to the editor or, in some cases, a letter to the specific columnist. Sometimes columnists print reader letters as Royko did, but more often the letters are printed in a special letters-to-the-editor section of the paper (often found on the editorial page). When those letters are printed, the readers are communicating not only to the newspaper, but also to other readers.

Evaluating Comments in an Editorial

In the columns in this lesson, Mike Royko expresses his feelings about teen suicide. The result of his opinion is a controversy over whether teen suicide is a tragic event or a vain, selfish act.

Royko's opinion is that teen suicide is a vain, selfish act. In his first column, Royko states his reasons for that opinion, all of which have to do with the small amount of pain he thinks teenagers have experienced compared to older people who have suffered a great deal. In the second column, some of his readers give their reasons for agreeing or disagreeing with him.

Royko frequently states his opinion using a caustic, nearly taunting tone. Some of his comments say the exact opposite of what he means; the reader must recognize his tone to understand his real intent. Some of his comments exaggerate. Some depend on being outrageous.

Listed below are some of Royko's statements from the columns. In the space provided after each statement, write a sentence or phrase telling what Royko really means. In some cases, the statement says what Royko means to say. In those cases, simply put a checkmark on the blank. Refer to the columns to see the statements in context if necessary.

1. Life is too painful. Or they aren't popular enough in school: Life is too painful. Or their parents don't listen when they talk: Life is too painful.

_____

_____

2. Of course, you'll cause considerable grief for your parents, sisters, and brothers, which might be your motive.

_____

_____

3. Yes, earlier generations did have it easier than you over-burdened North Shore teenagers.

_____

_____

4. Then they fought World War II—a lark compared with your problem of making friends and being popular.

_____

_____

5. As a youth, I, too, knew many young people who were close to death. But not by their own hand.

_____

_____

6. I can see how the pressures on you might be unbearable, and I don't know how you can stand it.

_____

_____

Using Your Newspaper

Look in your newspaper for a column or a letter to the editor on a topic that interests you. You may find columns in sections of the newspaper other than the editorial section. The sports page and the living section, for example. often use opinion columns. Letters to the editor can usually be found on the editorial pages.

Read the column or letter and determine the main idea, the basic opinion that the columnist or letter writer wants to express. On a separate sheet of paper, write that opinion in your own words. Under the opinion, list two to four support-ing reasons from the column or letter. Then, in a sentence, state whether you agree or disagree with the opinion. If you agree, pick at least one of the supporting reasons and tell briefly why you find that reason persuasive. If you disagree, list three or four reasons supporting your opposing stance.

Practicing Newspaper Skills

Together with a friend, settle on a topic that would be news in your high school paper or your local paper. Per-haps you can choose a topic that your friends are currently discussing.

Examine the topic. If the two of you do not have clear opinions that are in opposition, assign sides, debate-team style, for and against.

Outline your opinions. Make a list of the reasons that support your opinions. One or both of you may need to go to the library to do some research for more information.

Again, assign roles. One of you write either a column or letter to the editor stating your main opinion and your supporting reasons. The other's task then is to write a response to the other's column or letter. Discuss the topic once more after you have both written your opinions.

You have read other stories in Unit One and Unit Two that deal with special interest topics. Such stories are usually written by feature writers on fashion, discovery, biography, and so on. They are also written by columnists, who write more explanatory pieces and who are often specialists in an area such as sports, psychology, or gardening.

Such specialty service and advice columns are often further classified as *how-to articles.* In a how-to, the writer provides the reader not only with some interesting information but also with directions to do the activity that is the subject of the article. The two special interest features you will read in this lesson focus on a well-known American food—the sandwich. In each case the writer uses the how-to format of a recipe to give readers some new information they can put to their own use in the pursuit of "super sandwiches."

BURGERS

Strong Opinions on Fixing America's Favorite

By TOM SIETSEMA
Special to the Washington Post

The common hamburger has friends in high places—and they're adamant about how the sandwich should be prepared and served.

Julia Child prefers her hamburgers "fairly thick, nice and juicy," and calls them "one of our greatest contributions to civilization." Marion Cunningham, aka Fannie Farmer, is a fan who thinks "a hamburger should fit the mouth." One way the late James Beard cheered distraught friends was to make a bacon cheeseburger and serve it "with a fine, old, first-growth bordeaux—like a '64 Lafitte," recalls a longtime associate.

Foremost, say cooking experts, the model hamburger is built on good, fresh meat. The exact cut seems to depend on one's taste and budget. Ideally, says Cunningham, a hamburger should be made from "the trimmings of prime beef roast"—which even she admits is probably not very practical for the majority of burger enthusiasts. Among the many cuts available, ground sirloin is apt to provide the meatiest, most full-flavored sandwich, while those with more fat—regular or chuck, for example—are likely to be juicier, depending, of course, upon their degree of doneness. "Hamburger is not diet food," says Child, who likes hamburger with a 25- to 30-percent fat content. Fat, she adds, lends both flavor and tenderness. Nevertheless, if you want very lean meat ground for hamburger, opt for round, flank, chuck, neck or shank; a pound of ground beef is enough for four generous patties.

Some like 'em thick and some like 'em thin. But the cooking pros all tend to agree about how the hamburger should be handled: Pat—but do not squeeze—the meat, cautioned Beard. "I've learned that patting too firmly makes hamburgers rubbery and tougher," notes Cunningham, who recommends lightly molding the meat into patties. (A tip: if you dip your fingers in cold water before handling the meat, they won't stick.)

At this point, one might consider adding a sprinkle of grated onion, a dash of tomato juice, cream or some butter to keep the patty moist. Also, a beaten egg added to each pound of meat helps the meat adhere better to itself. And should you find it necessary to stretch hamburger, try blending ½ cup of soft bread crumbs (soaked momentarily in about 1/3 cup milk) to each pound of meat, or add ½ cup chopped bean sprouts, grated raw carrot, or ¼ cup of ground nuts, wheat germ, or pre-moistened cracked bulgur.

When grilling hamburgers, remember to grease the grill with some vegetable oil before laying on the patties—this prevents them from sticking. Unlike with other cooking methods, it's impossible to retrieve juices lost from hamburgers grilled over a fire. So to avoid dryness, sear the meat first: Place the grill close to the coals and lay on the burgers. Flip and sear the other side. Then raise the grill about 3 inches from the flame and cook until desired doneness. (The length of time will vary according to the meat and the fire's intensity.) But "cook no faster than necessary," says Cunningham, who also warns against compacting the patties with a spatula, which pushes out the juices. And remember that a well-done hamburger is rarely juicy.

The most important part of a hamburger—aside from an icy soft drink, some might argue—is the bun. A good bun is not

Continued on following page

Continued from preceding page

too hard and not too soft. And it shouldn't fall apart with the first few bites. As alternatives to the flimsy, mass-produced hamburger buns, Child suggests using either French or sourdough bread. Alternately, try English muffin halves, grilled dark bread or even bagels. Warming or lightly toasting buns makes for a better sandwich, too.

Garnishes and accompaniments are used for two reasons: to enhance a good burger and disguise an inferior one. While the meat should be the star of any well-made hamburger—"if it's really good meat, don't put anything on it," offers Child—there are an infinite number of ways to dress one up: Cunningham, who insists on a moist hamburger, adds sweet relish, shaved lettuce (never whole leaves) and finely chopped onion held in place with plenty of mayonnaise. Child might add grated onion, thyme and pureed garlic to meat that is unexceptional. And in response to that all-important question, both of them think catsup is acceptable.

Like garnishes, additions to the meat can include almost anything. For a twist on the usual, you might consider incorporating seasonings such as nutmeg or allspice into the meat, or topping finished burgers with shredded cheese and walnut pieces, sour cream with horseradish, or guacamole. The stellar hamburgers at Alexandria's Union Street Public House, served with slices of grilled rye bread and melted cheddar, are accented with caraway and beer (to one pound of meat, add about 3 ounces ale, 1 teaspoon caraway seeds and 2 teaspoons worcestershire sauce). Still, the accompaniments should never detract from the *raison d'etre:* "I strongly object to restaurants that serve 33 different hamburgers," says Cunningham of all the clutter.

Lastly, any good hamburger is improved with the addition of the following, Fannie Farmer's homemade buns:

FANNIE FARMER'S HAMBURGER BUNS

(Makes about 16 3½-inch buns)

"Rich buns with a fine texture," writes Marion Cunningham, "they pass all the hamburger bun tests—they hold the meat drippings, catsup, mayonnaise, mustard and relish without collapsing or becoming soggy. The same dough can also be shaped into hot dog buns."

1½ cups warm water	3 tablespoons sugar
²/₃ cup instant nonfat dry milk	2 packages dry yeast
¹/₃ cup lard	1 egg
1½ teaspoons salt	About 5 cups all-purpose flour

Combine water, dry milk, lard, salt, and sugar in a mixing bowl, and stir to blend. Sprinkle the yeast over, stir, then let stand to dissolve for a couple of minutes. Add the egg and 2 cups flour, and beat vigorously until thoroughly blended and smooth. Add enough of the remaining flour to make a manageable dough, then turn out onto a lightly floured surface and knead for a few minutes. Let rest for 10 minutes.

Add enough more flour so the dough is not sticky, and resume kneading until smooth and elastic. Place dough in a large greased bowl, cover, and let rise until double in bulk.

Grease several baking sheets. Punch the dough down and divide in half, then cut each half into 8 equal pieces. Roll each piece between your palms into a smooth ball and place about 3 inches apart on the baking sheets. Pressing down with the palm of your hand, flatten each ball into a circle about 3 inches in diameter. Cover lightly and let rise about 45 minutes, or until double in bulk. Bake in 425-degree oven 20 to 25 minutes, or until lightly browned. Remove from the baking sheets and cool on racks.

From "The Fannie Farmer Baking Book" by
Marion Cunningham (Knopf, 1984)

Checking Your Comprehension

Read the following questions. Put an *x* in the box beside the answer that best completes each one.

1. The first sentence reads: "The common hamburger has friends in high places—and they're adamant about how the sandwich should be prepared and served." To be *adamant* is to be
   - ☐ a. stiff.
   - ☐ b. insistent.
   - ☐ c. awful.

2. The story states that garnishes are used to "enhance a good burger and disguise an inferior one." The word *enhance* means to
   - ☐ a. improve.
   - ☐ b. repair.
   - ☐ c. beautify.

3. Many cooking experts agree that the key to a good hamburger is
   - ☐ a. not cooking it too long.
   - ☐ b. using salt to add to the taste.
   - ☐ c. using good, fresh meat.

4. The writer of the column says the most important thing besides the hamburger itself is
   - ☐ a. the bun.
   - ☐ b. the grill one uses to cook it.
   - ☐ c. the beverage one drinks with it.

5. If you were on a diet you would not want to eat many hamburgers because
   - ☐ a. you would be tempted to eat french fries, too.
   - ☐ b. hamburger has a high fat content.
   - ☐ c. you should not eat bread when you are on a diet.

6. When the writer says accompaniments should never detract from the *raison d'etre* he means
   - ☐ a. too many people soak their hamburgers with catsup.
   - ☐ b. accompaniments make the buns soggy.
   - ☐ c. the accompaniments could smother the taste of the hamburger.

Many newspapers run a weekly section devoted to food. The section will contain stories on restaurants, new food-preparation devices, nutrition, the particular qualities of a specific food, and so on.

Some of these articles are considered how-to's because they give the reader directions for cooking or tips for serving. One bit of specific advice in the hamburger story concerns how to make the best hamburger patty. The story also offers advice on how to grease the grill and how to sear the meat. In other words, if readers follow all of the article's directions, they will cook tasty hamburgers—that is the whole point.

The next story is about another popular sandwich. See why the two writers of "A Taste of America," a regular feature, also use a recipe.

A TASTE OF AMERICA

A sub by many other names

By JANE and MICHAEL STERN

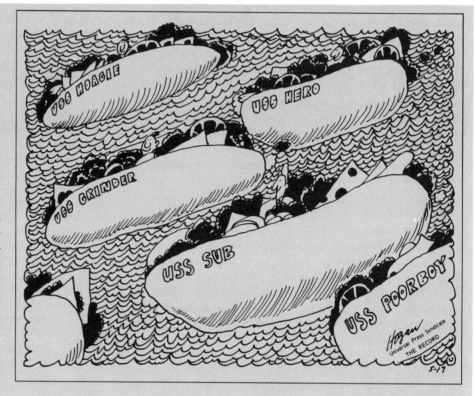

ATLANTIC CITY, N.J.—What do you call a long tube of crusty bread stuffed with cold cuts or meatballs? In many parts of the United States, it is known as a "hero." In New Orleans, it's a "poor boy." In Miami, they call it a "Cuban"; in much of the southern Midwest, it's an "Italian." In upstate New York, it's a "bomber"; downstate, a "wedge." In Connecticut, it's a "grinder." We've also seen menus listing "rockets," "Garibaldis," "zeps" (short for zeppelins) and "torpedos."

In the Delaware Valley, where behemoth sandwiches are a passion, the most common nicknames are "hoagie" and "sub." You don't have to be an etymologist to figure out that "sub" is short for submarine, a moniker derived from the sandwich's resemblance to an underwater ship.

Culinary historians credit the term "sub" to the White House of Atlantic City, a sandwich shop that has launched approximately 10 million submarines since it opened for business in 1946. Until that time, the term hereabouts was "hero," but to honor the silent service of World War II, Tony Basile of the White House started calling his heros "subs."

The White House is now a shrine for sub lovers. Pictures of celebrity clientele line the walls, inscribed with praise for the excellence of the White House. News clippings tell of the time the astronauts came to scarf down subs, and of Frank Sinatra craving them so much that he once had them shipped from New Jersey across the world to a movie location.

Despite its renown among sandwich connoisseurs, the White House remains a humble Naugahyde-and-Formica eatery with a row of booths along the wall and a six-stool counter up front. The lighting is neon, the napkins are paper, and the service is lightning fast: Who would want his submarine served any other way?

These sandwiches, let us tell you, are the elite of the corps. Each is about two feet long, loaded with ingredients that range from fancy white tuna fish to meatballs that are made right behind the counter while you watch. The "White House Special" is an armada of cold cuts —Genoa salami, ham, capicola and provolone cheese—all tightly packed inside the loaf, lubricated with olive oil, decorated with lettuce and bits of sweet pepper.

The ingredients are excellent, but submarine connoisseurs will tell you that it's what's outside that counts. The bread is the soul of a good sub sandwich. It must be absolutely fresh. It must have real body, enough oomph so it doesn't fall apart even when loaded with hot-sauced meatballs. And it must have a brittle crust that stays crisp.

The White House gets its bread from two nearby bakeries, the Rando and the Atlantic City. If you want to make first-rate subs and you don't live near a good Italian bakery, the only solution is to bake your own. It takes time, but these loaves are delicious—great for any supersandwich, hot or cold. If you really want to pile on the ingredients, scoop out some of the insides before constructing your sandwich.

SUBMARINE LOAVES

2 packages dry yeast
1 teaspoon sugar
2 cups warm water (110 degrees)
5 to 5½ cups all-purpose flour
2 teaspoons salt
2 tablespoons olive oil
  (plus a dash to oil bowl)
Yellow cornmeal

Combine yeast and sugar with ½ cup
Continued on following page

Continued from preceding page
of the water. In a separate bowl, mix 5 cups of flour, salt, olive oil and remaining water. When yeast is foamy, add it, stirring vigorously until dough pulls from sides of bowl. Turn dough onto floured board: clean and oil bowl.

Knead dough 10 minutes, adding flour if necessary. Return to bowl, rolling dough to cover with oil. Cover dough and let rise at room temperature 3 to 4 hours, until nearly triple in bulk. Punch down dough again. Let rise again, 1 to 2 hours.

Preheat oven to 400 degrees. Punch down dough. Divide it into quarters, then divide each quarter in half. Roll each piece into a torpedo-shaped cylinder and place on a baking sheet dusted with cornmeal. Slash top of each roll with sharp razor blade.

Using a plant atomizer filled with cold water, spray a mist onto rolls and pop them into hot oven. Five minutes later, open oven and spray rolls again, keeping door open as briefly as possible. Repeat once more after five more minutes.

Bake a total of 22 minutes, until rolls are nicely browned. Remove from baking sheet and cool on wire rack. Makes eight sub rolls.

Checking Your Comprehension

Read the following questions. Put an *x* in the box beside the answer that best completes each one.

1. The writers say that "you don't have to be an etymologist to figure out that 'sub' is short for submarine." An *etymologist* is
   □ a. an English major.
   □ b. a person who studies word histories.
   □ c. a compiler of dictionaries.

2. When it comes to ingredients, "submarine connoisseurs will tell you that it's what's outside that counts." A *connoisseur* is one who
   □ a. knows little about a subject.
   □ b. criticizes and analyzes as part of his job.
   □ c. knows about and enjoys something.

3. The first place to use the term *sub* for its sandwiches was
   □ a. the Delaware Valley.
   □ b. the White House of Atlantic City.
   □ c. a submarine base in Florida.

4. The recommended bread for a submarine sandwich must have each of the following characteristics except a
   □ a. brittle crust that stays crisp.
   □ b. real body that doesn't fall apart.
   □ c. thickness of at least four inches.

5. The specialty of the house at the White House is
   □ a. the service.
   □ b. a meatball sub.
   □ c. a cold Italian sub.

6. Given the emphasis on the bun and the White House's fame, we can conclude that the Rando and Atlantic City bakeries make
   □ a. two different types of buns.
   □ b. one type of bun for the White House.
   □ c. buns with scooped-out insides.

☆   ☆   ☆

Hobby and leisure-time activity columns have increased in number in most newspapers. That is because many people have more options for spending their free time, and newspapers, as we know, try to respond to the needs and wants of readers.

Food articles like the two you have just read are geared to appeal to people who like to eat out, people who like to cook, and people who like to do both. And those people—those readers—know that because of the how-to format they will read about something that interests them and learn a practical technique as well.

☆   ☆   ☆

Putting Steps in Order

The directions in a how-to article are designed to add to the appeal of the article and to give the reader a chance to be an active participant. Any article that includes directions depends for its effectiveness on the writer's ability to use sequence for the benefit of the reader. Then, if the directions are clear, it is up to the reader to follow them for the endeavor to be successful.

Following are directions from the two articles in this lesson. They cover the essential steps for fixing a hamburger and for baking submarine sandwich rolls. The steps, however, are not shown in the proper sequence. Read the steps. Then, without looking back at the articles, number them from one to five and put them in the proper order.

Fixing a Hamburger

_____ Add garnishes or accompaniments such as shredded lettuce or finely chopped onion.

_____ Lightly mold meat into patties.

_____ Grill hamburgers carefully to keep in the juices.

_____ Incorporate seasonings into the meat such as caraway seeds or worcestershire sauce.

_____ Place on a good bun with a fine texture.

Making Your Own Sub Rolls

_____ Preheat the oven to 400 degrees.

_____ Prepare the dough and allow it to rise and triple in bulk.

_____ Spray the rolls at least twice with a mist of cold water.

_____ Place the browned rolls on a wire rack to cool.

_____ Divide the dough into quarters and roll each into a torpedo-shaped cylinder; place on a baking sheet.

Using Your Newspaper

Look in your newspaper for a week or two. See how many different how-to articles or columns with directions for the reader you can find. Save the articles. To each one you collect attach a label indicating the people you think are the intended readers—they could be gardeners, athletes, home-owners, the general reader, and so on.

At the end of the two weeks, evaluate your collection. Do how-to articles seem to be directed at one group of people more than another? Are there more home repair how-to's than, say, how-to's for dancers? Are there many how-to's directed at the elderly? The very young? Are there more for women, or more for men? Are all the how-to's practical—can one really do them? If there is one that appeals to you, follow the steps and see how it works out.

Practicing Newspaper Skills

The story on submarine sandwiches tells the reader various names for the same sandwich in various parts of the country. What people know in New Orleans as a "poor boy," for example, is called an "Italian" in the Midwest. There are undoubtedly stories behind the names.

For this activity, research a food item in your area that has a distinctive name. Then write an account on how that name came to be. You might want to write about whatever it is you call the submarine sandwich. Or, maybe the people in your area are fond of "Coney Islands," or "Buffalo wings," or "potato crisps."

Query your parents and any people you know who have lived a long time in your area. Ask them if they remember when the food first became popular and if they remember how the name came to be. Then go to a restaurant, snack shop, or grocery store that sells the item and speak to the manager or a knowledgeable salesperson. Try to learn from that person how the food item came to be named, and anything else about its history.

Write a paragraph or two that traces the food item's history and the origin and evolution of its name.

The launch of the space shuttle *Challenger,* on January 28, 1986, was newsworthy because of the presence on board of Christa McAuliffe, who was to be the first private citizen of the United States to orbit the Earth. To the horror of the entire country, however, the launch turned into a disaster. Newspapers across the country and around the world were filled with stories and photographs of events surrounding not a triumph, but a tragedy.

The story below is about the *Challenger* disaster. As you can see, the *Boston Globe* printed a photograph and a drawing in addition to the story. Those visual elements help communicate the events to readers.

The second story in the lesson concerns the capsizing of a British car ferry off the coast of Belgium. Like the shuttle disaster, this story received worldwide coverage. The *Globe,* in reporting the ferry story, makes use of photographs, as was done for the shuttle story. As you read both reports, notice how the stories and visual elements work together to communicate information.

The Boston Globe

Vol. 229; No. 29   WEDNESDAY, JANUARY 29, 1986   80 Pages • 25 cents

Fiery blast destroys space shuttle; McAuliffe, six astronauts are killed

Challenger explodes in a ball of fire shortly after liftoff from Kennedy Space Center. Boosters leave trails of smoke (top and right center) as they separate from the shuttle.

Searchers find debris, no bodies

By MICHAEL KRANISH
and PETER MANCUSI
Globe Staff

CAPE CANAVERAL, FLA.—The space shuttle Challenger exploded into a huge fireball moments after liftoff yesterday morning, killing all seven crew members, including Christa McAuliffe, the New Hampshire high school teacher who was to be the country's first private citizen to orbit the Earth.

As Challenger rose spectacularly off its launch pad into clear blue skies at 11:38 a.m., all appeared normal, and a crowd that included McAuliffe's husband, two children and parents roared its approval.

Then, 75 seconds into the flight, as Challenger achieved full engine power for the thrust that would carry it into orbit, the spacecraft inexplicably exploded.

It was the country's worst space disaster, stunning the nation at a time when the shuttle program—and McAuliffe—had

Continued on following page

Continued from preceding page

succeeded in captivating the American public.

At first, thousands of spectators in VIP stands and press boxes assumed that the brilliant burst was the separation of the shuttle from its rocket boosters. But seconds later, a Mission Control official announced over loudspeakers: "We have a report that the vehicle has exploded."

As shocked onlookers stared in horror at the plumes of smoke that streaked the sky high above the Atlantic, NASA teams began rescue operations in hopes that some of the astronauts might be found at sea. But late yesterday afternoon, the space agency announced that all of the crew members had died in the explosion.

A Coast Guard spokesman said late last night that searchers at the crash site 18 miles offshore had recovered small pieces of debris.

"There has been some debris recovered but it has not been identified," said the spokesman, Chief Petty Officer Bob Baeten. "The wreckage was described as being several small chunks, but I don't know the exact size or where it was found."

He said that none of the bodies has been recovered, and that the search would resume at daybreak this morning.

In addition to McAuliffe, 37, the Challenger crew members killed in yesterday's explosion were mission commander Francis R. Scobee, 46; pilot Michael J. Smith, 40; Judith Resnik, 36; Ronald E. McNair, 35; Ellison S. Onizuka, 39; and Gregory B. Jarvis, 41.

At an outdoor press conference at the Kennedy Space Center overlooking the launch site, Jesse Moore, the director of the shuttle program, said the agency had no explanation for the explosion. In the distance, a flag flew at half staff, but a clock continued to tick off milliseconds as if the shuttle were still in flight.

"Flight controllers polled said they did not see anything unusual," Moore said.

Asked about a taped replay of the flight that appeared to show a leak in one of the shuttle's two fuel tanks, Moore said, "We will not speculate on the specific cause of the explosion based on that footage over this national tragedy."

Moore said that an interim NASA committee had been formed to begin investigating the explosion and that shuttle operations would be suspended "until we get a handle on what our problems are."

For a country accustomed to space flight and the routine launchings that have characterized the shuttle program, the explosion of the shuttle and deaths of the seven astronauts came as a national shock.

In Washington, President Reagan postponed his State of the Union speech, scheduled for delivery before Congress last night, and instead made a brief address to the nation from the Oval Office on the loss of the shuttle and its crew.

"We mourn seven heros," Reagan said.

"Nothing ends here"

The president, who learned of the explosion during a late-morning meeting with senior advisers, reaffirmed the government's commitment to space flight and the shuttle program. "The future doesn't belong to the faint-hearted," Reagan said. "It belongs to the brave." He added: "Nothing ends here. Our hopes and journeys continue."

Members of both houses of Congress said yesterday that they also expected committees with jurisdiction over the space program to investigate the explosion.

The disaster marked the first time in the American manned space program that astronauts had been killed in flight. It occurred a day after the 19th anniversary of the deaths of Air Force Lt. Col. Virgil I. (Gus) Grissom, Lt. Col. Edward H. White and Navy Lt. Cmdr. Robert B. Chaffee, killed when a fire broke out in their capsule atop a Saturn rocket being tested for the first manned Apollo flight.

Throughout the afternoon yesterday, the television networks, as they have during other national tragedies, linked the nation to the disaster, repeatedly replaying Challenger's brief flight and the horrifying footage of the explosion.

According to a transcript of the

Continued on following page

The Challenger disaster

THE FINAL WORDS

Launch Control: 10-9-8-7-6, we have main engine start; 4-3-2-1, and liftoff. Liftoff of the 25th space shuttle mission. And it has cleared the tower.

Pilot Mike Smith: Roll program.

Mission Control: Roger, roll, Challenger.

Mission Control: Roll program confirmed. Challenger now heading downrange. The engines are throttling down now at 94 percent. Normal throttle for most of the flight is 104 percent. We'll throttle down to 65 percent shortly. Engines at 65 percent. Three engines running normally. Three good fuel cells. Three good APUs (auxiliary power units). Velocity 2,257 feet per second (1,400 miles per hour), altitude 4.3 nautical miles (4.9 statute miles), downrange distance 3 nautical miles (3.4 statute miles). Engines throttling up, three engines now 104 percent.

Mission Control: Challenger, go at throttle up.

Smith: Roger, go at throttle up.

(Fireball occurs)

Mission Control: We're at a minute 15 seconds, velocity 2,900 feet per second (1,977 mph) altitude 9 nautical miles (10.35 statute miles), range distance 7 nautical miles (8.05 statute miles).

(Long silence)

Mission Control: Flight controllers are looking very carefully at the situation. Obviously a major malfunction. We have no downlink (communications).

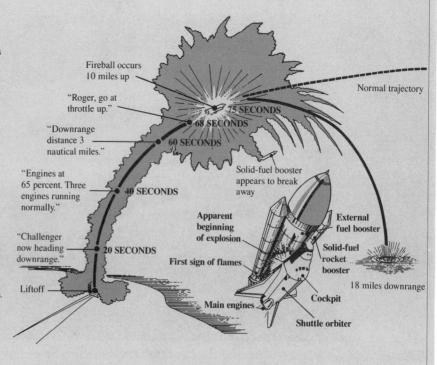

Normal trajectory

Fireball occurs 10 miles up

"Roger, go at throttle up."

75 SECONDS

68 SECONDS

"Downrange distance 3 nautical miles."

60 SECONDS

"Engines at 65 percent. Three engines running normally."

40 SECONDS

Solid-fuel booster appears to break away

Apparent beginning of explosion

External fuel booster

"Challenger now heading downrange."

20 SECONDS

First sign of flames

Solid-fuel rocket booster

18 miles downrange

Liftoff

Main engines

Cockpit

Shuttle orbiter

Continued from preceding page
conversations between Mission Control and the shuttle released late last night, flight controllers told the shuttle about one minute after launch, "Challenger, go, with throttle up."

The shuttle replied: "Roger, go, with throttle up."

Seventy-five seconds into the flight, at the time of the explosion, a NASA spokesman said: "One minute, 15 seconds, velocity 2,900 feet per second, altitude nine nautical miles, down-range distance seven nautical miles.

"Flight controllers here looking very carefully at the situation. Obviously a major malfunction. . . . We have a report from the flight dynamics' officer that the vehicle has exploded. The flight directory confirms that."

NASA's first public explanation on the explosion did not come until five hours after the disaster, and it provided few details. Videotape replays of the launch, however, led to speculation about what may have caused the explosion.

The tape appeared to show that within a minute of liftoff, a leak developed near the bottom of one of the two solid-fuel tanks that together contain 3.8 million pounds of propellant. Within seconds, another, larger leak seemed to appear in the same tank. Then the fiery explosion destroyed the shuttle.

Because the shuttle and the second fuel tank appeared unharmed until the explosion of the first tank, some observers speculated that the same leak had caused the entire explosion.

Tank was scraped

One of the two fuel tanks had been scraped last Saturday night in an incident that NASA dismissed then as insignificant. In that incident, according to a report issued by the space agency last night, a bolt protruding from a scaffolding platform scraped an area that connected the tank to the orbiter.

However, the report said that because the bolt protruded only one inch and penetrated a two-inch layer of foam insulation, "The scratch was determined to be of no consequence."

A major setback

For NASA, the explosion was a disastrous setback in the shuttle program, and raised immediate questions about whether the space agency could hold to its ambitious schedule to launch 13 flights on its three remaining orbiters this year.

The program was expected to receive a major boost from the flight of Challenger because of McAuliffe, the social studies teacher from Concord, N.H., who was picked to be the first private citizen in space.

McAuliffe was to have given two lessons on the Challenger mission to millions of students Friday from the shuttle, and her odyssey from the classroom to the shuttle had been followed closely by schoolchildren across the country.

At Concord High School yesterday, 1,200 students and 140 faculty, many with party hats and noise makers, eagerly awaited the launch on television. Gathered in the high school's auditorium, in the cafeteria, and in classrooms, they cheered loudly as Challenger lifted off after two minor delays.

"Awesome," said several students as they watched the 110-ton spacecraft slowly clear the pad and climb toward orbit.

When the shuttle exploded, many students burst into tears. Teachers escorted the students back to their homerooms and principal Charles Foley asked reporters to leave the building.

Checking Your Comprehension

Read the following questions. Put an x in the box beside the answer that best completes each one.

1. The report states the "spacecraft inexplicably exploded." *Inexplicably* means
   □ a. inexpressibly.
   □ b. inexplainably.
   □ c. inevitably.

2. The story says the accident came at a time when the shuttle program and McAuliffe "had succeeded in captivating the American public." As it is used here, *captivating* means
   □ a. capturing by force.
   □ b. holding within bounds.
   □ c. attracting by charm.

3. When the disaster occurred
   □ a. the astronauts were still on the ground waiting for lift-off.
   □ b. the astronauts were seventy-five seconds into the flight.
   □ c. the spacecraft had engines at 65 percent and running normally.

4. Had astronauts ever been killed before in the United States space program?
   □ a. The Challenger disaster was the first accident for the American space program.
   □ b. Three astronauts were killed by a fire in their Saturn capsule before lift-off.
   □ c. Yes, but the deaths went unreported.

5. Many people did not understand at first that something had gone wrong because
   □ a. a voice on the loudspeaker assured the crowd that everything was all right.
   □ b. they did not know exactly what a successful launch should look like.
   □ c. the explosion happened too high up to be seen well.

6. Which of the reasons below best justifies calling the accident "the country's worst space disaster"?
   □ a. The accident was unexpected because everything was going so smoothly.
   □ b. Seven people were killed in flight while the nation watched.
   □ c. The explosion would set the NASA program back.

The dramatic picture records the instant the space shuttle *Challenger* exploded. The image communicates disaster instantly to the reader.

The photographs in the following story also communicate disaster. Unlike the shuttle pictures, however, they do not record the British car ferry's moment of doom. Rather, they were taken hours after the vessel had capsized. The photos are compelling nonetheless, showing us a stricken ferry on its side in the ocean. We see those pictures and want to read the news report for more information.

As you read the story on the ferry disaster, notice how the photographs and the news story work together to explain the accident.

Ferry toll feared at 135

Query opens into disaster

By STEVEN ERLANGER
Globe Staff

ZEEBRUGGE, BELGIUM—More than 400 people have survived the capsizing of a British car ferry off the coast of Belgium Friday night, but at least 135 are dead or missing, with 51 bodies recovered from the icy North Sea, officials said yesterday.

Though diving teams searched through the ferry all day, Belgian Transport Minister Herman De Croo said there was little hope of finding more survivors. "I think we have to be pessimistic," he said. The divers suspended their search as night fell because of cold water and poor visibility.

A Belgian naval officer coordinating the rescue, said divers "found no life in the ship," except for three persons rescued from an air pocket about six hours after the accident.

The ship, *Herald of Free Enterprise,* lies more than half-submerged on its side on a sand bar outside this port at the southern end of the North Sea near the Strait of Dover. The straight connects the North Sea with the English Channel.

A Belgian official said 51 bodies had been recovered and 84 persons were missing and feared dead. He said there had been 543 on board.

Shipowners Townsend Thoresen, however, put the figures at 49 dead, 90 missing and 408 rescued, totaling 547.

British Transport Minister John Moore said there would be an investigation into how the 7-year-old, roll-on roll-off ferry could have capsized so quickly, by some accounts in only a minute. The 7,951-ton ship, which had 80 cars and 20 trucks on board, took on water and turned on its side 15 minutes after setting sail for Dover

The ferry *Herald of Free Enterprise* is surrounded by rescue workers as it lies on its side in the port of Zeebrugge, Belgium.

from Zeebrugge. The ship went down within a minute, the captain, David Lewry, is reported to have told a doctor at his hospital bed in Bruges—so quickly that he had no time to issue an SOS or institute the ship safety drill.

Late yesterday, the public prosecutor in Bruges impounded the ferry and said Lewry was unable to give a plausible explanation for the disaster, United Press International reported.

Officials believe the ship's huge bow doors, which provide access to the hold for the cars and trucks, somehow opened or perhaps were not completely shut. They say that earlier reports that the boat hit a harbor pier or wall were in error.

Peter Ford, managing director of Townsend Thoresen, said he had been told the bow doors had burst open, but said: "I just don't see how this could happen. [The doors] are operated by massive hydraulic rams—they just don't open by themselves."

But shipping experts in London said that any roll-on, roll-off ferry like the *Herald* is extremely dangerous if water gets into the hold, for there are no bulkheads inside the vehicle area, which is designed to be above the waterline.

A hole below the waterline could make the ship wallow, bringing the doors and the vehicle area under the water, lifting the ship and quickly sinking it. "No one in the industry will be surprised at the speed with which she sank," said one man who works for another ferry company.

But late last night, in an interview here, Valere Vautmans, Cabinet secretary to the Belgian public works minister, Louis Olivier, said: "Why this happened at all remains a mystery. The divers have found nothing, and the doors of the boat are normally three meters above the waterline. We can't see how enough water got into the ship to sink it."

The rescue of the passengers, most of whom are British, took place through a night of heroism and bravery, with help from British, Dutch and Belgian ships. A NATO minesweeping exercise was taking place at the time and helped speed the rescue efforts. The first helicopter was hovering over the ferry within six minutes.

Continued on following page

Continued from preceding page

Truckdriver William Cardwell, one of the survivors, said he was trapped on an upper deck when he saw a man, carrying a baby in his teeth, clamber to safety. "I saw this chap climbing over the tables and chairs holding the child in his clenched teeth—it was unbelievable."

Cardwell had been trying, with a group of adults and children, to break a window to escape onto the hull when the man with the baby joined them. "It was pitch-dark and freezing cold," he said. "We took it in turns to rub the baby to keep it warm." Finally, a helicopter succeeded in dropping a line to them.

Clifford Byrne, 22, and Andrew Simons, 30, together rescued a 2-year-old girl from their dark, flooded corridor. Simons, a mechanic from South London, said they were pulling themselves upward along a banister as the water quickly rose.

In a lounge of the ship, they saw a man in deep water holding the girl. "He was too cold to move," Simons said. "Cliff and I managed to get a hand to the baby and we got it out of the water."

Rescuers smashed a porthole, and the two friends passed through the girl, who was later reunited with her mother.

Such stories of sudden rescue were common yesterday. Emma Smith, 28, had left her husband, Robert, and son, Michael, 4, with their car when the ship began to sink. A man grabbed her and pulled her through a broken window, but her soldier husband and son had disappeared, and hospital checks proved fruitless.

"I don't know if they're alive," she said.

Royal Navy diver Eamonn Fullen, 19, described how he dived into the ship and swam, among bodies, through the cafeteria. He rescued three truck drivers, but a fourth could not be saved.

"He was so tired he could not hold on," Fullen said. The three who survived were so relieved, he said, "they couldn't stop laughing and joking."

Two diving teams, one British and one Belgian, conducted the search through the ferry.

Last night, a British captain stationed in Antwerp, who has been at work here since 10 p.m. Friday, described the ordeal of one truck driver. "He was in his lorry when another lorry crashed on top of it," the captain said. "He broke the door window with his suitcase and managed to climb up 15 feet and get out a window in the ship, but he doesn't know how. It was a horrendous experience, but he acts now as if it were all some sort of divine joke."

About 8 last night, Vautmans said, the Belgians called off the divers. "It's too dangerous in the dark and the higher sea," he said. "All the experts say that no one can still be alive. So there's no point putting the lives of the salvage people in danger just to look for bodies."

The search will continue today.

There was a crew of 85 aboard the ferry, but no final passenger list, because some travelers turned up at the last moment. At least 100 British military personnel were on board, returning to Britain on leave from West Germany. There were also at least 75 passengers on a day trip sponsored by the Sun newspaper. There were reportedly no Americans on board.

Townsend Thoresen officials began inspecting the ferry in detail yesterday, to try to understand why it foundered and to examine whether a salvage operation is possible today.

The bow of the *Herald of Free Enterprise* as seen yesterday morning at Zeebrugge, Belgium.

Checking Your Comprehension

Read the following questions. Put an *x* in the box beside the answer that best completes each one.

1. The ferry sank before the captain could "institute the ship's safety drill." By *institute*, he meant to
   - ☐ a. make official.
   - ☐ b. set into motion.
   - ☐ c. do something on the spur of the moment.

2. The report states that a hole lower than the ship's waterline "could make the ship wallow." To *wallow* means to
   - ☐ a. sink.
   - ☐ b. twirl around, end-to-end.
   - ☐ c. roll about.

3. By some accounts, the ship sank in approximately
   - ☐ a. one hour.
   - ☐ b. one minute.
   - ☐ c. five minutes.

4. Most of the people aboard the ferry were
   - ☐ a. British.
   - ☐ b. Belgian.
   - ☐ c. Dutch.

5. One man holding a baby was in deep water and was too cold to move. Two people grabbed the baby; the man was evidently
   - ☐ a. saved later.
   - ☐ b. able to free himself after handing over the child.
   - ☐ c. lost.

6. It is safe to conclude that, as the rescue operation went on into the night, the rescue workers themselves were
   - ☐ a. fearful.
   - ☐ b. putting their lives at risk.
   - ☐ c. disappointed at the small number of survivors.

☆　☆　☆

Photographers and artists perform non-writing roles that help newspapers report the news. In reporting the *Challenger* and British car ferry disasters, the photographers and artists communicate information to readers in ways that a reporter cannot. The photographs offer tangible glimpses of events that happened in other places at other times. The artist's rendering in the *Challenger* story shows the reader the essential parts of the shuttle, and the sequence of stages in the flight leading up to and including the terrible final moment in which the shuttle was destroyed. With the help of these pictures, readers form mental images that are complemented by the texts of the stories.

Of course, not all newspaper photographs are so dramatic. For every explosion or burning building or train crash picture, there are many shots of people simply talking, congregating at various social functions, even posing for the news photographer's camera. By the same token, artists' drawings are often used in service of stories that are quite tame in comparison to the car-ferry story. How-to's, sports stories, consumer information stories—all are the province of the newspaper artist.

☆　☆　☆

Recognizing Cause and Effect

The photographer's pictures capture the tragic results— or effects—of the two disasters. The smoke trails lingering in the sky after the shuttle explosion and the crippled ferry lying on its side in the ocean—both are effects, and both are eloquently communicated by the photographs. The stories elaborate on the pictures to report about the effects of the accidents in more detail. In addition to detailing the effects, both articles also report people's theories and guesses about the causes of the disasters.

Following are statements from both stories, the shuttle story first, followed by the car-ferry story. Read the statements. In the space provided before each one, write *cause* if the statement is a theory or guess about a possible cause of the disaster. Write *effect* if the statement reports an effect of the cause of the disaster.

Shuttle Disaster

_____ 1. The space shuttle Challenger exploded into a huge fireball moments after lift-off yesterday, killing all seven crew members. . . .

_____ 2. It was the country's worst space disaster, stunning the nation. . . .

_____ 3. As shocked onlookers stared in horror at the plumes of smoke . . . NASA teams began rescue operations in hopes that some of the astronauts might be found at sea.

Ferry Disaster

_____ 1. More than 400 people have survived the capsizing of a British car ferry . . . but at least 135 are dead or missing. . . .

_____ 2. The ship, Herald of Free Enterprise, lies more than half-submerged on its side on a sand bar outside this port. . . .

_____ 3. Officials believe the ship's huge bow doors, which provide access to the hold for the cars and trucks, somehow opened or perhaps were not completely shut.

_____ 4. Asked about a taped replay of the flight that appeared to show a leak in one of the shuttle's two fuel tanks, Moore said, "We will not speculate on the specific cause of the explosion based on that footage. . . . "

_____ 5. The tape appeared to show that within a minute of liftoff, a leak developed near the bottom of one of the two solid-fuel tanks. Within seconds, another, larger leak seemed to appear in the same tank.

_____ 6. Because the shuttle and the second fuel tank appeared unharmed until the explosion of the first tank, some observers speculated that the same leak had caused the entire explosion.

_____ 7. One of the two fuel tanks had been scraped [by a protruding bolt] in an incident that NASA dismissed as insignificant.

_____ 4. They say that earlier reports that the boat hit a harbor pier or wall were in error.

_____ 5. Peter Ford, managing director, said he had been told the bow doors had burst open, but said, "I just don't see how this could happen. [The doors] are operated by massive hydraulic rams, they just don't open by themselves."

_____ 6. But shipping experts in London said that any roll-on, roll-off ferry like the Herald is extremely dangerous if water gets into the hold. . . .

_____ 7. A hole below the waterline could make the ship wallow, bringing the doors and the vehicle area under the water, lifting the ship and quickly sinking it.

Using Your Newspaper

Survey your newspaper (or the photographs in this book) and collect ten photographs that you find interesting. Compare the photographs to the headline of the story. Which captures your attention most? Which holds your attention the longest?

Categorize the ten photographs that you have collected. You may want to categorize by grouping the photos into different types of pictures: human interest, seasonal, sports action, front page straight news, and so on. You may want to make up your own categories. Some categories will no doubt contain more pictures than others do. Do you think that might be because you are more interested in that category, or because many people are more interested in that category, causing newspapers to print more pictures of that type? Might there be another reason for the popularity of that type of picture?

Make a collage of your photographs or display them on the bulletin board. Encourage other students to add photographs to your collage or display.

Practicing Newspaper Skills

Become a newspaper photographer or artist by taking pictures or making drawings. If you can find a partner to be the reporter, you may wish to cover a news story together. Your partner can write the news story while you render the drawing or take the picture.

You may wish to cover a school sports event, play, or special class activity, or you could cover a community event—a city council meeting, for example. You might want to do a consumer report on the price of a popular item or service, or a feature story with a seasonal theme. The options are many and diverse.

Decide on a subject for your story and make arrangements to be on the scene. If you are working with a partner, make sure you have synchronized your schedules. Once at the event, take several photographs or make several sketches to illustrate what would make up the written information of the story. Again, if you have a partner, decide together what needs to be photographed or illustrated and how it should be done.

Get the photos developed and pick the best one or do a final draft of the best sketch. Write the story. (Write an abbreviated story if you are working alone. A partner should write a full-fledged news story.) Write captions, labels, steps, or whatever written information is needed for the photograph or drawing. Add a headline to the story and illustration.

Newspaper publishers first employed cartoonists because their comic strips helped sell papers. People today still love comics, and newspapers still feature them—on the sports page, in the business section, in the lifestyle section, and, of course, on the comics pages. Through their comic strips, cartoonists amuse us and divert us from the cares of the world even while they comment on everything from major news stories to the obstacles we all encounter in our daily routines.

In this lesson are two stories about comic-strip artists whose strips appear on the comics pages of newspapers around the country. The first story is an obituary for Chester Gould, who created one of the first strips that was not meant to be funny. Gould, in response to the crime and violence of Roaring Twenties-era Chicago, gave cartoon life to the square-jawed detective Dick Tracy. The strip is still published today.

The second story is a feature story on a young cartoonist named Cathy Guisewite whose cartoon character—also named Cathy—undergoes experiences similar to those of many young women today. In laughing at *Cathy,* readers can laugh at themselves.

Read the obituary for Chester Gould. It offers a look at the man who has guided readers through *Dick Tracy*'s world of evil and danger for decades.

'Dick Tracy' creator Chester Gould, 84

By WES SMITH
and KENAN HEISE

Cartoonist Chester Gould, 84, creator and artist of the "Dick Tracy" comic strip for 46 years, died of congestive heart failure at his farm home in Woodstock early Saturday.

He had been in poor health since suffering a heart attack last October, according to his daughter, Jean O'Connell, of Geneva.

Mr. Gould retired in 1977, but the strip's popularity endured. It currently is carried by about 500 newspapers throughout the world and is the basis of a movie about to begin production, in which Warren Beatty has signed to play Tracy.

Artist Dick Locher and writer Max Collins, proteges of Mr. Gould, now do the comic series for the Tribune Media Services Syndicate. Richard E. Fletcher drew the strip from December, 1977, until his death in March, 1983.

"He pioneered our field, we all owe him a debt of thanks," said Locher, a Pulitzer Prize-winning editorial cartoonist for The Tribune. "You could walk into his pictures and be part of his story and his strip. When Gravel Gertie talked to B.O. Plenty, you could smell B.O., and when he spit tobacco, you wanted to jump out of the way."

He virtually invented the adventure cartoon strip and he popularized the tough, two-fisted American detective," said Collins, who began corresponding with Mr. Gould at the age of 7.

Locher, who was attending the Association of American Editorial Cartoonists convention in Buena Vista, Fla., over

Chester Gould

the weekend, said he and his fellow cartoonists would observe a moment of silence for Mr. Gould. Dick Tracy himself will pay homage to his creator in the comic strip early this week, he said.

Mr. Gould's cartoon style was the first to graphically portray bullets spurting from brains and blood gushing from wounds—a fact that provoked the Meriden (Conn.) Record to cancel "Dick Tracy" in 1956 because its editors felt "crime is not entertainment."

It wasn't much fun for Tracy either. He was run over by cars, stabbed, gassed, chloroformed, pressurized, depressurized, mangled, fractured and shot 27 times in the first 24 years alone.

"When you combine realism with the fantastic, you've got a story every time," Mr. Gould said in his own defense in 1981.

It was in the panels of "Dick Tracy," not in scholarly journals, that the world first learned of two-way wrist radios, closed-circuit televison, space shuttles, and a lunar golf course, which appeared in Mr. Gould's comic strip two years before astronaut Alan Shepard hit a golf ball on the Moon. Olga, a Tracy villain, performed the first human heart transplant in 1963. Dr. Christiaan Barnard didn't do the first actual human heart transplant until four years later.

The most endearing quality of Mr. Gould's comic strip was his carnival of characters, from the shimmering Moonbeam and ever-endangered Tess Trueheart to the skulking scallywags B-B Eyes, Flattop, Gargles, Mumbles, Mrs. Pruneface, Peaches de Cream and Doc Hump.

"I wanted my villains to stand out definitely so that there would be no mistake who the villain was," said Mr. Gould,

Continued on following page

Continued from preceding page
who put up tombstones with the names of each of his villains on his 130-acre farm 60 miles northwest of Chicago.

He was 31 years old when he first drew the chisel-chinned cop [to resemble a "young Sherlock Holmes," he said] and proposed the strip "Plainclothes Tracy" for the Chicago Tribune-New York Daily News Syndicate.

Mr. Gould said he spent 10 years trying to sell a comic strip to Capt. Joseph Patterson, head of the syndicate, before the idea of a hard-nosed cartoon detective clicked.

Patterson, cousin of Tribune publisher Col. Robert McCormick, suggested calling the strip "Dick Tracy," with the first name drawn from the slang word for detective. The Tribune first printed the strip March 22, 1932. It had appeared before that in October, 1931, in the short-lived Detroit Mirror.

Mr. Gould, a farmboy from Pawnee, Okla., studied commerce at Oklahoma A&M for two years before packing off for Chicago with $50 in his pocket and larceny in his art. "I decided that if the police couldn't catch the gangsters, I'd create a fellow who would," he was quoted as saying in the book "The Celebrated Cases of Dick Tracy."

He was given the Reuben Award twice by the National Cartoonist Society and also an Edgar Award from the Mystery Writers of America.

He worked in the art departments of five Chicago dailies in the 1920s before arriving at The Tribune. He had lived in Woodstock since 1936.

Visitation will be held from 4 to 8 p.m. Monday in the Schneider, Leucht, Merwin & Cooney Funeral Home, 1211 N. Seminary St., Woodstock. Funeral services will be held at 2 p.m. Tuesday in the First United Methodist Church, 205 W. South St., Woodstock.

Besides his daughter, he is survived by his wife, Edna; two grandchildren; and a sister, Helen Upshaw.

Goodbye, My Friend ——— Dick Locher THE CHICAGO TRIBUNE

Checking Your Comprehension

Read the following questions. Put an *x* in the box beside the answer that best completes each one.

1. Dick Locher and Max Collins are described as being "protégés" of Chester Gould's A *protégé* is a
   - ☐ a. person who is helped in a career by an influential person.
   - ☐ b. main character in a fiction story; a hero or heroine.
   - ☐ c. creative person.

2. After Gould's death, Dick Tracy himself was to "pay homage to his creator in the comic strip." To pay *homage* is to
   - ☐ a. act humbly toward a person.
   - ☐ b. pay a tribute to a person.
   - ☐ c. pay off a debt owed to a benefactor.

3. Why did cartoonist Gould give his criminals names like B-B Eyes and Mrs. Pruneface?
   - ☐ a. He wanted readers to be sure who the villains were.
   - ☐ b. He couldn't draw very well and wanted to compensate for it.
   - ☐ c. He wanted funny names to disarm critics who accused him of using too much violence.

4. Why did Gould decide to draw a comic strip about crime?
   - ☐ a. He felt he didn't have a good enough sense of humor to do a funny strip.
   - ☐ b. He had always wanted to be a cartoonist, and crime strips were popular when he started his career.
   - ☐ c. He wanted to create a detective who could catch the gangsters, since the real police were having trouble doing so.

5. Why is Gould considered a pioneer in the field of comic strips?
   - ☐ a. He invented the adventure strip.
   - ☐ b. His cartoon style was graphic, showing bullets and blood.
   - ☐ c. Both reasons above are correct.

6. An example of Gould's cartoon style combining realism and fantasy is
   - ☐ a. the graphic portrayal of bullets and blood.
   - ☐ b. the villainess Olga performing a heart transplant four years before Dr. Barnard did the first actual human transplant.
   - ☐ c. Both reasons above are correct.

☆ ☆ ☆

Dick Tracy creator Chester Gould stated that the stories for the comic strip came from a combination of fantasy and reality. Interestingly, many of the ideas that constituted fantasy actually came to pass years after Gould had envisioned them.

Read the story that follows to find out what serves as inspiration for cartoonist Cathy Guisewite. As you read, think about the process by which a cartoonist thinks of themes and topics. Do you think it would be difficult to come up with ideas day after day?

Life imitates art for Cathy the cartoonist

Cartoonist Cathy Guisewite with a life-size *Cathy* doll and her dog Trolley, on the deck of her Laurel Canyon home.

Continued on following page

Continued from preceding page

By BETH ANN KRIER
Times Staff Writer

cathy®   **by Cathy Guisewite**

The *Cathy* abode is typically a mess—a slob's paradise where the oven is a holding tank for dirty dishes, the dresser warehouses used panty hose containers and the refrigerator is a shrine to Sara Lee, who the cartoon character claims is "the one woman who will never abandon me."

But here, near the top of Laurel Canyon off Mulholland Drive, at the spacious, modern, and rather luxurious home/studio of cartoonist Cathy Guisewite, there appears to be nothing but pure peace and quiet. And—get this—*ultra-tidiness.* No clutter to mar the minimalist decor. Fresh flowers in nearly every room. And a knock-your-socks-off view of the canyon that you'd swear is closer to Colorado than Chinatown.

Chaos, or what passes for it, is confined to a corner of Guisewite's home where the *Cathy* empire is created and preserved. A portion of the hall serves as the unofficial *Cathy* museum, displaying dozens of products from mugs to appointment books to dolls—everything but *Cathy* underwear. Two other work rooms include a large, slightly disheveled office in which Guisewite draws the cartoon strips and works with a part-time secretary and graphic designer, the latter primarily for the licensed products and coloring of the Sunday strip.

Here, unlike the rest of the house, inspired discombobulation is encouraged if not required.

"I need a certain level of anxiety in my life to do my job. I depend on it," said Guisewite, 36, offering a tour of the more public spaces of her home.

It was a need for more confusion and craziness in her life that led Guisewite to leave Santa Barbara for Los Angeles 2½ years ago.

"I moved here because Santa Barbara was too perfect. . . . I felt I was settling into more of a vegetative state than I wanted to be in. . . . Santa Barbara is the most tension-free city. I really couldn't stand it. At least people get mad here. I remember calling a plumber in Santa Barbara who told me he couldn't help me because it wasn't his karma to do plumbing that day. I got angry and he very

nicely suggested I should 'mellow out.'

"L.A. offers a real feeling of creative competition. I like that spirit. There's nothing I dislike about L.A . . . except the 4.5 million stunning blondes. OK, that's a problem."

Guisewite, who was born in Dayton, Ohio, and reared in Midland, Mich., is well aware that her semi-reclusive, top-of-the-canyon existence has its similarities to Santa Barbara. She observed it may overly protect her from the everyday stresses her character *Cathy* and her readers routinely experience. And she pointed out she has little need to venture out into the real world for much more than research. So she's devised a handy cure: "I sometimes on purpose go out in rush-hour traffic just to get aggravated."

Life Hasn't Changed

But to hear Guisewite tell it, all her success—the cartoon strip in more than 500 newspapers, an animated TV special which airs May 15 on CBS, books of her cartoon collections, a monthly strip in Glamour magazine, profits from the licensing of *Cathy* products and even a recently published advice book by her mother (for which she provided illustrations)—hasn't changed her life that much.

Appearances would indicate otherwise. She is considerably richer than her cartoon alter ego. (Success magazine estimated her annual income to be about $200,000 in 1983; she and her syndicate editor refuse to comment on what it is now.) And she is far thinner than *Cathy* (Guisewite is 5 feet 2 and 105 pounds—about 50 pounds lighter than when she more closely resembled her namesake).

But Guisewite insists she's still the same, often insecure, ever vulnerable creature that she was 11 years ago when she was vice president of a Detroit

advertising agency and drawing the strip on the side. The last impression she wants to leave her public with is that she is one of those women who has Got It All Together.

"When I read about a woman who has it totally together, my reaction is to go home and eat a carton of Cool Whip," she said, adding that she and *Cathy* still "turn to food to solve every problem. The difference is that *Cathy* will eat an entire cheesecake, whereas I'll only eat half of one."

But what about this thriving *Cathy* industry? And the stunning surroundings in which it's allowed its creator to live? Isn't this a rather major change?

"I don't feel that different than when I was living in an apartment like *Cathy,*" Guisewite said. "Then I was paying rent. Now I'm paying a mortgage. If anything I've found that the more successful I get, the more pressures there are on me to accomplish things and the more I get behind in my own schedule. And it seems like the anxieties just expand to match your personality. And the basic insecurities never change: Do I look OK? Am I capable of going on a date and being anything but totally incoherent?"

It is only in the area of personal, intimate relationships that the creator seems to be less successful than the product. Asked how the two compare, Guisewite replied, "[*Cathy*] is actually more settled than I am. . . . She's talking about living with Irving. . . . I've never lived with anybody, but I'm interested in trying it out in the strip."

Own Relationship Problems

Irving, she added, is a compilation of many men and the character on whom she conveniently drops all relationship problems.

Continued on following page

Continued from preceding page

And what about her own relationship problems? Is she presently involved in one?

"I think I've said enough," she responded, laughing. Later, however, she emphasized that she maintains a strict policy of not using the men she dates as fodder for the strip. At least not for a while. "Certainly, I would never draw anything about a current relationship. . . . I would never illustrate last week's date in the comic strip. . . . I'm very honest in the strip about my own insecurities. That's plenty."

Her parents, however, are open game. "I quote them about anything. I'm flat out about the parents."

But because Guisewite would like to keep both generations reading her cartoon strip, it's unlikely readers will see *Cathy* and Irving in bed together, the cartoonist said. "I sort of like keeping it vague so both generations are able to interpret it their own ways."

There have already been a few complaints from readers objecting to the fact that *Cathy* is even considering living with Irving, said Lee Salem, Guisewite's editor at Universal Press Syndicate. But not as many, he said, as there were in *Cathy's* early days when feminists routinely wrote in to say *Cathy* didn't represent them.

Hard, Hostile Line

As Guisewite sees it, "*Cathy* never took the hard, hostile line. The message [from complaining readers] pretty much was, 'The last thing that the world needs is another vulnerable woman' and they were particularly amazed that a woman would create a character who was vulnerable in the ways women are stereotypically vulnerable."

Yet *Cathy* continues to be super vulnerable. Consider Guisewite's description of the plot of her upcoming animated special: "Cathy is up for the Employee of the Year Award, Irving's out of town and she's basically groveling for a date."

Guisewite is well aware that it is precisely that sort of vulnerability that has created the loyal *Cathy* following.

"My real art is my ability to torture myself in my head. The strip is how I work out my anxieties. . . . The most important thing is to write from the heart, not guess what could be sold. Without exception, the ones [strips] that I like best are ones that have that. They're the ones where it looks like the person who drew it had no choice but to draw it."

Checking Your Comprehension

Read the following questions. Put an x in the box beside the answer that best completes each one.

1. Because of her success, cartoonist Cathy Guisewite is "considerably richer than her cartoon alter ego." An *alter ego* is a
   □ a. second self.
   □ b. changed person.
   □ c. comic character.

2. Guisewite says that, in spite of her success, she is the same "vulnerable creature" she was before. *Vulnerable* means
   □ a. disgusting or vulgar.
   □ b. open to attack.
   □ c. thick-skinned and insensitive.

3. Guisewite began drawing the comic strip
   □ a. while working on a TV special.
   □ b. while working for an advertising agency.
   □ c. after the breakup of a long-term serious relationship.

4. What people from Guisewite's life become characters in her comic strip?
   □ a. her current boyfriends
   □ b. her neighbors
   □ c. her parents

5. According to the story, do all readers think the *Cathy* character is a good role model for today's young women?
   □ a. No, some readers think *Cathy* presents a negative, regressive image of women.
   □ b. Yes, readers unanimously like the relationship between *Cathy* and Irving.
   □ c. No, some readers feel that *Cathy's* problems are too silly and don't reflect the hard realities of life.

6. When Guisewite creates a story for the *Cathy* strip, she
   □ a. anticipates what would sell and make the most money.
   □ b. remains true to herself by drawing on her own feelings and ideas.
   □ c. checks to see what other cartoonists are doing.

☆ ☆ ☆

Chester Gould commented on life as he saw it, blended with a healthy dose of fantasy, to create an imaginary world of crime and punishment in *Dick Tracy*. Using his considerable powers of invention, Gould dealt with good and evil while at the same time entertaining readers.

Cathy Guisewite uses a traditional gag-oriented approach to comment on life as she knows it. Her humorous situations entertain readers, but they also strike a chord. People recognize, in the continuing saga of *Cathy's* dilemmas, their own problems and predicaments.

☆ ☆ ☆

Biographical Sequence in Obituaries and Features

The articles about Chester Gould and Cathy Guisewite discuss their careers as cartoonists. The story on Gould is an obituary, or an announcement of his death. In the manner of a biography, the obituary tells readers how Gould came to be a cartoonist, what early problems he encountered, where he took his inspiration for the strip, and what he achieved as a cartoonist.

The feature article about the young cartoonist Cathy Guisewite tells readers how she became a cartoonist. But, since Guisewite is only thirty-six years old, the feature writer concentrates more on her current work habits than on detailing her past, as Gould's biographer has done. The story does include, however, some pertinent biographical information.

Listed below are statements taken from the obituary on Gould and the feature article on Guisewite. Read the statements. Then, in the spaces provided, number the statements in biographical sequence, or the order in which the events happened in Gould's and Guisewite's lives. Refer to the stories as necessary.

Chester Gould

_____ 1. Cartoonist Chester Gould, 84, creator and artist of the *Dick Tracy* comic strip for 46 years, died early Saturday.

_____ 2. Mr. Gould retired in 1977 but the strip's popularity endured.

_____ 3. Mr. Gould's cartoon style was the first to graphically portray bullets spurting from brains . . . a fact that provoked the *Meriden* [Conn.] *Record* to cancel "Dick Tracy" in 1956. . . .

_____ 4. He was 31 years old when he first drew the chisel-chinned cop [to resemble a "young Sherlock Holmes," he said] and proposed the strip "Plainclothes Tracy" for the *Chicago Tribune-New York Daily News* Syndicate.

_____ 5. The *Tribune* first printed the strip March 22, 1932.

_____ 6. Mr. Gould, a farmboy from Pawnee, Okla., studied commerce at Oklahoma A&M for two years before packing off for Chicago with $50 in his pocket and larceny in his art.

_____ 7. He worked in the art departments of five Chicago dailies in the 1920s before arriving at the *Tribune*.

Cathy Guisewite

_____ 1. Guisewite was born in Dayton, Ohio, and reared in Midland, Michigan.

_____ 2. . . . all her success—the cartoon strip in more than 500 newspapers, an animated TV special . . . books of her cartoon collections . . . profits from the licensing of *Cathy* products . . .

_____ 3. . . . 11 years ago when she was vice president of a Detroit advertising agency and drawing the strip on the side. . . .

_____ 4. . . . in *Cathy*'s early days . . . feminists routinely wrote in to say *Cathy* didn't represent them.

Using Your Newspaper

Skim the comics pages of your newspaper to find a daily cartoon you enjoy. Over the course of a week or two, save several of the strips (or one-frame comics, if that is your preference).

Write a letter to the cartoonist. Based on your reading of the comics you have collected, express your reactions to and enjoyment of the comic-strip artist's work. Be specific in your comments so that the cartoonist knows you've read the cartoons. You might also ask the kinds of questions that the two stories in this lesson deal with: How did the person become a cartoonist? How does he or she work? Where do ideas come from? Also, if you sketch cartoons yourself, you might want to include a few.

Call or write to your newspaper to get the cartoonist's address, then send your letter. Perhaps your cartoonist will answer, just as Chester Gould responded to Max Collins's letter when Collins was seven years old.

Practicing Newspaper Skills

Become a cartoonist yourself. Use your sense of humor to tell a story or to comment on everyday experiences. You can work alone or with a partner. If you find a partner, split the drawing and writing jobs as Max Collins and Dick Locher do on *Dick Tracy.*

Before you make your cartoon, brainstorm a list of topics you would like to comment on or stories you can tell. If you are commenting on everyday life, you may wish to use typical teenage experiences in much the same way that Cathy Guisewite uses life experiences in *Cathy.*

You could, for example, poke fun at the latest fad, an embarrassing situation, a topical school issue or a news-making community event.

After brainstorming a list of topics, choose one for a one-frame cartoon or a comic strip. Try out several sketches and write several versions of the dialogue. Look over your first drafts and select one that you feel can be made into the best cartoon. Draw a final version in pen and ink on good-quality art paper. Display your cartoon on the bulletin board.

How We Use the News

UNIT OVERVIEW

I n Unit One we examined values that help determine the content of the news. In Unit Two we studied the roles of the newspaper people who present the news. In Unit Three we will look at the newspaper—the product of information assembled by journalists following certain guidelines—from the point of view of the readership.

We turn to the newspaper for information about our world. Thus we "use the news" to the degree that the newspaper influences our daily lives and serves us in our need for up-to-date knowledge of ourselves.

The five lessons in Unit Three look at how the newpaper serves the readership through reader appeal, special papers, news datelines, daily record, and historical record.

To show how a local newspaper and a national news-paper take into consideration the idea of *reader appeal,* Lesson 1 contains two articles about the same idea—the high school spring prom. A city paper, *The Providence Journal-Bulletin,* ran a local prom story because the story held interest for readers in the Providence, Rhode Island, area. People there were intrigued by controversy over the prom at a local school. In contrast, the editors at the national newspaper USA TODAY chose to present the story of a typical, all-American prom, evidently on the premise that the way to reach a broad readership is by printing a story that has broad appeal.

Thus, a local paper appeals to its readers by devoting a good deal of attention to local issues. A national paper like USA TODAY, having no real local base, covers stories that different types of people in different parts of the country will be drawn to and will understand.

We saw in Unit One that proximity plays a part in determining the news. Similarly, newspapers consider not only where their readers live but also what their readers' interests are. Special papers are newspapers written for particular readers with special interests. A *special paper* may contain news reports, editorials, how-to columns, and feature articles, as do local or national papers. But the special paper uses these forms to report on subjects that are of interest only to a specific group of readers.

In Lesson 2, there are two examples of special papers. The first is a special bilingual section from the *Los Angeles Times.* When recent immigration laws were passed, the editors of the *Times* knew that specific readers—Hispanic immigrants—would need information about the new legis-lation. Accordingly, the paper ran a bilingual supplement for Spanish-speaking as well as English-speaking readers. The second example is a high school newspaper, the *Little Green,* published by students at Central High in Manchester, New Hampshire. The typical reader of the newspaper is a Central High student. Not everyone who lives in Manchester, then, is interested in the paper. Each of these special papers clearly serves a particular group of people.

In Lesson 3 we deal with *news datelines.* A dateline gives the date and place of an issue of a newspaper or magazine. Most newspapers have a daily dateline because they are published once a day. Many magazines have weekly date-lines—they contain the most important news stories of the past week. (*Time* and *Newsweek* come to mind immediately.) There are also newspapers with weekly datelines and maga-zines with monthly or quarterly datelines. Whatever the date-line, the news source will include only the important stories that have come to light in the period since the last issue.

As you will see in Lesson 3, it is useful to compare the news datelines of two different news sources and the amount of information each conveys. A newspaper, with its daily dateline, offers news stories of several paragraphs containing highlights and supporting details. A magazine, with its weekly dateline, can include an article several pages long covering the important events of the entire week. Readers often determine which source of news to consult by how much information they wish to learn.

In reporting the news, the newspaper serves as a *daily record* of what has happened in a town, in the city, in the nation, in the world. In the United States, this daily record of events is considered so important that its continuing existence is guaranteed in the First Amendment to the Constitution. Thanks to that First Amendment protection, no one can prevent a newspaper from covering a story and reporting information. Simply put, the public has a right to know the news.

In Lesson 4 two news stories report on censorship in South Africa. There the newspapers, and the daily record they form, are managed by the government. As you read the stories, think about a daily record that has been selectively controlled by a government acting in its own interest. Can such a record be complete? Can it be accurate? Fair? Truthful?

Because newspapers record the events of each day, with time they become a *historical record* of what has happened in the past. If a historian wants to research the American Civil War, for example, he or she can study newspapers from the 1860s and learn how the events of that era were reported day by day.

In Lesson 5, the newspaper stories report on the changes that have occurred over the years in labor unions. The first story recounts the status of laborers and labor unions when the organizations were new to the United States. The second article reports the status of workers and unions in society today. Thus the newspaper stories chronicle a chapter in history, becoming in the process chapters in the historical record.

In reading Unit Three, consider the ways the newspaper serves the public. What might life be like without the newspaper as a dominant source of information?

The two stories in this lesson were printed one day apart in two different newspapers. The first appeared in *USA TODAY,* a nationally circulated daily paper that is written for a broad readership, and the second graced the pages of the *Providence Journal-Bulletin,* a daily paper that reaches the people who live in the small state of Rhode Island.

Both of the stories are on the senior prom, a familiar seasonal event that many people enjoy reading about. But as you will see, the two stories chronicle two different approaches to the ultimate high school dance, one traditional and accepted, the other unconventional and hotly contested.

CHERYL AND DON: She was chosen to be queen.

THE GIRLS: Terri Denton, 17, left, and Marie Davis, 15, make some adjustments during a break at Eastbrook High's prom.

The crowning event of high school

By CRAIG WILSON
USA TODAY

VAN BUREN, IND.—By 3 in the afternoon she has bathed and is carefully touching up her make-up at the kitchen table.

She studies her perfectly coiffed hair in a portable lighted mirror.

"It won't move in the wind, so that's good," Cheryl Bryant says. "I think (the hairdresser) put on two cans of spray."

Her date, Don Fitzgerald, won't pick her up for another hour, but Cheryl has been ready for days.

She didn't sleep well last night and admits to being a bundle of nerves. She's up for prom queen at Eastbrook High School.

She's checked and rechecked her dress.

After weeks of getting ready, teens celebrate 'Now and Forever'

Her nails have been filed and polished to a deep, deep red.

"They used to be longer but I kept scratching Don," she says, adjusting the baby's breath sprouting from her curls.

"Do you like the glitter she put in?" she asks. "I kind of like it." A brush full of blusher goes across the cheek.

"I've looked forward to the prom since my sisters were going," says the sixth of eight children.

Like millions of teens who live the crowning moment of their adolescence this month, she's wearing the gown today.

"I had it made. I showed her a picture from *Bride's* magazine and it looks *just* like the picture. She did an excellent job. It's satin, and real shiny and has lace and pearls. It's a real old-fashioned dress with a big skirt and big hoop."

One more brush of the cheek and she's gone, up the stairs with her mother.

Don, senior class president and Cheryl's boyfriend of eight months, couldn't wait. In white tie and black tails, he appears at the door, a half-hour early.

Family members joke about his tux. "It's not real, you know," he says, one hand tugging his bow tie. The other grips a white box holding a wrist corsage: "Red

Continued on following page

Continued from preceding page
roses and stuff. It's what she wanted."

He fidgets until Cheryl finally appears. "Oh, man, you look absolutely incredible," he says, leaping to his feet.

She beams. He beams.

"She cleans up pretty good, doesn't she, Don?" Cheryl's mother says proudly.

The living room becomes a jumble of scents. Don is wearing Quattro. "It's by Mary Kay," he says. Cheryl is wearing Krystle. "I love it. I got it for Christmas," she says. "It's really elegant."

Photos are taken—first Cheryl alone, reflected in the front hall mirror, then the two together, immortalized on the front porch and under a front-lawn tree where prom-going Bryants have been photographed for years.

Don's 1975 Grand Prix waits in the driveway. Cheryl's voluminous dress, although protesting, is finally subdued by a closed car door.

The Eastbrook High tradition is dinner before the prom. Don is squiring his date to The Wharf in Fort Wayne, more than an hour away. He wanted to do it up right. Cheryl's only request: No Italian restaurants—she's afraid of spilling sauce on her dress.

They disappear down the road.

The prom doesn't start till 8, but couples are already arriving by 7:45.

"There's nothing about being socially late *here*," says Carolyn Beardsley, a junior class sponsor and English teacher. By 8:30 the 300 people expected are all where they should be.

The Grant County 4-H building is transformed into a sea of lavender and silver. A huge garage door is raised to expose a sideroom carpeted with Astroturf, with plants, a fountain and tiny white lights. "Now and Forever," the theme, is emblazoned in aluminum foil across one wall.

The women arrive in waves of purple and pink polyester, taffeta and satin; the men in white tails trimmed in pink and gray tails trimmed in white. More often than not, the only precious metals displayed are a mouth full of braces.

Immediately couples line up to be photographed. For $16.50 you could get two 8-by-10 and 24 wallet-sized photos, better known as Package F.

Don and Cheryl take Package D, $9.50.

"There are couples who don't want their pictures taken together. They just needed someone to get here," says Nancy

DANCING INTO HISTORY: Cheryl Bryant, 17, and Don Fitzgerald, 18, at the Eastbrook High School prom—held in a 4-H building decorated in lavender and silver, with 300 attending.

Myers as her husband, Bill, positions couples on a plastic bench. "But a lot of them cling up so good."

Cheryl and Don cling up real good.

"He asked me every day in the fourth grade to go with him," she says.

"And she'd always say no," says Don.

Cheryl, junior class president, is doing the rounds, checking on a number of details. Disc jockey Don Payne from WZPL in Indianapolis had promised fog and she hasn't seen any yet. A minor panic.

Two couples arrive in a limousine—a navy Cadillac, rented from a Kokomo firm. The limo included a bar, a TV and a phone, but the quartet made no calls.

"We didn't know how," says Brad Pinkerton. They did watch TV, although "it was kind of static-y," says Cassi Wright.

The limo works well, though, delivering them to the prom's front door after a dinner at Ponderosa Steak House.

Linda Leas, the local seamstress who made Cheryl's dress, is at the front door, waiting for "her girls." She made 15 of the dresses appearing at the prom. "I'll have one here with lights in it."

Enter Peggy Trout, in gold lame with black lace overlay and battery-operated lights sparkling across her skirt.

"Turn yourself on Peggy," someone
Continued on following page

Continued from preceding page
says. An unnecessary request. Peggy seems to be on all the time, twirling, laughing and hoisting up the top of her strapless gown. She manages to do all three at once.

James Vielee manages more. He has brought two girls to the prom. "He went for it because he used to like her and everything, too," says Shanna Miller, James' date, who convinced him to bring along her best friend.

"It's been a little bit of a hassle, but we'll see how the night turns out," he says. He was a sport and took both to dinner at Toysun, a Chinese restaurant.

Couples stroll in and out—working their way into dark recesses of the parking lot to smooch while leaning against vans. Police patrol with flashlights, making sure nothing more happens.

The hour draws near to crown a queen, or as the emcee of the event declares, "It's time to queen the queen."

The court is introduced and when the announcer says Cheryl Bryant is the new queen, a cheer goes up.

The crown—which her hairdresser assured her "could be smashed down" into her hair if she won—is put in place.

Cheryl puts one hand on Don's face, he puts his arms around her waist, and the strains of *Now and Forever* fill the room.

They dance off into the fog.

Checking Your Comprehension

Read the following questions. Put an x in the box beside the answer that best completes each one.

1. Cheryl and Don are "immortalized on the front porch . . . where prom-going Bryants have been photographed for years." As it is used here, *immortalized* means
   - ☐ a. made exempt from death.
   - ☐ b. made imperishable.
   - ☐ c. preserved for all time.

2. At the prom, "Now and Forever," the theme, is emblazoned in aluminum foil across one wall. *Emblazoned* means
   - ☐ a. set ablaze.
   - ☐ b. inscribed.
   - ☐ c. illuminated.

3. All of the following are examples of nervousness on the part of prom couples except
   - ☐ a. Don appearing a half hour early.
   - ☐ b. Cheryl admitting that she didn't sleep last night.
   - ☐ c. couples not wanting their pictures taken together.

4. A tradition at Eastbrook High is
   - ☐ a. dinner before the prom.
   - ☐ b. having the dance at the Grant County 4-H building.
   - ☐ c. police patrolling with flashlights.

5. The decorations, with a fountain and tiny white lights and fog created by the disc jockey, are examples of the students' attempts to
   - ☐ a. create a romantic atmosphere.
   - ☐ b. act rowdy.
   - ☐ c. act very sophisticated.

6. James Vielee could be considered a sport on this prom night for all of the following reasons except he
   - ☐ a. took two girls to a Chinese restaurant for dinner.
   - ☐ b. was good at dancing.
   - ☐ c. brought his girlfriend and her best friend to the senior prom.

☆　☆　☆

"The crowning event of high school" focuses on the senior prom as one of the high points in adolescence. The story emphasizes the traditions and rituals associated with the senior prom, which is an institution in high schools across the United States. Some of the traditions the writer mentions are: boys wearing tuxes and girls wearing fancy gowns; boys presenting their dates with corsages; couples going out to a nice restaurant for dinner.

The *Providence Journal-Bulletin* story that follows is not a typical prom story celebrating tradition and celebration. As you will see, it deals with tradition in order to report a mildly sensational issue of particular interest to people in Rhode Island.

Going 'stag' to the senior prom
Five Rogers girls are asking to attend dance without dates

By STEPHEN HEFFNER
Journal-Bulletin Staff Writer

NEWPORT—They're the best of friends and they'd like to go to their senior prom together, but alone. Without dates, that is. Gowns without tuxedos. Corsages without boutonnieres. Unescorted. Stag.

Five Rogers High School girls—four seniors and a junior, all 17—presented that idea three weeks ago to their school principal, Terrence Burns, who turned them down.

Tradition was at stake, Burns told them.

Tuesday night, they took their request to the Newport School Committee. The committee declined to act, and instead referred the girls to judgment by their peers.

Today, Sue Arouth, Robin Fanala,

Continued on following page

Continued from preceding page
Allison Gray, Cam McKenney and Charlee Spath might have to present their case to the Student Council and the senior class officers. Debate over the issue has divided the school, and the girls say they fear that the members of the council and the class officers are part of the opposing camp.

"All we're saying is: If you don't have a date, you shouldn't be banned from the prom," Miss Spath said yesterday. "We thought it was a simple issue and that we were asking a simple question."

"There are people in the school who can't get dates for the prom," said Miss Gray, the junior in the group. "They're not pretty or handsome, they're not really popular for some reason, and they're turned into outcasts by not being allowed to go to their own prom."

None of the girls considers herself one of these outcasts, and they say they could have had dates for the prom if they chose. Miss Fanala and Miss McKenney, in fact, will attend the junior prom tomorrow night, and several of the five say they've already turned down invitations to the senior prom.

The issue for them is one of principle—and of wanting to attend the biggest social event of their young lives with the people they like best.

"The prom is the last day of 12 years of school," said Miss Fanala. "It's the last time you'll be together with your class. We like our class; it was a great class, and the prom could be a great time. It should be a time to remember. We want to spend it with our best friends, and not have to worry about some guy who wants to leave early, or doesn't want to dance, or who isn't going to like it when we don't want to spend the whole prom holding hands with him."

The Rogers prom, to be held June 2, should be, indeed, a time to remember, if for no other reason than its venue, the ballroom at the Rosecliff Mansion on Bellevue Avenue. But if principal Burns has his way, the only students who'll get a chance at the memory will be those who arrive in boy-girl pairs.

"I think they're just looking for publicity," Burns said yesterday. "Unless the senior class officers come to me and say they've changed their minds, the issue is closed."

The girls denied yesterday that publicity was their motive.

Continued on following page

ON THEIR OWN: These four young women want to attend their senior prom at Rogers High School without dates. They are, from left, Sue Arouth, Cam McKenney, Allison Gray and Robin Fanala. Miss Arouth says, "We don't want to steal anybody's boyfriend. When the slow dances come on, we'll go over to the food table."

Continued from preceding page

"All we want to do is go to our prom," Miss Arouth said. "We don't want to cause any trouble. We don't want to steal anybody's boyfriend. When the slow dances come on, we'll go over to the food table. It's not like we're doing this to hurt anybody else."

"This has been really hard on us," said Miss McKenney. "We've lost friends over it. There's been a petition circulated against us. We've had debates about it in three of my classes. The issue for us is freedom of choice. But people just keep on coming up to us and saying, 'Why don't you just get a date?' "

"There were about 10 of us at first who were going to do this," said Miss Fanala. "But after Mr. Burns said no, they got scared. It's the same with the teachers. I think about half of them are with us, but a lot don't want to say it in public and go against their boss. They'll pull us over and say, 'Between you and me, I think you're doing the right thing.' "

Legal opinion may take over

Most of the girls say they feel they have the backing of their parents. Miss Fanala said her mother spoke in their favor at the School Committee meeting. Miss Gray said her mother encouraged her to pursue the issue.

"My mother told me to take it to the Supreme Court if I have to," said Miss Gray.

She might not have to go that far, and she and her comrades might not even have to face a decision by the Student Council or the senior class officers. School Committee chairman J. Clement Cicilline said last night that he had turned the matter over to Neil Galvin, the legal counsel for the committee.

"These students may have rights here that would supercede tradition and make any vote by the other students unnecessary," said Cicilline. "There's no need to polarize the school with a vote if we don't have to. That's what we will be finding out in the next couple of days."

Checking Your Comprehension

Read the following questions. Put an *x* in the box beside the answer that best completes each one.

1. Miss Spath said, "If you don't have a date, you shouldn't be banned from the prom." By *banned,* she meant
   - ☐ a. bullied.
   - ☐ b. cursed.
   - ☐ c. prohibited.

2. School Committee chairman Cicilline said, "There's no need to polarize the school with a vote if we don't have to." To *polarize* means to
   - ☐ a. magnetize.
   - ☐ b. divide into opposites.
   - ☐ c. bring opposing factions together.

3. The real issue for the five Rogers girls who are asking to go stag to their prom is
   - ☐ a. freedom of choice.
   - ☐ b. unpopularity.
   - ☐ c. publicity.

4. The girls' request to attend the prom unescorted was first turned down by the
   - ☐ a. student council.
   - ☐ b. principal.
   - ☐ c. school committee.

5. The girls may not have to face a final vote by their peers because
   - ☐ a. the school committee will decide the issue.
   - ☐ b. their parents are supporting them.
   - ☐ c. the matter could be a legal issue, with their rights protected by law.

6. Which of the following is *not* a negative outcome of the principal's initial refusal to let the girls attend the prom unescorted?
   - ☐ a. Some of the original ten petitioners dropped out in fear.
   - ☐ b. Neil Galvin, legal counsel for the school committee, is considering the issue.
   - ☐ c. Teachers won't publicly support the girls.

☆ ☆ ☆

What one reads in a particular newspaper on a given day is a matter not only of availability, but also of selection. Reporters write about what they think constitutes news; editors in turn include those stories they think are news.

The editors of USA TODAY evidently felt that a traditional prom story was news and would appeal to readers. The editors of the *Providence Journal-Bulletin* may have felt that a story essentially about students' rights was doubly newsworthy and appealing because it revolved around the prom.

☆ ☆ ☆

Arranging Events in Chronological Order

Each of the two stories presents a sequence of events. The *USA TODAY* story treats the prom as a traditional, seasonal event that readers are familiar with. The story, accordingly, offers no surprises, presenting mainly events that occurred on prom day and at the prom itself.

The *Providence Journal-Bulletin* story, on the other hand, covers the events that led to a standoff between five Rogers High girls and the school principal, as well as what is happening while the girls wait to learn whether they can attend their prom.

The events below are reported in the two prom stories. Number the events for each story according to the order in which they happened in time. Refer to the stories as necessary.

The crowning event of high school

_____ Couples dance to music provided by disc jockey Don Payne, and stroll in and out of the dance.

_____ Cheryl has her hair done and applies her makeup.

_____ Don gives Cheryl a red rose wrist corsage.

_____ Don and Cheryl have dinner at The Wharf in Fort Wayne.

_____ The court is introduced and Cheryl Bryant is crowned queen.

Going 'stag' to the senior prom

_____ Miss Fanala and Miss McKenney will attend the junior prom tomorrow.

_____ The school principal turned down the girls' request to attend their senior prom stag.

_____ The girls went to the Newport School Committee for a decision on Tuesday night.

_____ The Rogers prom will be held in the ballroom of the famed Rosecliff Mansion on June 2.

_____ Last night Neil Galvin, the legal counsel for the school committee, was asked to review the matter.

Using Your Newspaper

Find same-day issues of a town or community paper, a city daily, and a nationally distributed newspaper that are available in your area. (You may need to go to the library to find one or more of the newspapers.) Survey the front page of each paper to see what news items have been given front page coverage. Front page coverage usually falls into three areas: local and state news, national news, and international news.

Title a blank sheet of paper *Local Newspaper.* Title another sheet *City Daily,* and a third *National Newspaper.* Then make these three columns under each title: *Local and State News, National News,* and *International News.*

On the *Local Newspaper* sheet, list the front page stories from that paper in the appropriate columns. Do the same for the *City Daily* sheet and the *National Newspaper* sheets. Then examine the columns. How many stories from each of the three categories are found on the front page of each paper? Does the balance of local, national, and international news vary from paper to paper? How are the stories treated differently in the different papers?

Practicing Newspaper Skills

Write a feature story on a couple going to a prom or another big high school dance, or report on a controversial topic that concerns your school.

If you choose to write about a prom couple, arrange to accompany them from the beginning of the evening to a time well into the dance. Take notes throughout. When the boy arrives to pick up the girl (or vice versa), jot down details about their outfits, what they say to each other, and so on. If they go out to eat, note the restaurant, the food, whatever is appropriate. Do the same for the dance and its decorations, theme, and music. Unless your couple is willing to let you tag along all night, let them enjoy the end of the dance and the return trip alone (remember to arrange for a ride home in this case). From your notes, put together a feature story like the one on Cheryl and Don in *USA TODAY.*

You may want to report on a controversial issue, ruling, or topic that affects people at your school. The subject of your story might be a developing story like the Rogers High prom story, a dress code or school procedure, or even something that concerns only teachers.

To report the story, find all the facts you can. You will want to do some research, conduct some interviews, take notes— all the steps that reporters follow. After you have gathered your facts, write a straight news story. Begin with a lead paragraph that answers the questions *Who? What? When? Where? Why?* and *How?* Then fill out the rest of the story in subsequent paragraphs. Mix in quotes from people you have interviewed. Do not include your opinions.

Special-interest newspapers and special supplements to general-interest newspapers are designed to appeal to specific segments of the readership. A special-interest paper might employ a variety of writers in the roles described in Unit Two—reporter, feature writer, and so on. But for a special-interest paper those roles are more narrowly defined because the news is being presented to a particular group of people.

In this lesson you will read the introductory section of a special supplement to a large general-interest paper, the *Los Angeles Times.* You will also read a humorous commentary from the *Little Green,* a school newspaper put out by the students of Central High in Manchester, New Hampshire. Think about the readership of each of these papers. Decide whether you think either story meets an important need, namely, that of providing information, service, or entertainment to a particular readership.

BECOMING Legal

A Guide to the New Immigration Law

Guía para la nueva ley de inmigración

By FRANK DEL OLMO
Times Editorial Writer

Late last year, after a decade of often-emotional political debate, Congress approved, and President Reagan signed into law, a major revision of the nation's immigration laws. This week, millions of people across the nation will begin to feel the impact of those changes.

Under provisions of the Immigration Reform and Control Act of 1986, illegal aliens who have been in the United States for

Continued on following page

A fines del año pasado, después de una década de debate político frecuentemente emotivo, el Congreso aprobó y el presidente Reagan promulgó una importante revisión de las leyes de inmigración del país. Esta semana millones de personas de toda la nación comenzarán a sentir el impacto de esos cambios.

Según las estipulaciones del Acta de Reforma y Control de Inmigración de 1986, los indocumentados que han radicado en Estados Unidos por lo menos cinco años pueden comenzar el proceso de legalización de su situación migratoria el martes. Las

Continuación en la proxima pagina

Continued from preceding page

at least five years can begin the process of legalizing their status on Tuesday. The doors to legalization will remain open for a year afterward.

It is estimated that 3,000,000 to 4,000,000 people may qualify for legalization, or "amnesty," as it is often referred to. And the U.S. Immigration and Naturalization Service expects the largest number of applications it receives to come from Los Angeles and elsewhere in Southern California.

The amnesty program will provide an important opportunity for many illegal immigrants to emerge from the "shadow society" in which they now live, according to Los Angeles' Roman Catholic Archbishop Roger M. Mahony. The Catholic church here is helping hundreds of thousands of people apply for legalization.

But such a massive and unprecedented undertaking also brings with it potential for confusion, misunderstanding and even abuse. For that reason, the *Los Angeles Times* and *La Opinion* (the biggest English- and Spanish-language newspapers in Southern California) are collaborating in publishing this special supplement, "Becoming Legal," as a public service to the residents of this region.

This supplement does not attempt to judge the new law, nor to discuss any of its merits or shortcomings. Such discussions belong in other sections of *The Times* and *La Opinion.* Instead, this section aims to be mostly informational. It is an effort to explain—as simply as possible and as clearly as can be determined at this time—how the law will work, particularly with regards to amnesty.

As with any new law that is both complex and controversial, it must be emphasized that some facets of the Immigration Reform and Control Act could change in the coming months and years. Congress could decide to amend the new law if it decides that sections of it need to be refined. Some members of Congress are already discussing this possibility.

The law is also likely to be challenged in the courts, which could result in major or minor modifications. The government has already made some modifications in response to lawsuits. Thus, what is published here is based on the regulations that have been made public by the U.S. Justice Department and the Immigration and Naturalization Service as of May 1, 1987. It should remain valid for several months.

It should also be noted that two other important sections of the law will not be fully implemented until next month.

These include the section that will govern how agricultural laborers can apply for amnesty under the law. Congress decided that farm workers do not have to meet the same residency requirements that urban workers do. By the same token, ranchers and farmers must meet different labor requirements than employers in urban industries.

This supplement also contains only limited information about another important section of the new law—the penalties that are designed to discourage U.S. employers from hiring illegal aliens as workers.

Still unpublished are the regulations outlining how any person who feels that he or she has been discriminated against under the new law can file complaints with the federal government. This supplement briefly outlines what is known of

Continued on following page

Continuación de la pagina anterior

puertas de la legalización permanecerán abiertas por un año a partir de esa fecha.

Se estima que de tres a cuatro millones de personas califican para la legalización, o amnistía, como comúnmente se conoce el programa. El Servicio de Inmigración y Naturalización de Estados Unidos espera recibir el número más grande de solicitudes de legalización en Los Angeles y otros puntos del sur de California.

El programa de amnistía brindará una importante oportunidad a numerosos inmigrantes ilegales de salir de la "socieded de la sombra" en que ahora viven, de acuerdo con el arzobispo católico-romano de Los Angeles, Roger Mahony. La Iglesia católica está ayudando a centenares de millares de personas a solicitar la legalización. Pero dicha tarea masiva y sin precedentes conlleva también la posibilidad de confusión, malentendidos e incluso abusos.

Por ese motivo, *The Los Angeles Times* y *La Opinión* (los periódicos en inglés y español más grandes del sur de California) han decidido colaborar en la publicación de este suplemento especial, *Becoming Legal/Legalización,* como servicio público a los residentes de esta región.

Este suplemento no pretende juzgar la nueva ley, ni discutir ninguno de sus méritos o defectos. Dichas discusiones pertenecen a otras secciones de *The Times* y de *La Opinión.* En su lugar, esta sección se propone ser meramente informativa. Es un intento de explicar en la forma más simple posible, y en una forma clara en cuanto se puede determinar hasta ahora, cómo funcionará la ley, en particular en lo que se refiere a la amnistía.

Como con cualquier otra ley que es a la vez compleja y controvertida, debe enfatizarse que algunos aspectos del Acta de Reforma y Control de Inmigración pueden cambiar en los meses y años venideros. El Congreso podría decidir enmendar la nueva ley si decide que algunas secciones de la misma necesitan ser alteradas. Algunos miembros del Congreso están ya discutiendo esta posibilidad.

Es muy posible también que la ley sea llevada a los tribunales, lo cual podría también dar por resultado modificaciones de mayor o menor importanci. El Gobierno ha hecho ya algunas modificaciones en respuesta a demandas judiciales. Por ello, lo que se publica hoy aquí está basado en las normas que, hasta el 1 de mayo de 1987, han sido hechas públicas por el departamento de Justicia y el Servicio de Inmigración y Naturalización. Deberia seguir siendo válido por varios meses.

Se debe hacer notar también que otras dos secciones importantes de la ley serán implementadas hasta el mes entrante. Estas incluyen la sección que gobernará la forma en que los trabajadores del campo pueden presentar solicitudes de amnistía. El Congreso decidió que los trabajadores agrícolas no deben ajustarse a los mismos requisitos de residencia de los de zonas urbanas. Al mismo tiempo, los rancheros y agricultores deben cumplir diferentes requisitos laborales que los empleadores en las industrias urbanas.

Este suplemento contiene también únicamente información limitada sobre otra importante sección de la nueva ley—las sanciones que han sido creadas para desalentar a los empleadores estadounidenses a contratar indocumentados como trabajadores.

Continúan sin publicarse las normas que detallarán cómo cualquier persona que se sienta discriminada a tenor de las estipulaciones de esta ley puede presentar denuncias ante el Gobierno federal. Este suplemento presenta un breve bosquejo de lo que se conoce de estas tres áreas hasta ahora, pero debe

Continuación en la proxima pagina

Continued from preceding page
these three areas up to now, but it must be emphasized that it is subject to change.

By providing clear, up-to-date information on the new law, this section should help illegal immigrants avoid any unnecessary costs or trouble in dealing with the new law. Already there have been reports of unscrupulous individuals using the confusion and fear generated by the immigration reforms to extort money from immigrants and otherwise try to swindle them. We hope this section will help people avoid such rip-offs.

By the same token, it is hoped that this section will help steer those persons who do need special assistance in dealing with the new law, perhaps because their case is particularly complicated, to the reputable community agencies that can meet their needs most efficiently.

It will be noted that the format of this section is bilingual, in English and Spanish. That is because the majority of persons who will be affected by the law in Southern California are immigrants from Latin America. By publishing in both languages, we hope that this section will be helpful to all segments of society in Southern California—not just to workers who want to legalize their status, but also to any employers who want to help employees who are in this country illegally.

Continuación de la pagina anterior
enfatizarse que ambas están sujetas a cambios.

Al proporcionar información clara y oportuna sobre la nueva ley, esta sección debe también ayudar a los indocumentados a evitar costos innecesarios o problemas en lo relacionado con la nueva ley. Ya circulan informes de personas inescrupulosas que usan la confusión y el miedo generado por las reformas migratorias para extorsionar dinero de los inmigrantes y tratar de estafarlos. Esperamos que esta sección ayude a los inmigrantes a evitar dichas estafas. Al mismo tiempo, esperamos que esta sección ayude a guiar a esas personas que necesitan ayuda especial con la nueva ley, tal vez porque su caso es particularmente complicado, hacia las agencias comunitarias de buena reputación que pueden ayudarles en sus necesidades en una forma más eficiente.

Se notará que el formato de esta sección es bilingüe, en inglés y español. Ello obedece a que la mayoría de las personas que se verán afectadas en el sur de California son inmigrantes de América Latina. Al publicarlo en los dos idiomas, esperamos que esta sección ayudará a todos los segmentos de la sociedad del sur de California—no solamente a los trabajadores que quieran legalizar su estancia en el pais, sino también a cualquier empleador que quiera ayudar a sus trabajadores que se encuentran ilegalmente en este país.

Checking Your Comprehension

Read the following questions. Put an *x* in the box beside the answer that best completes each one.

1. The introduction calls the amnesty program a "massive and unprecedented undertaking." *Unprecedented* means
   □ a. unimportant.
   □ b. novel; new.
   □ c. unplanned; spontaneous.

2. The introduction cites "reports of unscrupulous individuals using the confusion and fear . . . to extort money from immigrants." To be *unscrupulous* is to be
   □ a. dishonest.
   □ b. dangerous.
   □ c. disloyal.

3. This section of the *Los Angeles Times* is bilingual because
   □ a. the editors want a sophisticated image for their newspaper.
   □ b. there is a large Latin American readership in Southern California.
   □ c. the writer, Frank del Olmo, is Spanish.

4. The Immigration Reform and Control Act of 1986 does *not* ensure that
   □ a. people who have been illegal aliens in the United States for at least five years can begin the legalization process.
   □ b. the door to legalization will remain open for a year.
   □ c. employers hiring illegal aliens will be penalized.

5. The introduction indicates that its main purpose is to help illegal immigrants
   □ a. apply for amnesty with as few problems as possible.
   □ b. file discrimination suits or complaints.
   □ c. know how to avoid people who would try to cheat them.

6. When the Los Angeles Roman Catholic Archbishop talks about people emerging from a "shadow society" he means that they have
   □ a. been engaged in criminal behavior.
   □ b. belonged to a secret Catholic society.
   □ c. had to cover up the fact that they live and work in the United States.

☆ ☆ ☆

Many general-interest newspapers carry a special supplement when there is a situation that demands one. The supplement to the *Los Angeles Times* meets a need in the Southern California area, that of making information available to the Spanish-speaking population through a bilingual format.

Next you will read a commentary from a Manchester, New Hampshire, high school newspaper, Central High's *Little Green*. As you read, think about the editorial's targeted readership. What is it about the subject of nerds that is so important to high schoolers?

Nerds: The inside story

nerd/'nərd/ *n.*
[origin unknown] *slang*
(1965): an unpleasant,
unattractive, or insig-
nificant person

—WEBSTER'S SEVENTH
COLLEGIATE DICTIONARY

By STEPH McLAUGHLIN

How do you define a nerd?
"You can't really define one
but if you saw one you'd say
'Yeah, that's a nerd,'" said sophomore
Joe Sicherman. Junior Rob Young had a
different opinion: "A nerd is a guy that
tries to act like me but never succeeds,"
he said quite confidently.

Commentary

Although nerds are hard to define, they
are easily identified. Nerds are either tall
and skinny or short and fat, and do not appear to care about physical appearance.
They seem perfectly happy with their
greasy hair and blemished complexions.
Nerds play the oboe and have nicknames
like Spaz.

Nerds wear the infamous black-rimmed
glasses with masking tape on the bridge of
the nose, a calculator watch and the familiar white socks, plaid pants, a striped shirt
and slide a pen guard in their shirt pocket.
Of course they always have a full back-
pack with an added load of books under
their arm.

Other nerd characteristics are: a strange
laugh, a whiny voice, highwater pants, an
undershirt showing through an oxford
shirt buttoned to the very top button, and
parents who own a big, age-old station
wagon. Nerds also frequently end up attending a well-known Cambridge tech-
nological institute where they spend most
of their time in the library.

After spending at least four years, pref-
erably six or eight, in a dusty lab at this
lofty institute, and graduating magna cum
laude, nerds begin a lucrative career in
the field of high technology. They then
make up the scant population of people
who understand the data.

While experiencing the "swinging singles" scene, they hang out with all the
other high-tech people. Nerds are often
affluent individuals, for they have no reason to spend money. With a number of
esoteric successes in their fields, they
eventually settle down to raise a family
so the whole cycle can start again.

However, before reaching the all-
important Cambridge-based university,
nerds can be found roaming the halls at
the local high school. When not in the
halls, they are most definitely dwelling in
the nearest computer lab.

Nerds subscribe to such magazines as
"Calculator Repair and Maintenance,"
"Fun with Logarithms," and "Students for
Better Eyeglass Care." They partake in
after-school and extracurricular activities
including the elite Accordion Orchestra,
the Yahtzee Club, and the Varsity Bingo
Team. The competition at Badminton
games, the All-State Tetherball Championship, and the State Chess Tournament is
composed almost entirely of nerds, who sit
and watch the girls rather than the game.

This brings up an interesting question:
Are there female nerds? Is nerdery just a
male curse?

Actually no one, male or female, will
admit to feeling like a nerd. "Everyone
feels like a nerd at one point or another,"
said one sophomore, "especially during
your freshman year," she added.

Freshman Bob Gaumont feels like a
nerd when "I tell a joke and I'm the only
one laughing." Another freshman feels
nerdy when he's with a nerd and someone
"cool" sees him.

Then again, all freshmen are nerds.

Checking Your Comprehension

Read the following questions. Put an *x* in the box beside the answer that best
completes each one.

1. The writer, Steph McLaughlin, says that many
   nerds undertake "a lucrative career in the field
   of high technology." By *lucrative,* she means
   ☐ a. satisfying.
   ☐ b. long-term.
   ☐ c. profitable.

2. McLaughlin observes that nerds "wear the
   infamous black-rimmed glasses." As it is used
   here, *infamous* means
   ☐ a. having a negative reputation.
   ☐ b. not at all well known; obscure.
   ☐ c. famous.

3. According to the article, nerds are hard to define
   but easy to
   ☐ a. dislike.
   ☐ b. imitate.
   ☐ c. identify.

4. Which of the following is not mentioned as an indicator
   of nerds' interests?
   ☐ a. They read magazines like "Calculator Repair
   and Maintenance."
   ☐ b. They watch mystery shows on TV.
   ☐ c. They participate in extracurricular activities like
   the Varsity Bingo Team.

5. Using the dictionary definition at the beginning of the commentary, you can conclude that freshmen in high school are often considered nerds because they
   ☐ a. are not taken seriously by upperclassmen.
   ☐ b. have nerdy reputations before they even arrive from junior high school.
   ☐ c. often have whining voices and are physically smaller.

6. The article implies that students referred to as nerds are often very smart. An example of this is that they
   ☐ a. hang out with high-tech people.
   ☐ b. graduate magna cum laude from a certain lofty institution.
   ☐ c. spend most of their time in the library.

☆　☆　☆

You have read two articles, one from a supplement designed to inform readers on an important topic, and one meant as entertainment for a distinct segment of the population. Think about the issue raised on page 114. Do you think both stories meet an important need by providing information, service, or entertainment to a particular readership?

Political considerations aside, the *Los Angeles Times* acted in the interests of the readership in publishing the supplement on immigration: many illegal aliens live in Southern California, and the Immigration Reform and Control Act is a fact. Newspapers must sometimes respond to news-making situations by doing more than simply reporting the news.

On the lighthearted side, the *Little Green* commentary deals with the questions of image and self-image that are so crucial to high-school people. To anyone other than the specific readers it addresses, perhaps "Nerds: The inside story" is just a funny piece in a school paper. But to a high schooler who's a nerd and is happy that way, or to a student who isn't a nerd and is clearly relieved not to be, it's important. In the best tradition of special-interest papers, the story and the readers connect.

☆　☆　☆

Recognizing Main Ideas and Supporting Details

The two articles in the lesson, one from a supplement to a major daily and the other from a special-interest newspaper, focus on the needs and interests of particular readers. The *Los Angeles Times* supplement carries the subheading "A Guide to the New Immigration Law." The readers most interested in this law would probably be illegal aliens residing in Southern California.

The commentary from the *Little Green* was also written for a particular population, namely, high school students. The topic under discussion, nerds, is familiar and interesting to school-age people.

Read the articles again. In each, find at least five details that support the main idea. Write the details on the lines provided beneath the statements of the main ideas.

Main idea: The Immigration Reform and Control Act of 1986 will be making its impact felt in the months to come.

1. _____

_____

_____

2. _____

_____

_____

Main idea: Nerds display a variety of identifiable characteristics.

1. _____

_____

_____

2. _____

_____

_____

3. _____

_____

_____

4. _____

_____

_____

5. _____

_____

_____

3. _____

_____

_____

4. _____

_____

_____

5. _____

_____

_____

Using Your Newspaper

Go to a newsstand or magazine store in your area and find the special-interest newspapers. Pick one that appeals to you and buy it. (You might try to find it in a public library, also.)

Read the newspaper from cover to cover, stories, advertisements, cartoons, everything. Identify the intended readership of the newspaper.

Write a paragraph or two describing the paper. Tell how the special interests of the readers are reflected in the name of the paper, the content, and the tone. For example, say the paper is called the *Senior Times*. The name gives you a pretty good idea that the paper is for senior citizens. The stories might have to do with retirement plans, age-discrimination laws, second-career ideas, and so on. The language could be sober and factual, or it could be newsy and folksy. Cover all such items and any others that you observe. Also, mention specific features in the paper that a general-interest newspaper would not carry.

End your description by telling how—and how well—you think the paper might serve its readership.

Practicing Newspaper Skills

The *purpose* of the *Los Angeles Times* supplement is to help new residents of the United States. The *form* of the *Little Green* piece is that of a commentary. For your article, combine the helpful purpose with the commentary form: write a piece intended to help a new student cope with something at your school that he or she might not anticipate.

The "something at your school" might be library procedures, course or teacher eccentricities, or special events or traditions. It could involve areas that are off-limits at special times, or rules that are peculiar to your school.

Address the piece to a hypothetical new student. Point out the special situation that he or she must be made aware of. Then describe the situation in detail, outlining its characteristics and the effect it has on the students, the teachers, or both. Use quotes when possible, speak from personal experience if relevant, and offer a concrete solution or plan. If the issue calls for a serious approach, state your opinions and support them with facts in a straightforward, direct style. If you find the situation funny or in need of lampooning, you might want to use humor or satire. But if you aim for laughs, don't lose sight of your purpose: to help.

Show the piece to a fellow student who knows of the situation. Ask for an evaluation of the helpfulness of your commentary.

The dateline for the *USA TODAY* story below is September 1. A *dateline* gives the date of a news story or an issue of a newspaper or magazine. The story reports on United States athlete Jackie Joyner-Kersee's record-setting day at the World Track and Field Championships in Rome, Italy. The newspaper reporter tells readers of Joyner-Kersee's accomplishments on the first day of competition and how she is preparing for the rest of the championships.

The *Sports Illustrated* article in this lesson was published two weeks later, on September 14. In writing his story, the magazine writer could sift through information on an event that was over. He could select data from the broadest scope—the entire story was there in his notes.

Read the *USA TODAY* story to see what Jackie Joyner-Kersee accomplished in one day at the World Championships. Given the facts you learn, try to project how she might fare over the whole competition.

10C • TUESDAY, SEPTEMBER 1, 1987 • USA TODAY

WORLD TRACK & FIELD CHAMPIONSHIPS

Joyner-Kersee on world-record pace
USA athlete leads Soviet in heptathlon

TOPPING HERSELF: Jackie Joyner-Kersee, leader in the women's heptathlon, clears 6-2¾ in the high jump Monday, beating her previous best of 6-2.

By DICK PATRICK
USA TODAY

ROME—Bob Kersee was pacing on the top row of the Stadio Olimpico, screaming at his wife, Jackie Joyner-Kersee, who was competing in the heptathlon high jump.

"She slept like a log last night," Kersee said. "And she's still asleep."

The wakeup call Monday arrived in the form of a miss at 6 feet, ½ inch.

"In the high jump, I was there, but not competing," said Joyner-Kersee. "I didn't feel fired up. When I missed, I got upset at myself. I said, 'What are you doing?'"

Joyner-Kersee went on to clear 6-2¾, a personal best by three-fourths of an inch. By the end of the day, after four of the seven events, she was on a pace to break her world record of 7,158 points.

With the long jump, javelin and 800 remaining, Joyner-Kersee has 4,256 points, 105 more than her best first-day effort ever and 338 more than second-place Larisa Nikitina of the Soviet Union.

Just another typical performance by Joyner-Kersee, who felt dehydrated and dizzy afterward.

"It's hard to compare Jackie with anyone else," said the USA's Cindy Greiner, who is 13th. "She's a very, very amazing athlete."

What pleased Joyner-Kersee the most Monday was the shot put, where she threw 52 feet 6 inches, a personal best by almost 2 feet.

"I'm finally starting to understand what I'm supposed to do in the ring,"

Continued on following page

Continued from preceding page
Joyner-Kersee said. "I could visualize it. It was a good feeling."

Shortly before the meet, she spent some time at a training camp, working on the shot put with her throws coach, Art Venegas of UCLA, and John Brenner, third in Saturday's shot put.

As is her custom, she wrote down key phrases on technique in a notebook she keeps. She studied it Sunday night and between events Monday.

"I have to remind myself not to go too fast across the ring," she said. "I end up not using my legs, where all the strength comes from."

She didn't rave about her 100 high hurdles (12.91) or 200 meter (22.95), but her husband-coach was impressed.

"I was pleased because of the lack of work in those events," he said. "We've been concentrating on the throws."

The result: Joyner-Kersee is in a familiar position, holding a big lead and threatening her record. She was on a record pace in June's national championship before botching the javelin.

"I wanted to score 7,161–7,200 points coming in," she said. "But first, I have to concentrate on the competition and think about winning. If I think about records, then I can end up missing first place."

So, Monday night she planned to make her notebook her bedtime reading. She'll read over technical reminders as well as her inspirational section.

She isn't taking first place or the record for granted. But nobody else will be surprised if she puts the record out of sight.

"Jackie set a world record in Moscow (last year)," Greiner said. "If you can set a record there, you can set it anywhere."

Checking Your Comprehension

Read the following questions. Put an x in the box beside the answer that best completes each one.

1. "I'm finally starting to understand what I'm supposed to do in the ring," Joyner-Kersee said. "I could visualize it." *Visualize* means
   - ☐ a. accomplish.
   - ☐ b. practice.
   - ☐ c. see.

2. Joyner-Kersee's bedtime reading includes "technical reminders as well as her inspirational section." *Inspirational* means
   - ☐ a. motivational.
   - ☐ b. practical.
   - ☐ c. cheerful.

3. Who holds the world record for total points in the heptathlon?
   - ☐ a. Larisa Nikitina
   - ☐ b. Jackie Joyner-Kersee
   - ☐ c. Cindy Greiner

4. Joyner-Kersee is on a world-record pace because she
   - ☐ a. has the best first-day score in history.
   - ☐ b. is 338 points ahead of the second-place athlete.
   - ☐ c. has only three events left.

5. Why does Joyner-Kersee write to herself in a notebook?
   - ☐ a. She can't remember the differences among the events in the heptathlon.
   - ☐ b. She takes notes on how to improve both athletically and spiritually.
   - ☐ c. She writes down how her opponents did and how many points she has amassed.

6. How does Joyner-Kersee plan to set a world record for the heptathlon?
   - ☐ a. By reading her technique book and by concentrating on winning each event.
   - ☐ b. If she concentrates on having a total score of between 7,161 and 7,200 points, she will automatically attain a record score.
   - ☐ c. If she concentrates on the javelin, which she botched in the national championship, she will improve one of her weaknesses and probably set a record.

☆ ☆ ☆

The headlines for the USA TODAY story are in the present tense, reinforcing the idea of the breaking story. "Joyner-Kersee on world-record pace," is the main headline, followed by "USA athlete leads Soviet in heptathlon." There is a sense of immediacy imparted by those headlines. Seeing them, readers would feel they were getting the newest information on an important event as it is unfolding. It would not be unnatural for readers to buy the newspaper to read the stories. And, the publisher hopes, readers who were interested in the story would buy the paper in the following days to keep up with the rest of the story.

Now look at the past-tense blurb directly under the headline of the Sports Illustrated story: "Jackie Joyner-Kersee won the heptathlon . . ." Obviously, the competition has ended, the runners-up and also-rans have come up short, and the winner has emerged. How did she do it? Was it luck, skill, hard work, all three? Those are the questions many readers will ask, and many will satisfy their curiosity by buying the magazine and reading the article. Sports fans know that they will get as complete an account as possible from a news-magazine story that uses the news event from start to finish as raw material.

ON TOP OF THE WORLDS

Jackie Joyner-Kersee won the heptathlon and long jump at the World Track and Field Championships

TRACK AND FIELD

"Her gift is her open joy in practiced, powerful movement, in improvement for its own sake."

By KENNY MOORE

Joyner-Kersee triumphed in her favorite event, the long jump, with a leap of 24′ 1¾″.

As Rome's Olympic stadium resounded through the nine hot days and thunderous nights of the World Track and Field Championships, it came to seem a small planet unto itself, glowing in the pine-scented air over the Tiber like a javelin-proof bubble. It was inhabited by the fastest, strongest, toughest, most arrogantly confident men and women, and when the meet was over this luminescent world belonged to Jackie Joyner-Kersee, who took possession of it with unaffected grace.

She first won the heptathlon by a staggering 564 points, 7,128 to 6,564 for runner-up Larisa Nikitina of the U.S.S.R. She rang up the highest first-day total (4,256 points) in history, with a 12.91-second clocking (worth 1,138 points) in the 100 hurdles, a 6′2¾″ (1,106) high jump, a 52′6″ (928) put of the shot and a time of 22.95 (1,084) in the 200, and all were accomplished with an eagerness that bespoke goals transcending mere victory.

Joyner-Kersee, like her name, is a blend. Her years of hard, thoughtful training are the Kersee part, the expression of husband-coach Bob Kersee's hatred of talent lying fallow. The Joyner half is Jackie in competition. She wants to win, but having won, wants to go on. She wants to impress, but having performed gloriously, still wants to go on. The Joyner gift is her open joy in practiced, powerful movement, in improvement for its own sake, and it causes observers to presume, in error, that what she does is without personal cost.

The second day of the heptathlon, she continued with a 23′5¼″ long jump (1,220 points) and a modest 149′10″ throw in the javelin (777). Somehow Joyner-Kersee doesn't seem warlike enough for the javelin. Even so, she was 64 points ahead of the world-record pace she had set last year in Houston.

But as she warmed up for the final event, the 800 meters, Joyner-Kersee suddenly felt tight and dizzy. "I drank some water and hoped not to die," she said. A 2:14 would break the record, and 2:11 would put her over 7,200 points. Her goal was 2:10.

Continued on following page

Continued from preceding page

When the gun sounded, Anke Behmer of East Germany seized the lead and controlled the pace. "It felt fast," said Joyner-Kersee. But the going was slow; the time at 400 meters was 68 seconds. "I got into a pace I just couldn't get out of," she said. She finished in 2:16.29. She had missed her world record by 30 points.

Both Jackie and Bob were puzzled by her fade. "I felt more was there, but ... it wasn't," she said. "We adjusted her training to allow her to long-jump at the Pan Am Games [where Joyner-Kersee tied East Germany's Heike Drechsler's world record of 24′5½″]," he said. "Maybe that had an effect."

It was left to fellow heptathlete Jane Frederick, 35, whose bronze medal was her first World or Olympic hardware in a devoted 22-year career, to make certain truths clear. "In the heptathlon, you have to be completely *free* to dig into yourself to the limit, to gut out that last bit in the 800," she said. "But Jackie knew she had the individual long jump still to come, and she knew she had the heptathlon won. So I'll bet that try as she would, her body was holding something back."

Joyner-Kersee's archrival in the long jump also was marshaling her strength. Drechsler had finished second in the 100 meters to teammate Silke Gladisch, but she skipped the 200 (a race in which she is ranked No. 1 in the world) to be rested for Joyner-Kersee's challenge in the long jump.

The women's long jump began in light rain. After two rounds, Joyner-Kersee led with a leap of 23′4½″. On her third jump she reached great height and landed about a foot beyond her earlier mark—but the electronic sensors in the takeoff board flashed that she'd fouled. The crowd whistled, disbelieving. Then the giant TV replay screens showed an irrefutable quarter of an inch of daylight between her toe and the foul line. The whistles became howls. The officials reversed themselves. The imprint of her landing, which had not been raked from the sand, was measured. She had gone 24′1¾″

Drechsler took the runway like an aroused Valkyrie, her eyes on fire. She pounded through her run but attained far less height than Joyner-Kersee and reached only 23′4¾″. Walking back, brushing off the wet sand, Drechsler knew

it was over. The pain behind her left knee, which she had been concealing, had become worse. On her next jump she could only run through the pit. She passed her last two jumps, and Joyner-Kersee had her second gold medal in the event that means the most to her.

On the victory stand, the two preeminent women track and field athletes of the day shared a long embrace, after which Drechsler tenderly rearranged her rival's hair. They both knew that the wreckage competitors cause each other is unavoidable. "I've been in her situation," said Joyner-Kersee, "and the athlete who beat me when I was hurt was happy. So *I'm* happy."

"It's amazing to me that Jackie can be in the heptathlon and still be so good in the long jump," said Drechsler later, and then she allowed the possibility of an even more sustained battle between them. "I'd like to do a heptathlon once just to see how I would fare. But my family would kill me."

The meet that swirled on around Joyner-Kersee and Drechsler was restless, shifting. Dynasties trembled and new orders rose, all with fine disregard for the infuriating officiating.

Checking Your Comprehension

Read the following questions. Put an *x* in the box beside the answer that best completes each one.

1. The opening paragraph states that, "when the meet was over this luminescent world belonged to Jackie Joyner-Kersee." *Luminescent* means
   □ a. dark.
   □ b. glowing with a self-generated light.
   □ c. dimmed by nightfall.

2. The writer calls Joyner-Kersee and Heike Drechsler the "two preeminent women track and field athletes of the day." *Preeminent* means
   □ a. competitive.
   □ b. well known.
   □ c. dominant.

3. In which events did Jackie Joyner-Kersee win gold medals?
   □ a. She won gold medals for setting a world-record pace on the first day and for the entire heptathlon event.
   □ b. She won gold medals for the heptathlon and the individual long jump.
   □ c. She won gold medals for the individual long jump and her record-setting first-day score.

4. Joyner-Kersee's special gift as an athlete is her
   □ a. winning gold medals and world records.
   □ b. consistent training and desire to beat her opponents.
   □ c. joy in practiced, powerful movement and in improvement for its own sake.

5. Which reason does *not* explain why Joyner-Kersee failed to break her own world record in the heptathlon?
   □ a. Anke Behmer seized the lead and controlled the pace of the 800-meter race.
   □ b. Her body and mind unconsciously knew she still had to compete in the individual long jump.
   □ c. The hot weather in Rome sapped her strength, leaving her dehydrated.

6. Which statement best describes the relationship between USA's Jackie Joyner-Kersee and East Germany's Heike Drechsler?
   □ a. They are fierce competitors who will meet each other in the upcoming heptathlon.
   □ b. They are fellow competitors who understand the pain and joy that their competitiveness results in.
   □ c. Joyner-Kersee dominates Drechsler in skills.

Many people read magazines to learn more detailed information about an area of special interest than can be printed in the newspaper. Sports fans, for example, read *Sports Illustrated.* People interested in entertainment read *Variety* or *Billboard.*

The stories in such magazines are more extensive and detailed than are newspaper stories on the same subjects. That is because magazine stories are often written after the news event is over, when all the facts are in. The stories do not necessarily report breaking or developing stories, as newspaper stories do. That difference results in two types of articles, often on the same topic: the daily, up-to-the-deadline newspaper story, and the in-depth magazine story that describes in detail an event that may already be a matter of public record. Neither the newspaper nor the magazine, then, provides what the other offers: timeliness on the part of the newspaper and depth of coverage on the part of the magazine. People who are interested in both timeliness and depth of coverage in a specific area of interest will often read the newspaper *and* a special-interest magazine to satisfy their need for complete information.

☆ ☆ ☆

Recognizing Time References in Newspaper and Magazine Stories

A dateline gives the date of an issue of a newspaper or magazine. Readers can read the dateline to be certain that they are looking at up-to-date news.

Writing for a daily newspaper with a dateline of Tuesday, September 1, the newspaper reporter chronicles Joyner-Kersee's accomplishments of the day before. In his story, the reporter repeatedly refers to that day, Monday, the references serving to anchor the story in time for the reader.

Reporting for a weekly magazine with a dateline of September 14, the magazine reporter writes his article after Joyner-Kersee has finished all her competitive events. He makes time references that keep the reader aware of the fact that he is reporting events that took place over many days.

Listed below are statements from the newspaper story and the magazine article. Read the statements. In the space provided under each statement, write the word or phrase that constitutes a time reference. After each word or phrase, write *newspaper* if the reference is from the newspaper story, or *magazine* if the reference is from the magazine article. Do not look back at the articles.

1. The wakeup call arrived Monday in the form of a miss at 6 feet, ½ inch.

   _____

   _____

2. By the end of the day, after four of the seven events, she was on a pace to break her world record of 7,158 points.

   _____

   _____

3. With the long jump, javelin, and 800 remaining, Joyner-Kersee has 4,256 points, 105 more than her best first-day effort ever. . . .

   _____

   _____

4. The second day of the heptathlon, she continued with a 23′ 5¼″ long jump. . . .

   _____

   _____

5. What pleased Joyner-Kersee the most Monday was the shot put . . . .

   _____

   _____

6. As Rome's Olympic Stadium resounded through the nine hot days and thunderous nights of the World Track and Field Championships . . .

   _____

   _____

7. . . . and when the meet was over this luminescent world belonged to Jackie Joyner-Kersee. . . .

   _____

   _____

8. So Monday night she planned to make her notebook her bedtime reading.

   _____

   _____

Practicing Newspaper Skills

Jackie Joyner-Kersee keeps a journal in which she records how to improve her physical movements and how to inspire her mind. Her journal is a tool she uses to express her gift of "open joy in practiced, powerful movement, in improvement for its own sake."

Many people write notes to themselves in order to be more successful or efficient in their hobbies or jobs. A naturalist like Jane Goodall (Unit One, Lesson 7) keeps *field notes* to record her observations of chimpanzee behavior. Using a *journal,* a fiction writer records observations of people and events, plot ideas, and partial drafts of stories. Calling it a *sketchbook,* an artist records images and preliminary drafts of later creations.

Occasionally you will see a newspaper or magazine feature story written from a reporter's journal entries: the reporter, on assignment in a distant place, keeps a diary, and that diary becomes the basis for an unplanned, more personal story. Other reporters decide consciously to do a journal story. Taking on a challenge such as quitting smoking or losing weight, the reporter keeps a journal for a specific period, then writes up the journal entries as a feature. Such stories sometimes demand weekly or monthly updates as the writer reports his or her progress.

Write a journal story about your attempts to improve your performance in a favorite activity or your efforts to meet a challenge. In the first case, you could record progress in one of your special interests, be it playing a musical instrument, modeling, or even studying. In the second case, you might record your efforts to make the basketball team, keep your room neat, or quit eating junk food.

Keep a journal for two weeks (or more, if you are really serious). In the case of the special interest, describe in the first entry how you do the activity. Then give yourself a specific suggestion for how you can improve on the second day. As the days go by, repeat the process and record how well you do as you implement your suggestions. You may choose to have an inspirational section like Joyner-Kersee's if you wish.

If you set a challenge, describe in the first entry the nature of the challenge and why you have taken it on. Record your successes and failures every day. Use humor if the situation calls for it, or be serious if the challenge is a serious one (you could use this activity to deal with a real problem).

At the end of the two weeks, write a feature story based on your journal entries that chronicles your self-improvement campaign or your response to a challenge. To begin the story, write an introduction that explains who you are, what you have done, when you did it, and why and how you did it. Follow that with the journal entries, heading each one with its day and date. They will make up the body of the story. After the last journal entry, write a concluding paragraph that sums up your feelings about your experience and your evaluation of how helpful it was.

In the United States, newspapers contain so much information about daily events that we take news for granted. Our newspapers are our daily record of events that happen each day. This right to print the news is guaranteed by the First Amendment to the Constitution, which states the rights of United States citizens to free speech and a free press.

This freedom to print a daily record of events is not guaranteed by the government of every nation in the world. For example, in June, 1986, South African readers of Johannesburg's newspaper *The Star* found blank spaces where the government had censored the information the newspaper was reporting.

As you will read, the South African apartheid government had ordered emergency regulations restricting the people and the press. President P. W. Botha ordered the clampdown to thwart the plans of antiapartheid groups who were organizing protests and a strike to commemorate the Soweto riots of 1976, in which black schoolchildren were killed by police. Since protests are news, reporters would certainly cover the march. President Botha did not relish the thought of these protests, just as he did not enjoy the idea of newspaper reporters telling the world that there are South Africans driven to street protests by government policies.

Both of the articles in this lesson are from a United States paper, the *Boston Globe,* and so are not censored like the South African newspaper. The first story reports President Botha's announcement of the emergency restrictions and the arrests of political opponents and people opposed to apartheid. The second story describes the problems that newspaper reporters encountered when they tried to report news under the press restrictions. As you read about the lack of freedom of the press in South Africa, think about the important role of newspapers in the United States: to inform citizens by reporting many events and various opinions.

As you read the story below, take care to notice what the government's restrictions on reporters were.

The Boston Globe

Vol. 229; No. 164   FRIDAY, JUNE 13, 1986   92 Pages ● 25 cents

Pretoria imposes state of emergency, arrests over 1,000

By PHILIP VAN NIEKERK
Special to the Globe

JOHANNESBURG—The government imposed a nationwide state of emergency yesterday, launching a crackdown on antiapartheid organizations and arresting more than 1,000 of its political opponents.

The emergency, declared by President P. W. Botha, gave police broad powers to detain people without charge and imposed severe restrictions on media coverage of political violence.

The White House yesterday denounced South Africa's imposition of a state of emergency but said the Reagan administration has no intention of supporting new economic sanctions against the Pretoria government. Page 8

Botha said in an address to Parliament that the emergency was necessary to stem plans by black organizations to stage large-scale protests and a general strike on Monday to commemorate the 10th anniversary of the Soweto uprising. On June 16, 1976, police shot dead black schoolchildren

President P. W. Botha addresses South African Parliament yesterday.

in the black township of Soweto who were protesting inferior education. The shootings touched off riots and boycotts that
Continued on following page

Continued from preceding page

swept South Africa for more than a year and claimed 575 lives, by official count.

Leaders of business and the white political opposition joined in condemning the new emergency as both futile and a serious danger to the battered economy.

Before the emergency was announced, security forces arrived in the night at the homes of antiapartheid activists, clergymen, church workers, student and labor leaders of all races. Black trade unionists were a particular target of the raids.

Hundreds of antiapartheid activists and leaders had already gone into hiding in anticipation of the crackdown. Political activists said that in response to the raids and the state of emergency, Monday's general strike might be extended through the week.

A nine-month partial state of emergency was lifted in March. It had been an attempt by the government to curtail almost two years of continuing rebellion in the country's black ghettos.

The emergency regulations published yesterday are tougher than those under the previous emergency. The new regulations apply to the entire country, whereas last year's restrictions were valid in only 36 magisterial areas, chiefly covering two regions—Johannesburg and the Eastern Cape.

There are also tighter controls on publications this time, including a prohibition on "subversive statements" and publications of a "subversive nature."

Botha told Parliament yesterday that

Government powers under emergency

Associated Press

JOHANNESBURG—Here are some of the regulations and special powers given to security forces under the nationwide state of emergency declared yesterday:

• Security force members may enter premises without warrant and "take such steps as a member may deem necessary for the maintenance of public order." They also may arrest without warrant anyone whom the arresting officer considers a threat to public order.

• People detained under the emergency regulations may be held for two weeks, but the minister of law and order, "without notice to any person and without hearing any person," may extend the detention for as long as the state of emergency continues.

• It is illegal to issue or report "subversive statements," including "encouraging or promoting disinvestment or the application of sanctions or foreign action

against the republic," promoting the aims of outlawed organizations, encouraging people to participate in boycotts or civil disobedience, discrediting the conscription system and engendering "feelings of hostility" toward the government or security forces.

• Members of the security forces and any other government officials or employees are exempted from any civil or criminal liability in connection with "good faith" efforts to enforce the emergency.

• Police permission is required to film, photograph, tape record or make drawings of unrest or of any action by the security forces. Permission also is needed to distribute or publish such pictures and recordings.

• Reporting the names of anyone arrested under the emergency regulations is prohibited unless authorized by the Ministry of Law and Order.

the outlawed African National Congress, the United Democratic Front, "and other radicals and anarchists" were planning large-scale unrest, acts of terror and sabotage between June 16 and 18.

Meanwhile, the first concrete signs of the crackdown inside South Africa came as police raided the homes of political activists in the early hours of yesterday.

Buildings housing antiapartheid organizations and trade unions in all the main

centers were sealed off by armed police and soldiers.

Those detained included whites, clergymen, trade unionists and grass-roots activists in scores of ghettos throughout the country.

A police unit took over the Johannesburg editorial offices of the black biweekly publication New Nation, ordered staff members to remain at their desks and spent two hours searching the files.

Checking Your Comprehension

Read the following questions. Put an *x* in the box beside the answer that best completes each one.

1. The report states that "Leaders of business and the white political opposition joined in condemning the new emergency as both futile and a serious danger to the economy." *Futile* means
   □ a. harmful.
   □ b. frivolous.
   □ c. useless.

2. The government exercised control over what it deemed "subversive statements." A *subversive* statement is one that
   □ a. advocates the overthrow of the government.
   □ b. is in opposition to the government.
   □ c. supports the government.

3. The state of emergency gave the police broad powers to
   □ a. arrest people and censor what news reporters could cover.
   □ b. detain people without charging them with a crime.
   □ c. do nothing but restrict media coverage.

4. The South African news media were required to obtain permission to
   □ a. report the names of anyone arrested under the emergency restrictions.
   □ b. film, photograph, tape record, or make drawings of unrest or police actions and to publish such pictures and recordings.
   □ c. do any of the things listed in answers *a* and *b*.

5. A newspaper that published an article about a march commemorating the deaths of Soweto children would probably be
   ☐ a. ignored by the government authorities.
   ☐ b. closed down by the government authorities.
   ☐ c. given permission to publish by the government authorities.

6. Which emergency power given below allowed the police to take over the offices of the newspaper *New Nation*?
   ☐ a. the power to detain people without charge
   ☐ b. the power to search without a warrant
   ☐ c. both of the above powers

☆ ☆ ☆

Review the list of emergency government powers that accompanies the first story. The two restrictions that most affect the ability of the press to report the news would seem to be (1) the stricture restraining the press from publishing the names of anyone arrested under emergency regulations, and (2) the requirement of police permission to film, photograph, tape record, or make drawings of unrest or action by security forces.

Now look at the headline of the next story. As you can see, one of the main results of emergency restrictions on the South African press was the tendency of newspeople to censor themselves. This can be seen as a by-product of government censorship—it is created by government censorship, but it is not, strictly speaking, *a part of* the government's censorship effort.

10   THE BOSTON GLOBE   TUESDAY, JUNE 17, 1986

New press restrictions lead to self-censorship

By PHILIP VAN NIEKERK
Globe Correspondent

JOHANNESBURG—The declaration of a state of emergency in South Africa last Thursday has led to the most extensive news blackout in the country's history.

As South African police continued to detain opponents of apartheid, leading to rumors that thousands of people were being held, the press has been prohibited from publishing any names of detainees.

So severe are the emergency regulations and the punishments for violating them that information has all but dried up. Local newspapers are having to censor themselves more than ever and foreign correspondents say that, for the first time, they are censoring their reports out of the country.

The police commissioner, Johan Coetzee, banned reporters from black townships yesterday and prohibited all news reports and comment on security force action. He said the only authorized news would be released by the government Bureau of Information.

The emergency regulations announced Thursday make it an offense to write, record, make or print any "subversive" statement.

No pictures of "unrest" may be published or sent abroad, and names and details of detainees may not be published. The government has also given itself the power to seize publications and ban them if they contain "subversive" statements.

To present the news in any other way than the authorized way is to risk fines of up to $8,000 or 10 years in jail, seizure or banning of publications and, for the foreign press, expulsion from the country.

"We are not kidding, we will not hesitate to take action," said David Stewart, the head of the Bureau of Information, which is charged with giving out information about "unrest" at daily press conferences in Pretoria.

At those press conferences, officials often simply refuse to answer questions. They give out much less information than was previously available from police reports and other state agencies.

Under the partial state of emergency declared last year and lifted in March, journalists were allowed to enter the black townships if they reported to police when violence broke out. There also was no prohibition on covering the political statements of the government's opponents.

Since Thursday, the offices of six newspapers or news organizations—the New Nation, the Sunday Tribune, City Press, Grassroots, Afrapix and Sash—have been raided, while Friday's issues of The Weekly Mail and the black daily, The Sowetan, were seized.

A cameraman for the CBS television station, Wim de Vos, was ordered out of the country and two foreign television crews were arrested filming "man in the street" interviews.

The television crews were released; de Vos appealed the order against him but was turned down yesterday and was told that he must leave the country by midnight today.

Courts could challenge some decisions of the government, said Jeff Budlender, a lawyer with the Legal Resources Center in Johannesburg. "But if the banning or seizure of a newspaper is challenged, all of its validity would depend on whether it was subversive 'in the minister's opinion,' " he said. "And if the answer was 'yes,' it would end the challenge."

Journalists are uncertain how to apply the regulations and have asked the Bureau for Information for clarification on various points. They were issued a statement

Continued on following page

Continued from preceding page
that they should speak to their lawyers.

No reason has been given for the raids and the seizures, and journalists say they do not know what they must avoid in order to publish lawfully.

Among five foreign correspondents interviewed during the weekend, none of whom wanted their names used, all but one of them said their reading of regulations made them feel compelled to censor copy, and most are seeking legal advice. The fifth correspondent said he would behave as if nothing had happened.

One of South Africa's leading press lawyers, who cannot be quoted for professional reasons, has advised his clients that the laws are in fact impossible to comply with. But he has warned that they are likely to be used selectively—meaning against the black press.

Checking Your Comprehension

Read the following questions. Put an *x* in the box beside the answer that best completes each one.

1. The police commissioner said the "only authorized news would be released by the government Bureau of Information." *Authorized* means
   - ☐ a. officially permitted.
   - ☐ b. news from experts or authorities.
   - ☐ c. written by a government-appointed author.

2. A leading press lawyer warned that the restrictions "are likely to be used selectively." By *selectively,* he means
   - ☐ a. applied equally to all.
   - ☐ b. used very seldom.
   - ☐ c. applied unequally.

3. Most foreign reporters have found that they are
   - ☐ a. behaving as if there were no restrictions.
   - ☐ b. compelled to censor reports and seek legal advice.
   - ☐ c. getting permission from the Bureau of Information.

4. Which police actions listed below have occurred since the declaration of the state of emergency?
   - ☐ a. The offices of South African newspapers have been raided and issues of papers seized.
   - ☐ b. Foreign correspondents have been arrested; one has been expelled from the country.
   - ☐ c. All of the above events have happened.

5. According to the South African government, which of the following is the only allowable source of information?
   - ☐ a. police reports
   - ☐ b. daily press conferences given by the Bureau of Information officials
   - ☐ c. man in the street interviews

6. We can conclude that a newspaper would not take its case to court in South Africa because a judge would be likely to base his decision concerning "subversive reporting" on the
   - ☐ a. laws about freedom of the press.
   - ☐ b. government minister's current opinion.
   - ☐ c. constitution of the country.

☆ ☆ ☆

After the declaration of the emergency regulations, the newspapers in South Africa were not a daily record of the events in that country. While people in other countries learned of protests and efforts to change the apartheid government, news reports were still censored. Therefore, reports in newspapers around the world could not tell all that has happened in South Africa.

However, South Africa is not the only country in the world that does not have a free press. Chile has press restrictions and has jailed reporters. In the Soviet Union, Premier Gorbachev has announced a relaxation of press restrictions, but the press is still controlled by the government.

The United States has a history of freedom of the press—that freedom is guaranteed by the First Amendment to the Constitution. Thus, newspapers in the United States print a daily record of "What Makes News," as we learned in Unit One.

☆ ☆ ☆

Identifying Cause and Effect in News Stories

Both stories report the South African government's actions and the reactions on the part of the people and the press. The root cause of the problems in South Africa is the apartheid system, but the immediate cause of the specific problems of June, 1986, was the declaration of emergency government powers. The effects of that cause can be seen in the lives of the people and in the altered work practices of members of the press.

The statements that follow are taken from the articles. In the space provided before each statement, write *cause* if the statement describes an element of the government's emergency regulations. Write *effect* if the statement describes what happened as a result of those regulations.

_____ 1. The government imposed a nationwide state of emergency yesterday. . . .

_____ 2. The emergency . . . gave the police broad powers to detain people . . . and imposed severe restrictions on media coverage of political violence.

_____ 3. Leaders of business and the white political opposition joined in condemning the new emergency as both futile and a serious danger to the battered economy.

_____ 4. Political activists said that in response to the raids and the state of emergency, Monday's general strike might be extended through the week.

_____ 5. There are also tighter controls on publications this time, including a prohibition on "subversive statements" and publications of a "subversive nature."

_____ 6. Those detained included whites, clergymen, trade unionists and grass-roots activists in scores of ghettos throughout the country.

_____ 7. Local newspapers are having to censor themselves more than ever and foreign correspondents say that, for the first time, they are censoring their reports out of the country.

_____ 8. No pictures of "unrest" may be published or sent abroad, and names and details of detainees may not be published.

_____ 9. At those press conferences, officials often simply refuse to answer questions. They give out much less information than was previously available from police reports.

_____ 10. Since Thursday, the offices of six newspapers or news organizations . . . have been raided, while Friday's issues of The Weekly Mail and the black daily, The Sowetan, were seized.

_____ 11. A cameraman for the CBS television station, Wim de Vos, was ordered out of the country and two foreign television crews were arrested for filming "man in the street" interviews.

Using Your Newspaper

Go to your library and look in the *Readers' Guide to Periodical Literature* or the *New York Times Index* for articles about people in the United States exercising their right to free speech. You could look up news reports on the civil rights demonstrations and marches of the 1950s and '60s or the 1970s protests against the war in Vietnam. Try to select an article that contains quotes from demonstrators or rally speakers—an article that contains, in other words, the opinions of participants. Make two photocopies of the article.

Imagine you are a government censor. Read the article carefully. Are there controversial statements? Do those statements make the government look bad? Are there reports of civil disobedience and unrest?

Cross out all the "subversive" information in one copy of the news report. Remember, as a government censor you feel that any and all news that reflects poorly on the government is a threat to the accepted order. And the accepted order includes everything from your country's political and economic systems to your job.

Display the censored copy and the original copy side-by-side on the bulletin board. Encourage class members to compare the two articles.

Practicing Newspaper Skills

Scan your local newspaper for a news story on a controversial issue in your community. For example, if your community needs a new dump or trash disposal method, city officials and neighborhood residents will probably favor different sites and systems. If a clash ensues, the local paper will report any confrontations as well as differing opinions.

Choose a story you like. Then call the paper to arrange an interview with the reporter of the story or an editor who is familiar with the story. Take a notebook and pencil or a tape recorder to the interview. Prepare your questions in advance. Ask the reporter or editor (let's say he's a man) how he handles controversial topics. What guidelines does he use for checking the accuracy of the information in news stories? Has he ever imposed self-censorship? In what situations might he censor his reports? Add to this list any questions you would like to ask in the interview.

Write an interview story. Introduce the story in a lead paragraph that identifies the person interviewed, where and when the interview took place, and what subject the interview covers. Then reproduce your first question, followed by your subject's first answer. Proceed in that fashion to assemble the written version of the interview.

As we have seen over the course of this book, the newspaper acts as a daily record of events. In recording events day by day, newspaper editors put emphasis on those they deem interesting and relevant to the readership. With the passing of time, that daily record becomes a historical record.

The two stories in this lesson are from the *Boston Globe*'s Labor Day edition. One deals with the early history of labor unions, and the other gives a glimpse of the status of working people in the late 1980s. If a person studying the labor movement in the year 2000 were to read one or both of these stories, that person would gain insight into the history of labor in the United States.

As you read each story keep its historical significance in mind. Also, see if you can detect each writer's view of labor unions.

A heroine for Labor Day

By JOHN GALVIN

Mary Kenney was born in Mark Twain's town, Hannibal, Mo., on Jan. 8, 1864, the daughter of Irish immigrant parents. As a child she was apprenticed to a dressmaker, but at 14, on the death of her father, she took a job as a bookbinder at $2 a week. Six years later, when her employer moved to Keokuk, Iowa, Mary—by then forewoman of the plant and earning $5 a week—went along, taking her invalid mother, who was to live with her for the rest of her life.

When the bindery failed, the Kenneys moved to Chicago, where Mary quickly found work. She was appalled at the squalor of the city, "the tragedies of meagerly paid workers, the haunting faces of undernourished children, the filth."

Rebelling against the long hours and wretched working conditions she had experienced, Mary Kenney organized the bookbinders union for women. As a result, she was elected to the Chicago Trades and Labor Assembly. Tall, comely, with wavy blonde hair, blue eyes and rosy cheeks, Mary Kenney was—as Wellesley professor Vida Dutton Scudder later described her—"a noble young woman on fire for her cause."

A friend of Jane Addams

She also had a quick Irish temper which she used effectively against factory owners who were breaking the law. When Jane Addams opened Hull House to union activities, Mary Kenney took her organizational meetings there, thus beginning her lifelong friendship with Addams and her Hull House co-founder, Ellen Gates Starr, whom Kenney regarded as an "older sister."

MARY KENNEY O'SULLIVAN
'A rare and powerful character'

Mary Kenney also organized the shirtwaist workers, and together with Florence Kelley, another persistent and fearless woman, prepared a widely read report on the shocking conditions in Chicago sweatshops. One consequence was the establishment of a Factory Inspection Department for the state of Illinois. In 1892, AFL president Samuel Gompers appointed Mary Kenney, age 28, the first national woman organizer of the American Federation of Labor. She traveled to upper New York State to organize women there, then went to Boston.

Here, Mary Kenney met and fell in love with a fellow labor organizer, widower John F. O'Sullivan, labor editor of The Globe. In 1893, she became executive secretary of the Union for Industrial Progress to investigate labor conditions in industry, a position she held for 10 years.

In 1894, she married John O'Sullivan. That same year, Mary O'Sullivan engaged in a public debate over the Haverhill shoe strike with attorney Louis D. Brandeis, later associate justice of the Supreme Court, O'Sullivan taking the labor side, Brandeis, the side of the manufacturer. Josephine Goldmark, Brandeis's sister-in-law, said of O'Sullivan: "She had been at the Carnegie Steel Company in Homestead in 1892 . . . she had been through the Haverhill shoe strike of 1894; she was active in all the textile strikes at Lawrence and Fall River. The workers' side of those struggles lost nothing in her telling, and in Mr. Brandeis she found an attentive listener." After the debate, according to one of his biographers, Brandeis began to realize "that trade unions were important to both labor and management."

One of Mary O'Sullivan's outstanding characteristics was her ability to make friends in all walks of life. Among them was Mrs. Glendower Evans of Otis Place, Beacon Hill, one of that extraordinary group of Brahmin women who became pioneer social workers in Boston's settlement houses. Mrs. Evans brought the O'Sullivans and Brandeis together, and he became a regular visitor to the O'Sullivan home on Carver Street in the South End, a gathering place for both American and British labor leaders.

Her mother and her oldest child died and her house burned to the ground, but through it all, Mary O'Sullivan's ardor for the labor movement never flagged. With their three remaining children, the O'Sullivans moved into an apartment in Denison House, a settlement house established in Boston's South Cove in 1893. In the spring of 1900, they moved to Beachmont. In 1902, John O'Sullivan was killed by a train. Influential friends like Philip Cabot then employed Mary O'Sullivan as agent for property in Roxbury and South Boston, enabling her to support her children and continue her reform work.

Continued on following page

Continued from preceding page

In 1903, Mary O'Sullivan and William English Walling, grandson of a Kentucky millionaire and a vigorous social reformer, organized the National Women's Trade Union League, which brought settlement house workers and trade union organizers together. O'Sullivan was also a founder of the Consumer's League and a member of the committee to draft a minimum wage law. After helping to organize the garment workers, she wound up president of the garment workers union, and her colleague, Helena Stuart Dudley, one of the most important leaders in the early settlement house movement, became treasurer.

Lawrence textile strike

In 1909, Mary O'Sullivan bought land and built a house in West Medford. In January 1912, "her enthusiasm and fighting spirit were revitalized" by the strike of 30,000 textile workers in Lawrence. Mary O'Sullivan went to investigate. "I had been in strikes in 1877 and had seen the poverty of underpaid workers in every form desirable," she wrote, "but never in my labor experience had I seen or known so many men, women and children as badly housed and undernourished."

"Under a greater strain than at any time in my life," Mary O'Sullivan sat down to plead the workers' cause for more than two hours with the intransigent president of American Woolen Mills, William M. Wood. She was there to see the strike settled and pay increases and other benefits granted to the workers. As an indirect result, thousands of textile mill workers elsewhere in New England got raises as well.

Partly as a consequence of the Lawrence strike, Massachusetts created a Division of Industrial Safety (now part of the Department of Labor and Industries). Mary O'Sullivan served as an inspector of industrial safety for the commonwealth from November 1914 to January 1934, when she retired from her 57 years of successful labor on behalf of working men and women. She died in West Medford on Jan. 18, 1943, and is buried in St. Joseph's Roman Catholic Cemetery, West Roxbury.

At the time of Mary O'Sullivan's death, Emily Greene Balch, the Wellesley College economics professor who was to share a Nobel Peace Prize with John R. Mott in 1946, wrote of her: "Her work . . . was devoted to the cause of Labor, but in no narrow spirit. She was not interested in one class to the neglect of others. All who were in need, all who suffered injustice, found her on their side. . . . She was a rare and powerful character who drew friends as the sun draws life-giving moisture.

"She endeared herself to all who knew her by her rich nature, vigorous and outgoing, generous, humorous, tempestuous and loyal, by her capacity for never flagging devotion, spontaneous and without thought of credit or reward. . . . She was a great comrade."

Just 50 years after her retirement as an ardent champion of working people, Mary Kenney O'Sullivan is someone worth remembering this Labor Day.

Checking Your Comprehension

Read the following questions. Put an *x* in the box beside the answer that best completes each one.

1. When Mary Kenney moved to Chicago, she was "appalled at the squalor of the city." To be *appalled* is to be
   - ☐ a. dismayed.
   - ☐ b. frightened.
   - ☐ c. amazed.

2. Writer John Galvin says that through all of Mary Kenney O'Sullivan's good times and bad, her "ardor for the labor movement never flagged." The word *ardor* means
   - ☐ a. impatience; restlessness.
   - ☐ b. anxiety.
   - ☐ c. zeal; loyalty.

3. As a young woman, Mary Kenney O'Sullivan held several jobs. Which of the following jobs did she not hold?
   - ☐ a. bookbinder
   - ☐ b. housekeeper
   - ☐ c. apprentice to a dressmaker

4. O'Sullivan's first organizing experience was with the
   - ☐ a. Garment Workers Union, Chicago Branch.
   - ☐ b. Union for Industrial Progress.
   - ☐ c. bookbinders union for women.

5. Galvin says that one of Mary O'Sullivan's outstanding characteristics was her ability to make friends in all walks of life. He means that
   - ☐ a. she was able to get along with people who were from very different backgrounds—the laborer, the socialite, the government official.
   - ☐ b. she took long walks to meet people and talk with them.
   - ☐ c. she made a lot of friends in her life, especially people who were just like her and were involved in similar activities.

6. The editorial writer feels Mary Kenney O'Sullivan is worth writing about because
   - ☐ a. she endeared herself to all who knew her.
   - ☐ b. a winner of the Nobel Peace Prize wrote about her.
   - ☐ c. she was a symbol of devotion to the cause of labor.

☆ ☆ ☆

The role of newspapers in society varies from paper to paper depending on the locale, the tenor of the times, and the readership toward which a paper is geared.

In this lesson you have been asked to focus on the newspaper's historical significance as it applies to two articles on labor in the United States. The biographical piece you have just read is clearly historical—it is a deliberate look at the past. But as the last paragraph in the article shows, part of the writer's intent is to link the past to the present.

In the following article, columnist David Nyhan outlines what he sees as the gloomy plight of working people today. Nyhan cites statistics to support the idea that since 1973, life has been an uphill struggle for the American working class.

For many, it's a gloomy holiday

By DAVID NYHAN

Labor Day, 1986. How fares the Working Man? He's getting croaked.

And unless he sends the little woman out to be Working Woman, he's not only not going to get ahead, he may not even be able to stay even. He might not know just how badly he's doing, but he's beginning to sense things are not going his way.

In households where both husband and wife work, half the men earn under $22,000, and half the wives under $9,000 a year. Throw in the rent, or a mortgage, if they're lucky, and a car payment or two and a couple of kids, and the mythical Working Person of Labor Day 1986 is up against it.

Not necessarily here. Massachusetts is one of the islands of prosperity in a sea of regional recessions; 31 states, with half the nation's population, are now in recession, pollster Albert Sindlinger concludes.

Anyone who wants to work in Massachusetts can now find work, as our supercharged economy barrels along. But we are the lucky ones, buoyed by a fortuitous mix that includes defense contractors, high-tech, boom-town construction, high-end services, such as hospitals, finance and insurance, and, undergirding it all, the marvelous academic network.

Across the land, these are hard times for the House of Labor. Faring poorly are those who make things: food, gasoline, steel, cars, ships, lumber, electrical gizmos, clothing, shoes, manufactured goods generally. Something like 1,100 farmers go bust every week.

The steelworkers union is half its former size and fading. US Steel just changed its name to USX Corp., typifying the distance the Pittsburgh titan is trying to put between itself and the fading steel industry. And 22,000 steelworkers are nonworkers, because USX braced them with a like-it-or-lump-it contract offer.

As the plight of farmers and nonunion oil workers demonstrates, it is not just unionized employees who are feeling the heat. But organized labor's plight is truly

Continued on following page

U.S. steelworkers, farmers across the nation have little reason to celebrate Labor Day.

Continued from preceding page

dismal. This has to be the worst Labor Day for the unions in decades. Only one of six nonfarm workers belongs to a union, and precious few of them are doing well.

The lucky ones are defense workers, construction workers in boom towns, airline pilots lucky enough not to have been thrown out of work, major league baseball players.

Name a recent economic trend, save for the lapse of inflation, and it has hurt the American worker: trade deficit, deregulation, rise in Social Security taxes, manufacturing decline, restrictions on union powers.

Along the way, labor's political clout has diminished in Washington, most spectacularly during the reign of Ronald Reagan, the first union president to reach the White House.

Consider: The year Ronald Reagan was born, the dominant imperial power on earth was the British Empire. In his lifespan, we've seen Britain, cradle of the industrial revolution, hatchery of Marxism, the world's preeminent power, reduced to economic strangulation, permanent 13 percent-plus unemployment and inability to compete in world markets.

If it can happen to the British worker, in one man's lifetime, it can happen here. And it's happening.

No one, with the possible exception of Rev. Jesse Jackson, a fiery orator who polarizes working class audiences, articulates the American worker's dilemma, which is precisely this: Other countries, with cheaper labor costs, now make most things as good or better than we do and sell them a lot cheaper.

President Reagan got reelected with his "It's morning again in America" TV spots, and his second term is concentrating on foreign affairs, not the economy.

Nicaragua, Libya, South Africa and the Soviets occupy the White House, as we are about to plunge into another recession. The new tax bill that will likely emerge from Congress rewrites economic rules for the future, with no immediate prospects for injecting adrenaline into the somnolent economy.

The Republican campaign for this fall is a 50-state patchwork of state-by-state issues. The GOP's by-now-traditional penchant for exploiting social issues— affirmative action, abortion, school prayer, private school aid, capital punishment—is designed to capture working-class and ethnic votes, without addressing the structural economic flaws that affect the bottom line for working people.

Between 1973 and 1984, the average real income of all families with children declined from the equivalent of $32,206 to $29,527. That statistic is given in 1984 dollars, and it demonstrates that families with kids lost 8.3 percent of their real income over that time. That's a lot of groceries.

The typical mortgage that took 21 percent of a male worker's income in 1973 soaked up 44 percent by 1984. Solution: Wives had to go to work. Side effect: Kids watch more TV.

There's more backsliding for the American worker. The pay increases negotiated this year in major labor contracts averaged only 1.2 percent in the first year, the lowest figure in the two decades Uncle Sam has kept track. But enough. It's Labor Day. Go for it, you happy workers. Your 1986 theme song is: "Been down so long it looks like up to me."

David Nyhan is a Globe columnist.

Checking Your Comprehension

Read the following questions. Put an *x* in the box beside the answer that best completes each one.

1. The writer calls the state of Massachusetts "one of the islands of prosperity in a sea of regional recessions." By *prosperity*, he means
   - ☐ a. well-being.
   - ☐ b. thrift.
   - ☐ c. popularity.

2. USX Corp. is referred to as a "titan." As it is used here, *titan* means
   - ☐ a. a type of metal alloy.
   - ☐ b. someone or something great in size and power.
   - ☐ c. a large company made up of many small companies.

3. According to the article, many things have contributed to the American worker's situation in the late 1980s. The only thing that has not hurt the worker is the
   - ☐ a. trade deficit.
   - ☐ b. lapse of inflation.
   - ☐ c. rise in Social Security taxes.

4. The article says that this is the worst Labor Day for unions in decades. One union cited as having a particularly hard time is that of
   - ☐ a. defense workers.
   - ☐ b. oil workers.
   - ☐ c. steelworkers.

5. The article implies that the reason so many housewives have taken jobs outside the home is that
   - ☐ a. people want more luxuries than they can afford on one salary.
   - ☐ b. women don't want to stay home with their kids.
   - ☐ c. almost half of the male worker's salary goes to a mortgage.

6. The article says that those workers who make things such as steel, cars, and electrical gizmos are faring poorly. This could be largely attributed to
   - ☐ a. President Reagan's concentration on foreign affairs.
   - ☐ b. competitive products and prices from other countries.
   - ☐ c. the new tax bill Congress is proposing.

☆ ☆ ☆

The two articles you have just read illustrate how the newspaper can serve as a historical record. "A heroine for Labor Day" chronicles Mary Kenney O'Sullivan's life and the events she lived through, becoming in the process part of what we regard as history. Similarly, the editorial "For many, it's a gloomy holiday" deals with current concerns that might well become part of the historical record as time goes on. People coming across the piece in the future would read why Labor Day in 1986 seemed gloomy to the writer. Having those statistics and opinions in hand, those future readers would be able to draw comparisons between the status and role of labor in 1986 and in their time, whatever it might be. In other words, we see material from the past as history; likewise, stories that document the events of our times will become a historical record for people in the future.

☆ ☆ ☆

Recognizing and Listing Details

The two articles deal with labor unions in the United States. The first is an account of Mary Kenney O'Sullivan's lifelong commitment to the establishment of unions and the betterment of working conditions. The second offers a rather dismal look at the current status of the working person. By reading the two articles one can get a view of labor from the late 1800s to the late 1900s.

Reread the two articles. In the first, look for examples of problems that laborers faced in the past. In the second, look for examples of problems that present-day laborers are facing or statistics that represent those problems. For each category, past and present, write the examples you find in the spaces provided below.

Problems for Laborers in the Past

1. _____

_____

2. _____

_____

3. _____

_____

4. _____

_____

5. _____

_____

Problems for Laborers in the Present

1. _____

_____

2. _____

_____

3. _____

_____

4. _____

_____

5. _____

_____

Using Your Newspaper

The biographical story of Mary Kenney O'Sullivan obviously had to do with the past, and Kenney O'Sullivan is long dead. But biographical sketches or articles on people who are still alive are also quite common. Survey your newspaper for the next week to find some features or editorials that are biographical in theme. You will often find such articles in the sports, arts, or entertainment sections of the newspaper.

Select an article about someone whose life and work will, in your opinion, have historical value.

Write a brief review of the piece. Include several sentences that state your reasons for believing that the subject of the article will be a person of lasting significance. In other words, tell why you think the person will become part of the historical record because of what he or she is accomplishing in life now.

Practicing Newspaper Skills

Pick a national holiday that interests you. Do some research and write a feature story on a person who was closely associated with the holiday in the past. Model your article after the piece in this lesson on Mary Kenney O'Sullivan.

Your purpose in writing the story will not be only to entertain readers but also to help them understand the holiday's place in history. A look at a particular person linked to the holiday might reveal information not known to readers who are unfamiliar with the person. O'Sullivan's history, for example, reveals many little-known facts about the development of labor unions in the United States.

Research the holiday at your library. You might want to start your research by checking the *Readers' Guide to Periodical Literature* or by looking in an encyclopedia. You will want to turn up someone on whom there is enough information to justify a feature story.

After selecting a subject, write a feature story that connects the person's life and work to the holiday or the events that inspired the holiday. Study the Mary Kenney O'Sullivan feature story or any of the feature stories in this book for guidelines on the feature-story form.

UNIT ONE: WHAT MAKES NEWS

LESSON 1

Checking Your Comprehension

1. a	1. b
2. c	2. a
3. b	3. b
4. a	4. c
5. b	5. a
6. a	6. c

Recognizing Cause and Effect

Saragosa Tornado	Stark Missile Attack
1. cause	1. effect
3. cause	2. effect
4. cause	4. effect
6. cause	5. effect

LESSON 2

Checking Your Comprehension

1. b	1. a
2. a	2. b
3. c	3. a
4. c	4. b
5. b	5. b
6. a	6. b

Recognizing Supporting Details in News Stories*

Tempestt Bledsoe is a name in the news who
1. recently signed autographs at Atlanta's Northside High School.
2. speaks on behalf of the President's Council on Physical Fitness and Sports.
3. sang in commercials for Applejacks and Good 'n' Plenty.
4. will appear in an ABC special with Della Reese.

Ted Kennedy, Jr. is a name in the news who
1. is the son of Senator Edward Kennedy.
2. wrote a cover story on the handicapped for *Parade* magazine.
3. heads a foundation, Facing the Challenge, whose purpose is to help the handicapped.
4. is the cousin of Joe Kennedy, who now occupies the House seat of former Speaker Tip O'Neill.
  * Wording may vary.

LESSON 3

Checking Your Comprehension

1. a	2. c	3. a	4. b	5. b	6. b	1. c	2. b	3. c	4. a	5. b	6. c

Linking Facts from a Feature Story to Charts and Graphs

Name	Country Emigrated From	Year of Immigration to United States	Major Event of that Year or Closest Year
1. Dino Hirsch	Germany	1941	U.S. enters World War II after Japanese bomb Pearl Harbor
2. Elias	El Salvador	1986	not shown
3. Peter DiFoggio	Italy	1920	The American Civil Liberties Union is founded
4. Victoria Sarfatti Fernandez	Macedonia	1916	Bolshevik Revolution in Russia—1917
5. Dung Mai	Vietnam	1981	not shown
6. Quen-Fen Chen	Taiwan	not shown	not shown
7. Rose Vanger	Russia	1910	The NAACP is founded
8. Carmen Lima	Mexico	1971	President Nixon orders U.S. troops into Cambodia
9. Arnold Ambler	England	1920	The American Civil Liberties Union is founded

LESSON 4

Checking Your Comprehension

1. b	1. a
2. a	2. c
3. c	3. b
4. b	4. a
5. a	5. b
6. c	6. c

Drawing Conclusions from Feature Stories

1. unsuccessful	5. successful
2. unsuccessful	6. unsuccessful
3. successful	7. successful
4. successful	8. unsuccessful

LESSON 5

Checking Your Comprehension

1. a	1. b
2. b	2. c
3. a	3. b
4. b	4. c
5. c	5. a
6. a	6. b

Recognizing Signal Words and Phrases in Feature Stories*

Sweaters
1. lightweight knits <u>are taking</u> center stage

2. <u>Nowadays,</u> men are wearing sweaters
3. Pallack <u>recently</u> sold a season's worth
4. came into Pallack's shop <u>not long ago</u>
5. <u>In the meantime,</u> men are finding

Sunglasses
1. The <u>current</u> version, with a nylon frame
2. In <u>1986, they're still hanging in</u>
3. <u>Still big</u> among the California surfing set
4. Cat-Eye offspring <u>now</u> fetch between $55 and $75
5. There's <u>now</u> a complete line

* Wording may vary.

LESSON 6

Checking Your Comprehension

1. b	1. c
2. a	2. b
3. b	3. c
4. a	4. a
5. b	5. c
6. c	6. a

Detecting Bias in Sports Writing

1. E	5. E
2. C	6. C
3. C	7. NB
4. E	8. E

LESSON 7

Checking Your Comprehension

1. c	1. c
2. a	2. a
3. a	3. b
4. b	4. b
5. c	5. c
6. a	6. c

Examining Sequence in Feature Story Biographies

Jane Goodall	**Vicky Neave**
1. 4	1. 4
2. 5	2. 1
3. 1	3. 3
4. 2	4. 2
5. 3	

LESSON 8

Checking Your Comprehension

1. a	1. a
2. b	2. c
3. c	3. c
4. b	4. b
5. b	5. b
6. b	6. a

Fact and Opinion in the Question-and-Answer Format

1. fact	5. opinion
2. fact	6. fact
3. both	7. opinion
4. both	8. both

UNIT TWO: WHO REPORTS THE NEWS

LESSON 1

Checking Your Comprehension

1. b	1. c
2. b	2. b
3. a	3. b
4. c	4. c
5. a	5. b
6. b	6. a

Interpreting Colorful Language in Sports Stories*

1. Runs in the last three innings defeated the Red Sox.
2. Fernandez replaced Darling as pitcher. No one scored a home run from him until the sixth inning and he struck out four Red Sox.
3. A straight, line drive hit that landed between the left fielder and center fielder.
4. Wasn't this the same pitcher who had controlled the Mets in previous games?
5. Knight hit a pitch really hard.
6. At the beginning of the season, Ray Knight did not have a bright future.
7. Knight will probably play for the Mets next season because of his hitting, fielding, and energy.
8. He can enjoy the World Series win and the MVP title.
*Wording may vary.

LESSON 2

Checking Your Comprehension

1. b	1. c
2. c	2. c
3. b	3. c
4. b	4. b
5. a	5. b
6. a	6. a

Recognizing Fact and Opinion in News Stories and Editorials

News Story	Editorial
1. fact	1. opinion
2. opinion	2. fact
3. fact	3. fact
4. opinion	4. opinion
5. fact	5. opinion
6. opinion	6. opinion

LESSON 3

Checking Your Comprehension

1. b	1. a
2. b	2. b
3. c	3. a
4. a	4. b
5. c	5. c
6. b	6. a

Fact and Opinion in Feature Stories and Reviews

1. fact	7. opinion
2. fact	8. both
3. fact	9. fact
4. opinion	10. fact
5. both	11. opinion
6. opinion	12. both

LESSON 4

Checking Your Comprehension

1. c	1. b
2. b	2. a
3. b	3. b
4. a	4. a
5. c	5. a
6. b	6. c

Evaluating Comments in an Editorial*

1. Life is not all that painful.
2. ✓
3. Earlier generations did not have it easier than North Shore teenagers.
4. World War II was much harder to live through than today's social scene.
5. ✓
6. The pressures are easy to bear.

*Wording may vary.

LESSON 5

Checking Your Comprehension

1. b	1. b
2. a	2. c
3. c	3. b
4. a	4. c
5. b	5. c
6. c	6. b

Putting Steps in Order

Fixing a Hamburger	Making Your Own Sub Rolls
5	2
2	1
3	4
1	5
4	3

LESSON 6

Checking Your Comprehension

1. b	1. b
2. c	2. c
3. b	3. b
4. b	4. a
5. b	5. c
6. b	6. b

Recognizing Cause and Effect

Shuttle Disaster	Ferry Disaster
1. effect	1. effect
2. effect	2. effect
3. effect	3. cause
4. cause	4. cause
5. cause	5. cause
6. cause	6. cause
7. cause	7. cause

LESSON 7

Checking Your Comprehension

1. a	1. a
2. b	2. b
3. a	3. b
4. c	4. c
5. c	5. a
6. b	6. b

Biographical Sequence in Obituaries and Features

Chester Gould		Cathy Guisewite
1. 7	5. 4	1. 1
2. 6	6. 1	2. 4
3. 5	7. 2	3. 2
4. 3		4. 3

UNIT THREE: HOW WE USE THE NEWS

LESSON 1

Checking Your Comprehension

1. c	1. c
2. b	2. b
3. c	3. a
4. a	4. b
5. a	5. c
6. b	6. b

Arranging Events in Chronological Order

The crowning event of high school	Going 'stag' to the senior prom
4, 1, 2, 3, 5	4, 1, 2, 5, 3

LESSON 2

Checking Your Comprehension

1. b	1. c
2. a	2. a
3. b	3. c
4. c	4. b
5. a	5. a
6. c	6. b

Recognizing Main Ideas and Supporting Details*

The Immigration Reform and Control Act of 1986 will be making its impact felt in the months to come.
1. Regulations made public on May, 1987, should remain valid for several months.

2. Three to four million people may qualify for amnesty.
3. Farmworkers do not have to meet the same residency requirements as urban workers.
4. There will be penalties to discourage employers from hiring illegal aliens.
5. There are community agencies prepared to meet the needs of illegal aliens and help solve their problems.

Nerds display a variety of identifiable characteristics.
1. Nerds do not seem to care about physical appearance.
2. They have a strange laugh and a whining voice.
3. They can be found in the computer lab and the library.
4. They subscribe to magazines like "Fun with Logarithms."
5. They participate in activities like the Varsity Bingo Team and the Yahtzee Club.
*Wording may vary.

LESSON 3

Checking Your Comprehension

1. c	1. b
2. a	2. c
3. b	3. b
4. a	4. c
5. b	5. a
6. a	6. b

Recognizing Time References in Newspaper and Magazine Stories

1. Monday/newspaper
2. By the end of the day/newspaper
3. best first-day effort ever/newspaper
4. second day/magazine
5. Monday/newspaper
6. nine hot days/magazine
7. when the meet was over/magazine
8. Monday night/newspaper

LESSON 4

Checking Your Comprehension

1. c	1. a
2. a	2. c
3. a	3. b
4. c	4. c
5. b	5. b
6. b	6. b

Identifying Cause and Effect in News Stories

1. cause	7. effect
2. cause	8. cause
3. effect	9. effect
4. effect	10. effect
5. cause	11. effect
6. effect	

LESSON 5

Checking Your Comprehension

1. a	1. a
2. c	2. b
3. b	3. b
4. c	4. c
5. a	5. c
6. c	6. b

Recognizing and Listing Details*

Problems for Laborers in the Past
1. Workers were poorly paid.

2. Workers' children were undernourished.
3. People worked long hours.
4. Working conditions were wretched.
5. Workers were poorly housed.

Problems for Laborers in the Present
1. Many recent economic trends have hurt workers.
2. Other countries sell products of equal quality at lower prices.
3. The average real income has declined.
4. Husbands and wives both have to work.
5. Recent pay raises were the lowest in two decades.
*Wording may vary.

GLOSSARY

beat   A subject, such as science or education, or particular buildings, such as city hall, police headquarters, and the courthouse, to which a reporter is assigned and which is that reporter's specialty.

blurb   A short notice or announcement, usually written to describe and create interest in what follows it.

by-line   The name of the writer of a news story, feature article, or special column. It usually appears just below the headline.

copy   The manuscript of any news story prepared for typesetting.

dateline   The line at the beginning of a news story that gives the date of a news story, or an issue of a newspaper or magazine.

deadline   The time after which copy is not accepted for a particular issue, or the time by which certain stages in the production process must be completed.

edition   Any issue of the newspaper; large newspapers issue several editions during the day or night.

editorial   A newspaper article that gives the newspaper's stance or the writer's personal thoughts on current events. An editorial may praise, criticize, or comment on an issue. It often encourages actions the paper or writer thinks may benefit the community.

feature story   A news story dealing with subjects that are of less immediate importance than the subjects of straight news stories. A feature story is often written to be both informative and entertaining.

five W's   The five W's—*Who? What? When? Where? Why?*—and *How?* They are the questions usually answered in the lead, or opening paragraph, of a news story. The five W's summarize the story's most important information.

lead   The opening paragraph of a news story. In most cases, it provides the important information in the story by relating the five W's.

subhead   A short heading used to break up the columns of a long news story.

ACKNOWLEDGMENTS

Acknowledgment is gratefully made for permission to reprint the following articles:

UNIT ONE

Lesson 1 Stark death toll rises to 37. Reprinted courtesy of the Associated Press. Tornadoes rare in stricken area, forecasters say. Reprinted with permission of *The Dallas Morning News.*

Lesson 2 Tempestt Bledsoe of 'Cosby' raising awareness about food. Courtesy of *Atlanta Journal.* Reprinted with permission. TV film tells of triumph amid tragedy. Copyright 1986, *USA TODAY.* Reprinted with permission. Defaming the realm? Reprinted courtesy of *The Boston Globe.* Roots of rock. Reprinted courtesy of *The Boston Globe.*

Lesson 3 Liberty at 100: Changing faces of immigration. Reprinted courtesy of *The Boston Globe.* Commercialism isn't ruining Miss Liberty. Copyright 1986, *USA TODAY.* Reprinted with permission.

Lesson 4 Invention is alive and swell in Houston. Copyright 1987, *The Houston Post.* Reprinted by permission. Company boasts it has a better mousetrap. Reprinted courtesy of *The Boston Globe.*

Lesson 5 Man's new uniform: Bold, bright knits. Copyright 1987, *USA TODAY.* Reprinted with permission. Saying it with sunglasses. Reprinted courtesy of *The Boston Globe.*

Lesson 6 Red-hot Lincoln dethrones King. Copyright 1987. Pulitzer Publishing Company. Reprinted with permission. Lincoln rocks King for Class AA title. © *Chicago Tribune.* Reprinted by permission: Tribune Media Services.

Lesson 7 Jane Goodall. Copyright 1986, *USA TODAY.* Reprinted with permission. Atypical neurosurgeon beats odds—her way. The *High Point* (N.C.) *Enterprise.*

Lesson 8 Q & A. Reprinted courtesy of *The Boston Globe.* Sex too soon. ©1987, Los Angeles Times Syndicate. Reprinted by permission.

UNIT TWO

Lesson 1 We're #1. Reprinted courtesy of *The New York Post.* MVP Knight becomes King of the Series. Reprinted courtesy of *The New York Post.*

Lesson 2 Teenagers emphasize need for jobs, antidrug messages. Reprinted courtesy of *The Boston Globe.* Limiting after-school work. Reprinted courtesy of *The Boston Globe.*

Lesson 3 Madonna—more than a material girl. Brett Milano/*Boston Globe.* Madonna hidden in Hollywood. Reprinted courtesy of *The Boston Globe.*

Lesson 4 When a 'tragedy' is only vanity. Reprinted by permission: Tribune Media Services. Death Wish? Then spare the self-pity. Reprinted by permission: Tribune Media Services.

Lesson 5 Burgers. Tom Sietsema/*The Washington Post.* A sub by many other names. Taken from "Taste of America" by Jane and Michael Stern. Copyright 1987 Universal Press Syndicate. Reprinted with permission. All rights reserved.

Lesson 6 Fiery blast destroys space shuttle; McAuliffe, six astronauts are killed. Reprinted courtesy of *The Boston Globe.* Ferry toll feared at 135. Reprinted courtesy of *The Boston Globe.*

Lesson 7 'Dick Tracy' creator Chester Gould, 84. ©Copyrighted 1985, Chicago Tribune Company, all rights reserved, used with permission. Life imitates art for Cathy the cartoonist. Copyright, 1987, *Los Angeles Times.* Reprinted by permission.

UNIT THREE

Lesson 1 The crowning event of high school. Copyright 1987, *USA TODAY.* Reprinted with permission. Going 'stag' to the senior prom. Reprinted by Permission of the Providence Journal Company ©1987.

Lesson 2 Introduction to Becoming Legal. Copyright, 1987, *Los Angeles Times.* Reprinted by permission. Nerds: The inside story. Reprinted courtesy of Stephanie McLaughlin, the *Little Green,* Central H.S., Manchester, N.H.

Lesson 3 Joyner-Kersee on world-record pace. Copyright 1987, *USA TODAY.* Reprinted with permission. On top of the Worlds. The following excerpts are reprinted courtesy from SPORTS ILLUSTRATED's September 14, 1987 issue. Copyright ©1987 Time Inc. "On Top of the Worlds" by Kenny Moore. ALL RIGHTS RESERVED.

Lesson 4 Pretoria imposes state of emergency, arrests over 1,000. New press restrictions lead to self-censorship. Phillip Van Niekerk/*Boston Globe.* Government powers under emergency. Reprinted courtesy of the Associated Press.

Lesson 5 A heroine for Labor Day. John Galvin/*Boston Globe.* For many, it's a gloomy holiday. Reprinted courtesy of *The Boston Globe.*

PICTURE CREDITS

UNIT ONE

Lesson 1   Londie Rhoden: John Pemberton/*Fla. Times-Union & Journal*. USS *Stark:* AP/WIDE WORLD PHOTOS. Illustrated map of Texas and illustrated map of Saragosa: Reprinted with permission of *The Dallas Morning News*.

Lesson 2   Tempestt Bledsoe: Photo courtesy of *Atlanta Journal*. Senator Ted Kennedy and Ted Kennedy, Jr.: Photo by Robert Deutsch, *USA TODAY*. Copyright 1986 *USA TODAY*. Used by permission. Dick Clark: AP/WIDE WORLD PHOTOS.

Lesson 3   All photographs and illustrated chart: Reprinted courtesy of *The Boston Globe*.

Lesson 4   All photographs: Manuel M. Chavez © *The Houston Post*. Reprinted by permission. Ken Bernard and Mice Cube: Boston Globe Photo.

Lesson 5   Sweater: Photo by Robert Deutsch, *USA TODAY*. Copyright 1987 *USA TODAY* Used by permission. Illustrated graphic, American Pop: Reprinted courtesy of the Associated Press. Jack Nicholson: UPI/Bettmann Newsphotos. Yoko Ono: Boston Globe Photo. Jackie Onassis: AP/WIDE WORLD PHOTOS. Sunglasses and trunk: Boston Globe Photo.

Lesson 6   Basketball game: Pamela Schuyler-Cowens/Stock, Boston.

Lesson 7   Jane Goodall: Photo by Barbara Ries, *USA TODAY*. Copyright 1986 *USA TODAY*. Used by permission. Vicky Neave: Photo by Woody Marshall/*High Point* (N.C.) *Enterprise*.

Lesson 8   Ask Beth: Los Angeles Times Syndicate.

UNIT TWO

Lesson 1   Ray Knight: AP/WIDE WORLD PHOTOS.

Lesson 3   Madonna close-up: Max Goldstein/Star File Photo. Madonna: Vinnie Zuffante/Star File Photo.

Lesson 4   Mike Royko: Photo courtesy of the *Chicago Tribune*.

Lesson 5   Illustration of burger: Reprinted courtesy of Martha Vaughan. Illustration of submarines: HOGAN COPYRIGHT 1987 THE RECORD. Reprinted with permission of UNIVERSAL PRESS SYNDICATE. All rights reserved.

Lesson 6   Explosion photo: Courtesy of *The Boston Globe*. Globe diagram by Bruce Sanders and Deborah Perugi. Herald of Free Enterprise: AP/WIDE WORLD PHOTOS. Bow of ferry: UPI/Bettmann Newsphotos.

Lesson 7   Chester Gould: AP/WIDE WORLD PHOTOS. *Dick Tracy* comic strips: Reprinted by permission: Tribune Media Services. Cathy Guisewite: ©1987 *Los Angeles Times*. *Cathy* comic strip: CATHY COPYRIGHT 1984 UNIVERSAL PRESS SYNDICATE. Reprinted with permission. All rights reserved.

UNIT THREE

Lesson 1   Prom: All photos by Barbara Ries, *USA TODAY*. Copyright 1987 *USA TODAY*. Used by permission. Going stag: *Providence Journal-Bulletin* photo by Rachel Ritchie.

Lesson 2   Illustration of immigrants by Richard Milholland.

Lesson 3   Jackie Joyner-Kersee: AP/WIDE WORLD PHOTOS. On top of the Worlds: ©ALL-SPORT USA/Tony Duffy, 1987.

Lesson 4   Botha: AP/WIDE WORLD PHOTOS.

Lesson 5   Farmer: J. C. Allen & Son, Inc., W. Lafayette, IN. Steelworkers: AP/WIDE WORLD PHOTOS.